Managing Industrial Change in Western Europe

Managing Industrial Change in Western Europe

Edited by François Duchêne
and Geoffrey Shepherd

Frances Pinter (Publishers), London and New York

First published in Great Britain in 1987 by
Frances Pinter (Publishers) Limited
25 Floral Street, London WC2E 9DS

British Library Cataloguing in Publication Data

Managing industrial change in Western
    Europe : policies towards industry in
    Germany, France, Italy and Britain.
    1. Industry and state—Europe—History
    —20th century
    I. Duchêne, François   II. Shepherd,
    Geoffrey, *1943*—
    338.94   HD3616.E82

ISBN 0-86187-281-9

Typeset by Florencetype Limited, Kewstoke, Avon
Printed by Biddles of Guildford Ltd

Contents

List of tables

List of figures

List of contributors

François Duchêne was until 1982 Director of the Sussex European Research Centre, University of Sussex.

Ernst-Jürgen Horn is an economist at the Kiel Institute of World Economics (Institut für Weltwirtschaft)

David Marsden is a lecturer in industrial relations at the London School of Economics and Political Science.

Patrick Messerlin is a professor of economics at the University of Paris XII and a research fellow at the Fondation Nationale des Sciences Politiques (Service de l'Etude de l'Activité Economique), Paris, and is currently (1986–8) on leave at the World Bank, Washington, DC.

Pippo Ranci is a professor of economics at the Catholic University of Milan and a member of the Istituto per la Ricerca Sociale, Milan.

Geoffrey Shepherd is a senior fellow at the Science Policy Research Unit, University of Sussex, currently (1986–7) on leave at the World Bank, Washington, DC.

Annual average units of national currency to the European Currency Unit (ECU), 1960–86

	West Germany	France	Italy	United Kingdom	United States
1960	4.4360	5.2145	660.1	0.37721	1.0562
1961	4.3074	5.2695	667.1	0.38119	1.0673
1962	4.2792	5.2817	668.6	0.38207	1.0698
1963	4.2792	5.2817	668.6	0.38207	1.0698
1964	4.2792	5.2817	668.6	0.38207	1.0698
1965	4.2792	5.2817	668.6	0.38207	1.0698
1966	4.2792	5.2817	668.6	0.38207	1.0698
1967	4.2592	5.2570	665.5	0.38765	1.0648
1968	4.1155	5.0797	643.1	0.42870	1.0289
1969	4.0262	5.2903	638.9	0.42591	1.0222
1970	3.7414	5.6777	638.9	0.42593	1.0222
1971	3.6457	5.7721	647.4	0.42858	1.0478
1972	3.5768	5.6572	654.3	0.44894	1.1218
1973	3.2764	5.4677	716.5	0.50232	1.2317
1974	3.0835	5.7339	775.7	0.50980	1.1927
1975	3.0494	5.3192	809.5	0.56003	1.2408
1976	2.8154	5.3449	930.1	0.62158	1.1181
1977	2.6483	5.6061	1006.8	0.65370	1.1411
1978	2.5561	5.7398	1080.2	0.66391	1.2741
1979	2.5109	5.8295	1138.5	0.64639	1.3706
1980	2.5242	5.8690	1189.2	0.59849	1.3923
1981	2.5139	6.0399	1263.2	0.55311	1.1164
1982	2.3760	6.4312	1323.8	0.56045	0.9797
1983	2.2705	6.7708	1349.9	0.58701	0.8902
1984	2.2381	6.8750	1381.8	0.59072	0.7877
1985	2.2320	6.8158	1458.0	0.58387	0.7477
1986	2.1944	6.8216	1555.2	0.58108	0.8522

Source: Table 41 of Commission of the European Communities, *European Economy*, No. 26, November 1985.

Preface

This is the second of two books reporting on a research project originally undertaken by the Sussex European Research Centre, University of Sussex, on Western European industry and industrial policy. The aims of the project were to identify the kinds of adjustment problems facing Western European industry, to understand public and private responses to these challenges better (and how and why these have differed across sectors and across countries), and to anticipate some of the adjustment problems and policy options that Western European countries, individually or collectively, would have to face in the near future.

The first book, *Europe's Industries: Public and Private Strategies for Change*, edited by Geoffrey Shepherd, François Duchêne and Christopher Saunders, was published (by Frances Pinter) in 1983. It examined the adjustment experience of a number of sectors in Germany, France, Italy and Britain and made some additional comparisons with Japan. The sectors covered were textiles, steel, shipbuilding, motor cars, electrical power plant, process plant contracting, machine tools and semiconductors. These studies showed that the pressures for adjustment were generally very strong, but that new processes and market opportunities also offered the more dynamic firms a number of opportunities for profitable survival, even in so-called mature sectors. These studies also suggested that, notwithstanding the specific characteristics and problems of each sector, the pattern of private and public response to adjustment pressures showed more common traits within countries (and across sectors) than within sectors (and across countries). The present volume leads on from these findings by looking more systematically at the characteristic approaches to coping with industrial change in Western Europe's four largest national economies.

A considerable amount of initial work went into the four country studies, as well as a study on labour markets in the four countries, at the time the original project was formally underway. This project was made possible by the foresight and generosity of the Anglo-German Foundation for the Study of Industrial Society, London, and the Volkswagen Foundation, Hanover. Their funds financed research at the Sussex European Research Centre from 1977 to 1984, as well as the special costs of international collaboration. Thanks for help in funding the time for the editing of the present volume are also due to the Science Policy Research Unit, University of Sussex (which has taken over the Sussex European Research Centre's work on industrial and technology policy in Western Europe since 1984).

The research in the four countries has given rise to earlier studies which appeared separately, and an earlier version of the German country study by Ernst-Jürgen Horn was published in 1982 as *Management of Industrial Change in Germany*, Sussex European Papers No. 13, Sussex European Research Centre. A study of industrial adjustment in the United Kingdom by Margaret Sharp and Geoffrey Shepherd appeared as an ILO working paper in 1983 (and will shortly be published by the ILO in an updated version as *Managing Change in British Industry*). In 1984 Patrick Messerlin completed an unpublished monograph, *Managing Industrial Change in France* (Sussex European Research Centre).

Given the time that has elapsed since the beginning of the research project, the studies in the present volume were completely reworked by their authors in 1986. In this task the authors owe a particular debt to Eric Midgley, who played a major role in cutting down and editing the lengthy manuscripts of the country studies and provided a number of very valuable insights.

We are also most grateful to Terrie Russell and Komola Ghose, who typed much of the manuscript.

Brighton
and
Washington, DC

François Duchêne
Geoffrey Shephard
May 1987

Introduction

Geoffrey Shepherd and François Duchêne

West Germany, France, Great Britain and Italy are the giants of Western Europe, accounting for over half of its population and for two-thirds of its domestic product. With the United States, they were at the centre of the world economy until two world wars sapped their vitality and industry expanded rapidly in other parts of the world. The governments of these four countries saw industrial performance as central to preserving their position in the world, first in the post-war economic recovery of the 1950s, then in the challenge posed by American technology and multinational corporations in the 1960s, and most recently in the threat of recession and Japanese competition in the 1970s and 1980s.

This book describes the way the governments of these four European countries have sought to influence the process of industrial change since World War II. The subject has a dual interest. First, differences in the national approaches to industrial change across four countries of similar size, economic structure and endowment—second-rankers in the Western industrial league after the United States and Japan—are instructive: can 'industrial policies' influence the way countries face industrial change? Second, these countries are at the core of Western Europe's economic integration process: their industrial strengths and weaknesses become those of the European Community, while the extent to which their policies are national or European determines the cohesion and progress of the Community.

As the challenges posed by the world economy have progressively borne in on Europe since the 1960s, the parallel response of the governments of the Four has been to formulate national 'industrial policies' designed to protect and promote manufacturing industry. The term 'industrial policy' is difficult to pin down. It usually refers to policies to promote industrial activity, but often refers—correctly or incorrectly—to policies with a more strictly social objective, such as saving jobs (through import protection, for instance) or promoting backward regions. Moreover, industry-promoting policies, narrowly defined, may cover only selective policies that act directly on firms or sectors; more broadly defined, they may also cover trade and anti-trust policy; in some cases they may additionally cover macro-economic policies (which, of course, always have micro-economic implications). It does not appear profitable to try to pursue a watertight definition, and the authors have been left to define their own field of policy coverage. While all the authors understand industrial policy more or less to cover the micro-economic policies applied to particular manufacturing industries, some go further and lay considerable stress on macro-economic policies.

Rather than in a definition of industrial policy, the commonality of the four country studies constituting the core of this book is to be found in the approach adopted. First, all four studies adopt an historical approach, des-cribing the development of policies towards industry since World War II, Europe's common watershed. Second, the studies show how these policies grew out of national perceptions of economic problems and how to deal with them. Third, the studies seek to place industrial policy in the broader context of the institutions—financial and labour markets, the structure and organization of firms, for instance—which influence the way manufacturing firms adapt to, or resist, change and which therefore constrain the effective-ness of policy. Fourth, the approach to looking at industrial policy is deliberately broad and largely non-quantitative in an effort to distinguish declaratory from real policies, policy concerns and policy instruments and to appreciate better the interaction of policies, history, institutions and producers.

Chapters 1 and 2 set the scene for the country studies. In Chapter 1, 'Sources of industrial policy', François Duchêne and Geoffrey Shepherd describe the context for industrial policy as one of complex and ill-understood social forces; a society's formula for industrial success is difficult to invent, may then have a long shelf-life, but will not be good for ever. Governments have been drawn into industrial policy for a number of reasons, notably their central role in fostering institutional development—in education and research for instance; the emergence of corporate forms of economic organization, including trades unions and large firms (these firms become planners in their own right as increasing technological complexity or capital intensity lengthen planning horizons); and the struggles over income distribution that occur both nationally and internationally. Industrial policy is often powerfully driven by mercantilist ambitions to increase world market share. Such mercantilism *may* be effective in earlier stages of development—and can be absorbed by the international system—but this system cannot tolerate too much mercantilism from its leading economies.

In Chapter 2, 'Western Europe: a family of contrasts', the same authors highlight some economic similarities among the four, in their economic structure, the importance (and growth) of the government's role in income redistribution, and the dominant role of government as an industrial customer. By and large these countries are similarly corporatist, but this corporatism takes distinct national forms which influence the character of industrial policy. Nationalist economic policy comes up against another preoccupation of these governments—the quest, on historical, political and economic grounds, for European integration. There is an increasingly European character to the competitive problems these countries face *vis-à-*

vis the world economy. There are also, despite the nationalism, signs of a slowly growing common response, with Germany—because she is Western Europe's key economy—playing the regulatory role.

Of the four countries, it is Germany that has most consciously opted for market-orientated industrial policies in the post-war period, creating a relatively strong consensus around the principles of the social market economy, an economy concerned with redistribution as well as the discipline of the market. Germany's industrial success is also often explained in part as the consequence of its particular institutional characteristics, notably the division of economic responsibilities between federal and state governments, the role of a powerful universal banking system, and procedures governing labour relations that generally lead to substantial consensus on economic issues. But as Ernst-Jürgen argues in Chapter 3, 'West Germany: a market-led process', closer inspection reveals a considerable degree of interventionist industrial policy. Even in the 1950s investments were to an extent directed through tax incentives and Marshall Aid funds, but it is since the revaluations of the Deutsche mark and the external shocks of the early 1970s that industrial policies have been at their strongest. In a sense the task of policy became more difficult as growth increasingly required innovation, rather than the imitation of best practice elsewhere in the world. The cumulative development of selective policies has distorted market forces, and these policies have very often contradicted each other. At best their contribution to solving Germany's adjustment problems has been mixed. At the same time, partly as a result of these policies, the economy appears to have become a good deal less flexible than in the 'miracle' years of the 1950s. Even so, its remaining strengths are considerable.

The French government is usually held up as the leading European exponent of deliberate and coherent policies to promote industrial growth. But Patrick Messerlin does not share the view of many of his countrymen: in Chapter 4, 'France: the ambitious state', he describes the government's efforts as a costly exercise in futility. The government's industrial ambitions, stemming from the near-extinction of the French state in World War II, were frustrated for two major reasons. First, no French consensus was achieved—indeed, the matter was hardly debated—on the framework of economic rules in which industry should operate: markets and interventions have coexisted uneasily, with successive French governments seeking to promote firms rather than markets. France's position stands in clear contrast to Germany's durable consensus on the social market economy. Second, the very multiplicity of French interventionist actions dissipated government efforts and reduced their effectiveness, at the same time leaving the government open to pressure groups soliciting particular concessions. If industrial policy was a failure, what accounts for France's impressive post-war growth? Over the long term, Messerlin argues, trade liberalization—at first in a European then in a world context—has increasingly provided the invisible hand of the market. Thus for France the extent to which the

European Community remains open to world trade will determine the extent to which national industrial policy will have an impact.

Italy's weak government—reflecting its unstable politics, overburdened legislature and weak administration—stands in contrast to the conventional view of France's strong government. In Chapter 5, 'Italy: the weak state', Pippo Ranci concludes that this was not entirely a bad thing. Certainly, a stronger government would be better at fulfilling the traditional public role in industry—in the infrastructural, educational and basic research facilities that are clearly deficient in Italy. Moreover, Italian industrial policies have achieved some success—in particular, trade liberalization in the 1950s, public investment in the 1950s and 1960s in basic industries such as steel and chemicals, and even the measures to bring industry to the Mezzogiorno. But otherwise, industrial policy has lacked a conscious design and has been unbalanced and ineffective; Italy is, for instance, a country where the price of haircuts is government-controlled, but where anti-trust policy is non-existent. Italy's industrial strengths have come from its small and medium enterprises—a sector promoted in part by the government's own benign neglect and inability to apply its tax laws—but also from the recovery in recent years of large firms in the public and private sector. In fact, there has been a remarkably successful return to market-orientated values in the mid-1980s. Time will tell whether this is a sea-change or just part of the political and economic cyclicality that has characterized post-war Italy.

In Chapter 6, 'United Kingdom: a resistance to change', Geoffrey Shepherd takes the view that the relative decline of British manufacturing industry since the latter part of the last century above all reflects deep-seated institutional problems, in particular a conservatism that is the inheritance of the nineteenth century. This conservatism shows, for instance, in labour relations, as well as in the slowness with which the modern, integrated multi-divisional corporation has emerged in Britain compared to the United States or Germany. Whatever its historical origins, this conservatism was reinforced by the emergence of a strong social consensus in post-war Britain that economic policies should give priority to redistribution over growth. The view that, in effect, growth would take care of itself if government assured demand, helped put off the full realization of the micro-economic problems underlying Britain's failure to compete internationally. The all-party consensus became increasingly frayed as economic failure persisted, but only with the advent of the 1979 Conservative government was this consensus seriously attacked. The swings in economic policy as successive governments sought to improve economic performance did little to bolster businessmen's expectations, while industrial relations became increasingly difficult. The selective industrial interventions that also developed in response to economic difficulties are best characterized, in Eric Midgley's words, as 'a bull in the ring charging in different directions at unattainable objectives and always perishing at the last'. The greatest stability in industrial policy has been provided, in fact, by the steady process of trade liberalization (as in France) and the growing strength of anti-trust policy.

Much as the four country studies have emphasized the importance of national institutional characteristics in managing industrial change, this area still remains an underdeveloped feature of economic policy analysis. For instance, the country studies do not pretend to do justice to the role of financial markets and institutions or of educational systems. Chapter 7, by David Marsden, 'Collective bargaining and industrial adjustment in Britain, France, Italy and West Germany', fills this gap in one area by comparing the way that labour markets and labour relations systems in the four countries provide different constraints and opportunities for industrial change—in effect, different kinds of flexibility. With fairly rigid wage structures in all four countries, labour market adaptations take place instead through quantitative and qualitative changes. Increasing levels of legislated and negotiated job security over time may further reduce labour market flexibility, though the extent of this can be exaggerated. The chapter distinguishes between occupational labour markets (where training essentially occurs externally to firms and workers have the attributes that allow them to move with relative ease between firms) and internal labour markets (where training and job redeployment tend to occur within the firm). At the margin at least, occupational labour markets are more prevalent in Germany and Britain, while internal labour markets are more prevalent in France and Italy. Both types of labour market have their own kind of flexibility, but on balance internal labour markets may be better at easing the problems of incremental technical change and appropriately changing the mix of skills.

In the final chapter, 'Policies for a wider world', François Duchêne compares the industrial policies and politics, the social and institutional environment, and the economic performance of the four countries, relying partly, but not wholly, on the findings of the four central chapters. This comparison stresses the following: the importance in Germany's economic success of its traditional industrial strengths (strengths which may not be as good in carrying Germany into the age of electronics, witnessed by its recent faltering economic performance); the illusion of inherited industrial strengths in the British case; the relative success of France's mixture of intervention and competition in bridging the gap with the world's industrial leaders; and the industrial success of Italy—economically the most underrated of the four countries—in spite of the incoherence of industrial policy in the 1960s and 1970s. The chapter argues that intervention can be effective for less industrially developed countries with highly developed institutions seeking to catch up; but once this has been more or less achieved and innovation takes over more squarely from imitation, intervention by blunting industry's responses to the market will increasingly obstruct the innovation process. Private responsiveness to market signals appears in turn to depend on a strong supporting environment where priority is given to skill formation and where, more generally, social attitudes (as reflected both in the culture and in government policies) support industrial values. This kind of environment is more readily found in Germany, and even Italy than in Britain or France. The chapter concludes that while the traditional policy concern with economies of scale has been exaggerated, it cannot be ignored. Neither the policies of 'national champions' with monopoly powers at home, nor forced marriages with United States or Japanese corporations have been able to promote efficient economies of scale for most European would-be multinationals. This points to the need for a European, rather than a national, approach to economies of scale. Otherwise, in many branches, European firms will take part in world economic integration from positions of weakness.

1 Sources of industrial policy

François Duchêne and Geoffrey Shepherd

Britain: 'Trade is so far from being inconsistent with a gentleman, that . . . trade in England makes gentlemen'.
Daniel Defoe, *The Complete English Tradesman*, 1726, p. 376
(cited in Perkin 1985, p. 59)

France: 'Why, when President Auriol at Donzère [a major hydro-electric dam] . . . claimed that this was the true face of France, was it not only malicious foreigners, but the man in the street himself who had the impression that the true face of France was that of a farm-cart stuck in the mud?'
Herbert Lüthy, *The State of France*, 1955, p. 297

Germany: 'At that time [1860], everyone looked on Germany as incapable of competing with France, England or America in any sort of organized energy'.
Henry Adams, *Education of Henry Adams*, 1918, p. 83

Japan: 'To see your men at work made me feel that you are a very satisfied, easy-going race who reckon time is no object . . . First-class managers . . . are required to wake things up and get out of the go-as-you-please style that seems universal at present'.
Australian expert, report on manufacturing
to the Japanese government, *Japan Times*,
18 August 1915 (Goh Keng-Swee, 1983, p. 41)

Whatever the signs that industry is beginning to follow agriculture and, with ever-increasing levels of output, employ fewer and fewer people, it remains the core of the productive system. Services may provide more jobs, but many of them depend on links with manufacturing. Services also have far less weight in foreign trade where the division of labour, as the basis of all wealth, is ultimately honed. This may change in future, but until it does, industry constitutes the heart of the economy.

It is not surprising, then, that governments, which are so deeply involved in modern society, should give prominence to industrial policies; nor that this term should be used so loosely that it can refer equally to efforts which exploit, and promote, industry. For instance, Italian policies designed to make industry invest in the less-developed South are inevitably industrial in many of their effects. So are lame-duck policies designed to protect employment. Yet these are better defined by regional or employment aims than by industrial ones that they can sometimes frustrate.

Even when industrial policies seek to promote manufacturing as such, they can embrace very disparate concerns. In a narrow sense, they cover 'micro-economic' measures applied to particular sectors, including, for instance firm structures, technology and manpower. But they are apt also to extend to any policies, such as those for aggregate demand or income distribution, which can shape industry. In particular, the link between aggregate demand and industrial production is vital to both. The two must balance, but they can do so at low or high levels. A major aim of industrial policy must therefore be to maximize the elasticity of supply in order to expand the potential of efforts to raise aggregate demand. Demand that cannot be followed by competitive production is soon undermined. Conversely, demand that falls below supply and starves producers of markets gradually restricts capacity.

Since industry is embedded in a milieu, one also has to take account of the ways in which the relevant institutions in society interact to achieve industrial ends. This may be termed industrial behaviour and includes all forms of activity by which the establishment in the widest sense can influence industrial management from outside the firm.

Finally, there is a still broader element that may best be called the industrial culture. This goes beyond industrial behaviour to the potential for response to industrial needs of the society as a whole. It includes all social and cultural forces, such as general values, and levels of education, including their patterns of distribution, which may condition both industrial behaviour and policy.

1.1 Competition

The field is as multi-layered as it is because industry permeates much of society and, like all dynamic social activities, is dialectic. Industrial performance results from the interactions of the various participants in a system. Each responds to what exists and to the stimuli from the environment. Every change that any party to the system introduces, however small, potentially affects the challenges and opportunities all the other parties face. Hence, activities in industry must always be generated in conditions which are to some extent new and specific. They will be specific in time because technology and competition evolve continually. They will also be specific to their culture, that is the institutions, shared or conflicting sectional outlooks, traditions and skills of the society that produces them.

Even if one takes a dialectic process ostensibly as simple as a football league, it is impossible to say conclusively why a given team succeeds or fails in a given game or season. Clubs gamble big sums on managers or players, but the gambles often go wrong, just as many successes are unexpected. Yet the gambles that go wrong often build on the very managers or players who previously succeeded.

Much the same mystery of human relations applies in industry. Industry may not be more embedded in society than football, nor harder in principle to analyse, but it covers an incomparably wider range of groups and a more decisive level of activity. In consequence, industrial achievement consists in the exploitation not only of ideas, technology and capital but of a given society's characteristics at the relevant time. The patterns behind the successful (or unsuccessful) industrial formula draw on the unconscious as well as conscious resources of society. They must do so, for many of the vital characteristics were formed long before modern industry existed and evolved for reasons totally ignorant of today's purposes. Every formula for economic success has depended on the exploitation of novel opportunities in idiosyncratic ways. The process is inherently unpredictable.

If the net and effective will of the strategic groups and individuals in society to promote manufacturing rather than, say, agriculture or leisure is low, no amount of policy will achieve the industrial success of countries where it is easier to mobilize energies in that direction. The problem could be to change societal attitudes. In practice, however, one can never be sure what potential performance could be, nor what, in the interaction of policy and society, can be laid at the door of the leaders of policy or of those in their wake.

A number of practical consequences seem to follow. First, because societies are highly complex organisms not easily led to collective goals which have yet to be absorbed as common habit, successful formulas cannot be invented very often. Failure is equally difficult to deal with, because it challenges the groups benefiting from the pre-existing social patterns (Olson 1982, p. 74).

A second consequence is that hierarchies of industrial power persist. They seem to become effective in association with new technologies, perhaps because these stimulate open competition where relative effectiveness at any given moment is most clearly revealed. Once set, they tend to crystallize until a new technology and new power come along. American and German firms came to the fore in the 1880s in electrical engineering and chemicals. They have predominated in these sectors ever since. They are now challenged by Japan through micro-electronics. It follows that some periods fix industrial hierarchies more than others. Because of current innovations, the 1980s seem to be one of them.

A third, related implication is that imitation of best practice may reduce the gap between an industrial leader and followers striving to catch up, but is unlikely to close it. Success has at least to some extent to be reinvented to suit the new practitioner as well as the time, environment and technology.

In classical economics, the difficulties posed in analysing these dialectical processes are approached through the theory of competition. Producers operate freely on an open market. Desire for profit incites them to supply products which customers find they want. Suppliers who are more lucky, innovative or efficient than others, in the sense that they cater better to potential demand by their new ideas, their quality or their price, will push out those who are less successful. New products will appear, costs will fall, quality will improve and general welfare rise.

If some countries compete better than others across the whole range, their currencies will sooner or later grow rarer and dearer in terms of the currencies of less-effective exporters. Their goods will also grow dearer on world markets and their competitive edge to that extent be blunted. Strong sellers cannot drive out weak in a stark, cumulative way, since the market, through exchange rates, will re-establish trade balances between them. Moreover, product cycle theory suggests how poorer economies can rise up the ladder of production, competition and wealth (Vernon 1966, pp. 190–207). Countries that have reached a higher combination of average incomes and size of total market than others begin to generate new demands. Their producers can respond by devising new lines and technologies. Where these are developing rapidly, the leaders will have a built-in advantage because they are able to exploit opportunities followers have not yet sighted. However, when technological change in a given field is decelerating, as sooner or later it must, followers have opportunities to catch up. With lower standards of living, their labour costs will be cheaper. If they can develop, buy, beg or steal the technology—and, more difficult, adapt it to their culture—their lower costs give them an edge over those who launched the activity in the first place but now must move on to higher things.

In theory, this provides a route by which all countries can climb the steps of the competitive industrial hierarchy. The historic evidence suggests this is often a realistic picture. Japan has climbed, though very rapidly, in a quite classic way up the ladder. Even South Korea and Taiwan, despite high growth and fears that electronics and 'multinational' firms might help them jump many of the rungs, have largely conformed to the pattern.

On this reading, it can well be asked why industrial activity needs to be shaped by 'policies' at all. Any intervention risks damaging the elastic adjustment of the millions of active participants who are closer to markets, and therefore better placed to do their job, than are outsiders. Yet historically, unvarnished competition has played a smaller, and public intervention a larger, part than market theory would suggest. Each one of the economies which have grown to industrial pre-eminence, even Britain, the progenitor of free-trade doctrines, has at some time in its industrial ascent been protectionist or interventionist. The United States and Germany were notoriously protectionist in their rise to industrial pre-eminence, and Japan's close internal organization is widely considered to be mercantilist today.

1.2 Motives for industrial policy

This gap between textbook capitalism and the practices which can be widely observed, seems to be due to three broad influences, all of them derived from the steadily growing scale of economic activity.

The first is the cumulative build up of the *institutional supports of manufacturing*. Historically, this first became important with Prussia, and then Germany, which in the nineteenth century developed manufacturing in a context dominated by British exporters. Britain, as first-comer, had developed the classic orthodoxy of free trade, characterized by well-functioning markets and perfect competition. Prussia now deliberately used state investment to stimulate industrial 'take-off'; she pioneered close links between science, education and manufacturing; and in the 1850s the banks assumed a major role because Prussian firms, unlike English, could not finance growth from ploughing back profits (Pollard 1981, p. 187).

Education was perhaps the quintessential instance because it could not offer sufficient prospect of private profit to respond as rapidly or fully as required to industrial need. Nearly everywhere, education of the masses, most of whom were too poor to afford it, has ultimately been the responsibility of public authorities, central or regional, though private funds have sometimes been significant, as in the United States and Britain. The role of state-supported technical education and of public research institutions in the rise of German industrial power, is one of the clichés of economic history.

The advantages of a coordinated effort to strengthen the institutional environment of industry, as revealed by Germany at the turn of the century, have been so great that no country has been able to ignore them since, though some are much better at achieving them than others.

The second factor has been the emergence from the late nineteenth century, first in the United States, then in Europe, of *the modern corporation*, which began to displace smaller, more specialized firms (Chandler 1977). The modern corporation sought through vertical integration to improve control of its supplies and its markets and to enlarge sales by cheaper mass production. It increasingly used scientific and technological knowledge to routinize its search for new processes, products and markets and to apply more scientific approaches to management. Economies of scale in production and marketing have proved to have an inexorable logic and the average size of firm and the degree of concentration have continued to grow, at least until the early 1970s.

Industrial systems have come to be dominated by small numbers of powerful actors, the largest firms, labour federations and the governments. These large actors seek cooperation as well as competition. Cooperation may actually be aimed at restricting competition. But it may also be more positive: to achieve better labour relations, to maximize the productivity of supplier–client relations, or to reduce the uncertainty about the future in a context of rapid industrial change.

Decision-making in business has also been affected by changing time-scales. As production develops on a larger scale and becomes more capital-intensive, investment may take a decade or more to bear fruit. It is no longer possible, if it ever was, to evolve by reacting to relatively simple, short-term price signals. Competition by price, the mainstay of textbook capitalism, becomes an uncertain guide, and advantage accrues to those who can devise appropriate longer-term strategies.

All such partly speculative activity implies forms of planning. It may be corporate planning, or planning by a cartel or banks or an arm of the state. But while there are important differences between these, they are not the difference of nature that is assumed between a bureaucratic state and a swarm of small capitalists reacting to an open market. If planning is wide-spread, the argument is no longer whether it should exist, but who should do it, how and to what ends. Distinctions between what belongs to the sphere of the firm or the state also become less sharp as the stakes involve larger and larger fractions of society, whoever takes the decisions. It is not inevitable, but it is far from unnatural for states to be drawn into such processes. In some countries, they were always associated with it: industry grew up in the shadow of state markets for communications and armaments. It is hard to overestimate the impetus given even in the last half century to 'high techno-logy' by the defence and space programmes of the US federal government. The state is the referee in quarrels over the distribution of benefits; it regulates concentrations of productive power that give openings to abuse; it has often taken over bankrupt firms and nationalized them. The list could be almost indefinitely extended.

In these conditions, to speak of industrial policies as a form of 'interven-tion', implying an exceptional or artificial intrusion into the natural workings of perfect markets and competition, is misleading. The purveyors of industrial policy today are not best seen as external to the decision-making system. They are not management and should, and usually do, stay distinct. But nowadays, governments, or administrations within them, along with associations of employers, banks, labour unions, think tanks, labora-tories in business or the universities and even other lesser institutions and *dramatis personae*, are all part of the normal decision-making complex behind industry. They are strands in the fabric, not foreign bodies crawling over it from outside. Therefore, industrial policies are best understood as all forms of activity by which the establishment in the widest sense tries to influence industrial management in directions collectively seen as desirable.

It follows from this interweaving of forces that the sources of initiative are not necessarily the most apparent ones. In particular, is the state pushing a given firm in a specific instance, or *vice versa*? Public procurement is a favourite area of uncertainty, implicit in Eisenhower's famous warning at the end of his Presidency against the 'military-industrial complex'. It is impossible to assume coherent national strategies if firms are manipulating programmes for their individual interests; or to base future expectations on political choices if forces at the societal root are paramount and have other goals. Furthermore, it becomes very difficult to know if state action in industry is a remedy for, or a sympton of, industrial weakness. Such ambiguities are familiar to all bureaucratic bargaining.

Conflicts over gains and losses from industry, which are marginal in market interpretations but omnipresent in Marxist ones, have been the third ingredient of divergence from the textbook model. Since advances in production depend on the division of labour and specialization, there are overwhelming odds against their occurring at equal rates as between either persons or localities. The inequalities between different groups which this implies operate even in an autarchic and centrally planned economy dedicated to equal distribution of benefits among the population. Certain categories of producers and regions will be better placed to generate some activities than others, the benefits of these activities will vary and so will peoples' practical (economic or political) access to them. Society and its institutions are usually slow to wake up to the implications. But sooner or later, pressures build up to reduce the privileges that result. When industry, as something new in a commercial-agricultural milieu, first took off, industrialists were relatively free in their decision-making. The same freedom can be detected today in the ability of multinational corporations to operate across frontiers because of the lack of common views or interests between governments on how to regulate them. But sooner or later, the political process catches up on the escaping wanderer, who is gradually shepherded back into the pen.

Historically, of course, the process began almost with industry itself as trade unions tried to moderate the abuse of manufacturers' near-monopoly of authority and incomes. Trade unions have developed to represent workers' claims to better wages, working conditions and job security and to give them a say in policy. Left-wing parties have moved from political to economic goals and there has been an enormous growth in government activities to redistribute incomes. Industrial issues have naturally reflected the course of domestic political struggles. For instance, the nationalizations after the last war corresponded at least in part to a change in the balance of political power in the respective countries.

However, some of the most dramatic conflicts have tended to appear through international markets where competition is keenest. This has proved the case again in contemporary Europe. Industrial policies have come to the top of the political agenda largely for international reasons. As in the past, they arise from competition for relative advantage, in this case in the form of a perception of the problems the growth of multinational corporations and of industrial power in East Asia pose for European economic security and standards of living. They surfaced in the 1960s with the 'technology gap' *vis-à-vis* the American 'multinationals', and then became increasingly fashionable after 1973 when the world-wide slump heightened international competition and dramatized the progress of Japan.

Free trade can give enormous rewards to efficient producers, on the principle that the winner takes all. Though across the board and in the long run this cannot be absolute, in the short run it can eliminate weaker firms and even whole sectors of industry. Since there is no world government responsible for redistributing the benefits of the competitive process—or enjoying the legitimacy to do so—states tend to step in to re-establish balances which they fear may be tilting against their power, their firms or jobs at home. Their judgements are subjective, of course. Industrial policy is easily dramatized as a proxy for political competition. The will of the state to promote industry is in many ways an echo of its traditional preoccupation with territory and survival.

In such conditions, and not surprisingly, a country's position in the hierarchy of industrial power tends to shape its attitude. Economic leaders— firms or countries—tend to preach free trade. They have some prospect of sweeping the board if only they can eliminate the political barriers built up around domestic markets by significant but weaker competitors. Followers, trying to compete with the strongest but conscious of labouring under disadvantages, tend to be interventionist. Even here there are distinctions. Small countries, with inadequate domestic markets of their own, and which rely on access to foreign markets to compete, are much more free-trading than middle-sized industrial powers with home markets large enough to confer on them a degree of choice, apparent or real. The present study, by the mere fact that it deals exclusively with four large economies, but not the largest, concentrates on countries where industrial intervention is more likely to be prominent.

Industrial policies are also influenced by the cyclical variations and long-term evolution of the industrial system. The most relevant cyclical variations are not the short phases of boom or slump usually called the 'business cycle', but longer ones, in principle of fifty years (though in practice with much variation) named after Kondratieff, the Soviet economist who first claimed, in the 1920s, to have detected them. Whether they really exist is controversial, but they provide a widely used hypothesis for considering the evidence.

In boom times, with room for everyone to improve mass living conditions, priorities tend to be couched in terms of the good running of the whole international system (sustaining growth, opening access to markets, etc.). In depressions, competition over shares of markets tends to take much greater precedence because governments think it determines who rakes in the better share of what growth is going. Boom periods tend to free-trade (the mid-Victorian and post-World War II booms), while depressions generate state intervention (1873–96, the 1930s and again today).

However, booms do not all lead to freer trade, nor does protectionism prohibit all booms. The period from 1873 to 1945 tended to sustain protectionism irrespective of boom (1896–1914 and 1924–29) or slump. Was this because throughout these years there was no single economic leader, as Britain was in the early Victorian period or the United States was after World War II? If so, one of the major problems for the world economy, and for industrial policies, may, now as then, be the lack of any country with the interest and power to define and underwrite its formal or informal rules.

The effect of the long-term evolution of the system on industrial policies can best be gathered from the contrast between the present situation and that of a century ago. In the 1890s, firms tended for the most part to be confined to their national base. The main form of international economic transaction was trade in goods. Manufacturers, politically dominant within the leading societies, wanted freedom from domestic controls as well as from foreign rivals in their home markets. Thus the main form protection of the home market took was customs duties limiting imports. These sheltered but did not regulate producers.

By the 1980s, international factors have become far more powerful and devalued traditional protection of domestic markets, at least in European conditions. An enormous increase in the differentiation of products since the last war has devalued price competition, and therefore customs duties, in favour of competition based on technology. The rise of huge so-called 'multinational' firms, which are present as producers in many economies across the world and have turnovers sometimes as large as the GDP of small states, and the partly associated emergence of virtually open international financial markets with sums moving across frontiers which dwarf the scale of the trade in goods mean that exchange rates can no longer function as they did to re-establish competitive balances between countries. The two main instruments of traditional protectionism and adjustment, customs duties on imports and exchange rate variations, have become much weakened.

International forces and markets are now paramount. The standards of competitive power are set in the leading industries by firms' positions on the world market. One famous precept propagated by the Boston Consulting Group asserts that only the first three suppliers of a product *world-wide* (often a highly specialized one) have a real chance of winning glittering prizes. Accordingly, the promotion of national industry has tended to shift from protection by trade measures affecting price, to an attempt by the state to promote firms, especially big ones, through direct support in winning larger market shares, at home (such as by government procurement reserved to domestic suppliers) and in the world (such as by export subsidies). The state has become part of the marketing campaigns of its favoured agents. Protectionism, dedicated merely to sheltering the domestic market, has duly been driven into the shade by a new mercantilism, which can be defined by its central aim to increase national market shares in the world.

1.3 What works?

The debate between free traders and mercantilists into which so many discussions of industrial and trade policy tend to resolve, is built on two antitheses that seem integral to the subject. In the first, free-trade arguments rest their case on the general, that is average, interest; mercantilist ones concentrate on relative losses and gains for individual interests around that average. In the second, free trade asserts the crucial role of the market (i.e. demand) in rewarding and punishing supply; mercantilism is apt to emphasize the gains from long-term strategic planning. Since all of these are inherent to industrial activity, they seem in the last resort not to be contradictions so much as poles that permanently define the field. If so, the relative merits and demerits of different approaches are not to be recognized in terms of abstract principles so much as in the balance sheets of their various practical effects. In this light, there are two vantage points from which industrial policies can be considered: that of the single actor; and that of the international economic system as a whole.

From the individual actor's—normally a country's—point of view, the criterion is how successfully the chosen path leads forward. Some countries, too small to have a choice, have developed very successfully in a virtually free trade environment. But most have begun by import substitution, that is, by protecting the domestic industries they launch, often on state initiative and with state support, against imports from abroad that undercut them at a time when they are young, fragile and uncompetitive.

This does not usually work for long, primarily because the needs of the new industries for inputs and equipment that cannot be competitively produced on the spot, create an immense appetite for imports. Most societies then seem to launch selective export drives, state-subsidized and supported and often accompanied by the continuation of many forms of protectionism (Stecher 1981; Donges & Müller-Ohlsen 1978). This is the classic mercantilist period, dedicated to the increase in the world market shares of the country's firms by state manipulation of the conditions of trade. The idea is to loosen, and as far as possible remove, the balance of payments as the main apparent constraint on domestic growth.

The evidence for the success of such a development strategy is very mixed. Many countries remain both mercantilist and a great deal less developed than they would like. On the other hand, every dominant economy has been protectionist or mercantilist at some point, and Germany before 1939 or Japan have been virtually models of the *genre*. In France or Spain since the war, mercantilism seems to have worked well enough in catching up on known technologies along well-blazed paths during boom periods. But even in France, results have begun to disappoint within sight of the frontiers of contemporary performance. At this point it seems that imitation fails and an indigenous capacity to extend qualitative frontiers must be developed. Countries aspiring to be among the industrial leaders must sooner or later show an acute sense of world markets, an ability of the firm and society to internalize change, and a capacity to innovate. Japan and Germany have always shown a capacity to combine cooperation and competition to an exceptional degree. This has seemed to be a functional equivalent, in their case, for the free-trade disciplines others find more necessary for excellence. From the point of view of the individual country, then, the contrast may be less between intervention and free trade in all circumstances, than between policies that work more or less for different kinds of societies at different stages of development.

The criteria shift partially but significantly when one turns from the individual practitioner's interests to those of the international system as a whole. The traditional assumption has been that what is most efficient in enhancing world growth and meeting (or revealing) effective demand is, on balance, desirable. This has underlain the basic case for free trade as the most elastic form of mutual adjustment between economies at different stages in their evolution and so of the general long-run welfare of the system *in toto*. But free trade's weakness, of course, has been that the winner-takes-all principle is not generally believed to address the problems of the distribution of the benefits of growth between members of the system.

In practice, industrial policies with a strong protectionist or mercantilist cast are tolerable and may even be positive if the practitioner does not account for too large a percentage of world trade; if those policies are associated with high domestic growth (especially in boom periods and the phase of catching-up); and if the country in question buys as much as it earns (usually but not always the case). In these conditions a self-centred industrial policy can also conduce to the general interest.

The same behaviour becomes costly and even intolerable if maintained once a country becomes a major, and still more a dominant, producer. Industrial policy can then reduce other societies' export and growth chances. This is not only a matter of trade. An emphasis on enlarging one's world market shares often implies a deliberate restriction of demand at home. This holds world growth below its potential, a condition from which weaker producers and competitors suffer most. Such an approach can undermine the sense of collective responsibility for a healthy world economy, aggravate the divisions of interest between countries and reduce confidence in common interests to be fulfilled.

The virtue of the overwhelming economic hegemony of the United States in the fifteen to twenty-five years after the war was that American policies provided both the credit for others and the markets in the United States to encourage world growth. As a result of rising prosperity and economic power elsewhere, this functional substitute for world government has broken down. When hegemonies are disputed, there is no guardian of the system possessing some of the power and legitimacy that, whatever their faults, governments enjoy inside the nations. World-wide recession today may be partly rooted in objective factors, such as that growth depends more on innovation in leading economies, which is relatively slow, than on catching-up, which is relatively rapid. But it is also partly due to the spread of power to economies that lay more stress on their world market shares than on sustaining the general system. Like recession, this encourages the political revival of Social Darwinism.

1.4 Levels of analysis

Beyond these complexities integral to industrial policies, analysis faces further ones of application. First, at what level should industrial policies be considered? Are states the proper focus? Might not regions, sectors or firms be more relevant? Second, and more basic still, how can one assess the impact of policies on performance?

Some economic historians have argued that one can be seriously misled by concentrating on the industrial policies of states. This assumes that national frontiers are the natural dividing lines between industrial development and backwardness, whereas historically industry has never spread evenly across the territory of any country and has on more than one occasion straddled frontiers (such as Northern France and Belgium or the Rhine network). The relevant understanding should be of regional factors and contrasts. It has, for instance, been suggested that France's nineteenth-century failure to keep up with Germany and Britain in manufacturing, despite some major assets, may have been linked to the extreme dispersion of her industry in peripheral regions (Pollard 1981, pp. 1–23 and 137–9).

It can also be argued that one should expect policies to resemble one another as much or more across frontiers within a given industrial sector as they do within frontiers between different sectors. In Western Europe there is considerably less difference in modes of intervention inside given sectors than one might suppose from divergent declaratory policies along national lines. The Germans, for instance, despite their emphasis on free trade, have not been immune from nationalizations (shipbuilding), subsidies and trade protection (textiles and steel), nor the promotion by state aid of 'infant' industries (semiconductors, aerospace, nuclear power plant). It is reasonable to conclude that some of these 'anomalies' are due to sectoral features, most obviously those of new branches with prospects of growth but lacking the scale to compete, or of old ones in socially painful decline.

Clearly, regional and sectoral influences—the latter the theme of the companion volume to this book (Shepherd, Duchêne and Saunders 1983)—have to be taken into account. But that book itself concluded that today national influences on policy were particularly strong. Contrasts in performance across the board between the various countries have also been striking. Germany, with some of the world's highest unit labour costs, is not just one of the world's largest exporters of capital goods but much more unexpectedly the second highest exporter of textiles as well (GATT 1985,

Table A15). France has gradually widened the range of her industries from an initially weak post-war position, but remains a fragile competitor on world markets. In Britain there has been a steady weakening in the competitive strength of what appeared to be a powerful industry after the war. Italian manufacturing has so far successfully concentrated in the labour-intensive end of the range and this tendency, far from fading in the past decade, seems to have become more marked. National patterns are not the only dimension of industrial policy and performance, but they are important and persist.

This leads into the basic difficulty of assessing the importance of industrial policies for actual industrial performance. At the most elementary level, are they cause or effect? There is evidence that policies do play a part in the apparently systematic differences between countries. Relatively low limits of government tolerance of subsidy do seem to be one reason why German textiles and steel adapted faster to changing conditions in the 1970s than counterparts in other European Community countries. But this does not explain why Japan, with very high barriers to imports of manufactures, has proved vastly more dynamic still. Nor is it possible to take at face value the claim of today's Germans to have outclassed post-war Britain because they practise free trade. Germany also outpaced Britain from the 1870s to 1931, when she was much the more protectionist of the two. Nor does it tell us why the United States, which has beaten the drum since the war so much for free trade, is an international leader mainly in sectors where the impetus has come from federal defence and space programmes.

In these conditions, declaratory industrial policies do not necessarily tell one very much. It follows either that policies which are, or have been, placed in the foreground are not as significant as they seem and others may be more appropriate and active, or that the milieu in which the policies are applied is for some reason more responsive in some cases than others.

In practice, the evidence suggests each of these possibilities may be relevant. The first is the justification for looking beneath the declaratory surface at national industrial policies, and comparing them, to see if there is a level at which different policies help to explain performance. The second possibility, though equally important, is a particularly difficult one to test. Industry is almost as broad as society itself. It is impossible to ignore the decision-making—that is societal—milieux in which industrial activities are undertaken. Yet the chains of cause and effect in this field are notoriously full of uncertainties and virtually incomputable. The tracing of links between performance and society, or culture in the broadest sense, is strewn with traps even for the wary. Hence the epigraphs to this chapter. And yet, given the nature of the case, it cannot suffice to pretend reality is confined to what is easily measured. The hinterland cannot be left out of the picture to which it acts not just as the frame but as an active influence.

References

Adams, H. (1928), *The Education of Henry Adams: an Autobiography*, Boston, Mass., Houghton Mifflin.

Chandler, A. (1977), *The Visible Hand*, Cambridge, Mass., Belknap Press.

Donges, J.B. and Müller-Ohlsen, L. (1978), *Aussenwirtschaftsstrategien und Industrialisierung in Entwicklungsländern*, Kieler Studien 157, Institut für Weltwirtschaft, Kiel.

GATT (1985), *International Trade 1984/85*, General Agreement on Tariffs and Trade, Geneva.

Goh Keng-Swee (1983), 'Public administration and economic development in LDCs', *World Economy*, Vol. 6, September (quoting *Japan Times*, 5 May 1977).

Lüthy, H. (1955), *The State of France*, London, Secker.

Olson, M. (1982), *The Rise and Decline of Nations: Economic Growth, Stagflation and Social Rigidities*, New Haven, Conn., Yale University Press.

Perkin, H. (1985), *Origins of Modern English Society*, Ark Paperback (1st edn, 1969), London, Routledge.

Pollard, S. (1981), *Peaceful Conquest: the Industrialization of Europe 1760–1970*, Oxford, Oxford University Press.

Saunders, C., ed. (1981), *The Political Economy of New and Old Industrial Countries*, London, Butterworths.

Shepherd, G., Duchêne, F. and Saunders, C., eds (1983), *Europe's Industries: Public and Private Strategies for Change*, London, Frances Pinter.

Stecher, B. (1981), 'The Role of Economic Policies' in Saunders, ed., 1981, op. cit.

Vernon, R.G. (1966), 'International Investment and International Trade in the Product Cycle', *Quarterly Journal of Economics*, Vol. 80, No. 2, May.

2 Western Europe: A family of contrasts

François Duchêne and Geoffrey Shepherd

Until 1939, and because the United States stood aside, world politics and economic competition still focused on European great powers. Europeans were, and by historic habit are, geared to competitive comparisons among themselves.

Europe's hegemony ended in rubble in 1945. During the 1950s, economic 'miracles' conveyed surprise that achievement was still possible in 'the old world'. The hope that, through European integration, the gap with the United States might be narrowed was heady but not wholly self-assured. When the new international economy began to break in on the region in the 1960s, the hint that the 'technology' gap across the Atlantic might instead be widening touched a raw nerve. So, later, did finding that Japan was closing gaps faster than Europe. Apparently third in the trilateral industrial competition of the slump since 1973, Europeans have agreed on the vital need to 'readjust', above all in manufacturing, with a tinge of 'Euro-pessimism' about succeeding. Post-war experience tends to underline the common predicament of Europeans, rather than the differences.

As a result, old rivalries and new resemblances are inextricably woven into comparisons of the major states of Western Europe.

2.1 Industry and power

Since manufacturing became the sinews of political power, the industrial history of Europe has been the yardstick of her rivalries. In the late eighteenth century, Britain rose to hegemony as the world's first industrial state. From 1870 onwards, the United States and Germany gradually overhauled her. France, still in Napoleon's day a demographic and military giant, was never an industrial front-runner. She paid for it at the hands of Germany between 1870 and 1945. Italy was virtually a pre-industrial economy till the turn of the century. Like France, she has fully industrialized only since the war.

Britain was much the biggest manufacturer in Europe in 1900 and ahead of Germany even as late as 1959 (OEEC 1960, p. 4, Table C). Germany's pre-war strength, however, was in the capital goods industries, while the British

Table 2.1.   Manufacturing in France, Germany, Italy, the United Kingdom and the United States, 1901–1985

Country	Growth in selected periods (base year in each column = 100)				Gross value added in manufacturing[‡] (Factor cost) (Germany = 100)	
	Booms 1901–29 (17 yrs)*	2 Wars + 1930–40s (32 yrs)[†]	Postwar 1950–85 (35 yrs)[‡]	1901–85 (84 yrs)	1970	1984
France	212	105	401	893	57	66
Germany	256	92	566	1,333	100	100
Italy	224	161	652	2,351	44	53
United Kingdom	155	194	217	653	57	56
United States[§]	234	279	363	2,369		

* 1901–13 and 1924–9.

† 1913–24 and 1929–50. Each war includes reconstruction.

‡ Current market prices and exchange rates.

§ Industry excluding construction but including water, gas, electricity. Includes construction for Italy and the United States, 1955–64.

Sources: OEEC 1960, Tables C and 4; OECD 1966, *Main Economic Indicators* (i) *Historical Series 1955–64* & 1984, *1964–83*; (ii) November 1986: Eurostat 1986a and 1986b.

relied more on older sectors like textiles (Musson 1978, pp. 273–96). This qualitative gap opened up after the 1950s into a quantitative one.

Table 2.1 shows some dramatic differences among the Four in the long-term rates of growth of manufacturing this century. Italy, above all, has grown fast, though no faster than the United States. By their standards, Germany's record is moderate. France and especially Britain have grown comparatively slowly. France has performed better than Britain because, in good years, she almost paced Italy and Germany. Britain did not. The two wars in effect deprived Germany and France, unlike Britain and Italy, of a full generation of growth. Germany has duly taken over leadership of the group, and France second place, from a Britain whose relative decline has been particularly steep since 1960. Britain is now roughly at the level of Italy, some years marginally ahead in the lists and some behind, depending on the exchange rates. Italy started so far down the scale that she is still one of the two smallest of the Four, and part of her progress has consisted of catching up, but in retrospect it is very impressive. Table 2.1 also shows a tendency for Germany's growth to slow down since 1970, relatively as well as absolutely.

Other comparisons also tend to confirm the first impressions. First, patterns of manufacturing show Germany in a class of her own in what one might call the core sectors of industrial chemicals and engineering. In these, in 1981, she produced about 44 per cent of the output (gross value added) of

Table 2.2. Labour productivity in manufacturing

Country	Output per man-hour (1973 $ PPP, US = 100)		Gross value added (factor cost) 1981 (ECU† 000s)
	1973	*1981*	
France	56	70	22.4
Germany	66	82	21.5
Italy	54	62	17.7
United Kingdom	35	37	18.9
EEC (10)			20.6
Japan	50	71	

* PPP = Purchasing Power Parities.
† ECU = EEC's European Currency Unit (of account).
Sources: A.D. Roy, 'Labour Productivity in 1980: An Internatonal Comparison', *National Institute Economic Review*, August 1982, Table 8 (for output) and Eurostat 1986a (for gross value added).

the Four, that is not much less than the other three put together. In 'traditional' sectors (along with 'other transport', including aerospace), she was far less dominant, with 30 per cent of the collective output. In 1981 over a quarter of Italy's *official* manufacturing employment was in the 'traditional' clothing, textile and leather goods sectors, where wages are low (against about a tenth in France and Germany), and Britain led in the food, drink and tobacco industry, where wages are fairly high. France was weak in mechanical, but fairly strong in electrical, engineering and, like Britain, rather specialized in aerospace (Eurostat 1986a, pp. 38–49; Eurostat 1986b, pp. 64–164).

Second, for reasons partly related to the structures just hinted at, Germany and France lead in labour productivity. Table 2.2 gives different estimates, one by the Commission of the European Community (EC) using ordinary exchange rates, the other by A. Roy, taking into account different price relationships in the four countries (purchasing power parities). The EC statistics put Germany and France virtually abreast in the lead and Britain and Italy 15–20 per cent behind, both on average and in most branches. Roy puts Germany first, with France 15–20 per cent behind. Both were closing the gap with the United States in the 1970s, but Japan was closing it half as fast again. Italy, equal to France in 1970, lagged thereafter, and Britain even more, at a level below half that of Germany.

Third, in 1983, Germany, along with Switzerland and Sweden, had levels of industry-financed R & D, both per head of population and relative to value added in manufacturing, about twice as high as Britain or France and three to four times as high as Italy. Germany's share of patenting in the United States in 1985 was three times that of Britain and France and seven times that of Italy (Patel and Pavitt 1986, Table 10). Growth rates of industry-financed R & D equalled Germany's in France and Italy between

Table 2.3.   Percentage distribution of world exports of manufactures (including intra-EEC trade) in 1913, 1937, 1973 and 1984

Year	US	Japan	UK	Germany	France	Italy	Others
1913	12.6	2.4	29.9	26.5	12.9	15.7	
1937	19.6	7.2	22.4	22.4	6.4	3.6	28.4
1973	12.9	10.0	7.4	17.4	7.5	5.4	39.4
1984	12.5	14.4	5.5	12.9	6.1	5.5	43.1

Sources: 1913 and 1937—Musson 1978, p. 265; Italy derived from Woytinski and Woytinski 1955, p. 123. 1984—GATT 1985, Tables A8 and 34—40; OECD 1985.

1967 and 1983 but not in Britain. Though it is tricky to draw conclusions from such measurements, the implication of this and other evidence is that Germany's technological strength is substantially greater than that of any of the other Three.

Fourth. production hierarchies tend to be reflected in foreign trade. Paradoxically, the outstanding message of Table 2.3 is that the 'minor' exporters, who hardly counted in 1913, now make a major impact on world trade in manufactures. Whereas Germany, Britain and the United States still accounted for nearly two-thirds of world manufactured exports in 1937, the leaders in 1984, Japan, Germany and the United States, barely represented two-fifths. Britain and Germany were the world's leading exporters of manufactures in 1937. After the war, the United States replaced them, then was overhauled by Germany in 1971, which gave way in turn to Japan in 1984.

New trends may be implicit in developments since 1973. Germany, even more than Britain and France (in that order), has lost world market shares in manufactures in recession. But despite these signs of weakening, she has remained, since the early 1950s, the one Western European country with almost continuous balance of trade surpluses. She is much the largest European exporter of engineering and high technology products. Unit values of her exports have been higher than those of France, let alone Britain (NEDO 1977, Table 1). Britain has fallen back into the second rank of traders, roughly on a par with France and Italy. Italy alone, though at first the smallest of the Four, has resisted the European trend and kept her world export share fully intact since 1973. Interestingly, she has done so despite the fact that her world market shares in 'high technology' exports are by far the smallest of any of the Four (see Table 2.10).

Several points emerge from these varied measurements. One is Germany's leadership in Europe, as manufacturer and exporter, but with a marked reverse in world market shares from 1973 to 1984. A second has been the spectacular British decline since the war. Yet in many ways the most remarkable and certainly the most underrated development has been the progress of Italy. Her industrial record this century should warn observers against the quite unwarranted neglect from which she often suffers in European comparisons.

2.2 Paths to industrial society

The differences between the four countries in rates of development are matched by the diversity of routes they have taken to enter modern society. Their idiosyncratic paths could well be the most important clue to their varied industrial policies and performances.

Britain, as the first-comer to factories, invented free-trade ideas, modern trades unions and an urban-centred world. There were a smaller proportion of people working on the land in Britain in 1851 than a century later in Germany, let alone France and Italy (Best 1971, p. 99). Many observers have suspected that her recent difficulties have been part of the price of pioneering industrial society.

Germany grew up, as an industrial power, in the shadow of Britain. There was an institutional input into her industrialization which reflected both the authoritarian traditions of the Prussian state and the need to fend off competition from dominant British exporters. Germany is associated with the first infant industry arguments for protection, the first close association of science and education with manufacturing, partly through the banks the first modern cartels and, in the 1880s, the first social insurance. It adds up in effect to an alternative model of development.

Unlike Britain and Germany, France and Italy have never known a period of industrial leadership. They were partially industrialized in 1945, but France had over a third, and Italy 45 per cent, of the working population still on the land. Even off it, society was an ocean of small shops, artisans and tiny businesses with only a few archipelagos of factories here and there. But France was substantially wealthier than Italy. Though both had a 'dual' economy, France lacked Italy's extreme contrast between the developed North and pre-industrial South. Property ownership was much more widely distributed, so that whereas Italy had a large landless rural proletariat, especially in the South, France's hallmark was the *petite bourgeoisie*. And whereas Italy, late in uniting and, like Belgium, long overshadowed by foreign masters, had a weak administration, France had one of Europe's most centralized states and civil services outside Russia.

2.3 Family resemblances

Thus, the contrasts between the Four in performance and in evolution have been, and are, very substantial. Yet the paradox, at this stage in a long and turbulent history, is that they are probably more equal to each other, in purely material terms, than they have ever been before or than four important neighbours are anywhere else today. This is not quite an accident. Until Germany's partition in 1945, it could not have been the case.

First, they are neighbours with almost equal populations, ranging from 55 million (France) to 61 million (West Germany) and so have about half the numbers of Japan and a quarter those of the United States. Demographically, they are more nearly static than any other region, even though all industrial societies are ageing. Population in West Germany has actually been declining by some 200,000 a year since 1981.

Second, Western Europe has negligible reserves of economic raw materials other than energy. Japan is still worse off and, in both cases, lack of them makes a sharp contrast with the superpowers. Europe and Japan depend on the capacity to import fuels and raw materials. This gives special significance to being competitive in industrial exports. The four are, with Japan and the United State, the leading exporters of manufactures, and the European Community is the biggest trading entity in the world, though if one excludes trade within regions, Japan has become a substantially larger exporter of manufacturers than either Western Europe or North America! (GATT 1985, Tables A36–7).

Third, all four are also bunched together in the world 'league tables' for manufacturing output, from the fourth rank (Germany, behind the United States, Japan and the Soviet Union) to the seventh (Italy or Britain). They are all major producers, but not in the class of the largest, partly because of smaller area and populations, and perhaps, in comparison with Japan, for qualitative reasons as well.

Fourth, in all four countries there has been a decisive shift of manpower since the war out of agriculture. Britain has long had one of the world's lowest proportions of people on the land (under 3 per cent of the working population), but now even in Italy it has fallen under 12 per cent, and in France 8 per cent. There is no longer the old distinction between industrial Britain and Germany, and semi-agricultural France and Italy. All now are essentially urban. That does not mean they are only industrial. In fact, services now account for between 50 and 60 per cent of all employment.

Fifth, all Four have become mass high-consumption societies since the war. Though Germany has a national income about half to three-quarters larger than that of Britain or Italy, the differences are much smaller when domestic purchasing powers and population are taken into account. The gap between top and bottom is then less than 30 per cent per head (*Financial Times*, 10 February 1987) and may be less than 15 per cent if Italy's 'black' economy really does amount to 20 per cent of the recorded one (Deaglio 1985).[1] These material similarities are significant shaping influences, reinforced by important parallels in the societal choices made by the Four since 1945. Further, the rapid emergence of a world economy which provides external points of comparisons has brought out the close family

Table 2.4. University students as a percentage of those taking subjects of direct relevance to industry, and numbers of scientists and engineers per 10,000 in the labour force in 1976/77 in EEC, United States and Japan

Country	Students as % of 19–24 age-group	% of students relevant to industry 1976*	Scientists engineers per 10,000 in labour force 1977
United States	56	21	57
Japan	33	20	50
EEC	24	26	
Germany			41
United Kingdom			31[†]
France			30[‡]

* Commerce, business administration, natural sciences, mathematics, computer sciences and engineering.
† 1975
‡ 1976
Source: Commission of the European Communities, *The Competitiveness of European Community Industry*, III/387/82, Brussels 1982, pp. 47–9, from UNESCO *Yearbook* and US National Science Board, *Science Indicators*, 1978.

resemblances between Europeans of which they themselves have been perhaps least conscious.

2.4 Mixed economy and welfare state

After the war the Western European countries adopted various types of 'social democratic' systems combining a market orientation with strong state responsibility for social welfare. Their mutual likeness, as well as difference from other countries, can most simply be gauged by the part of the national product consumed or redistributed by public budgets. Since 1960 this has risen from between 30 (Italy) and 35 per cent (France) to between 45 (Britain) and 58 per cent (Italy) in 1985 among the Four, as against 29 to 32 per cent from 1960 to 1985 in the United States (where defence spending is proportionately larger) and 19 to 29 per cent in Japan (*European Economy* 1986, Table 46; de Montbrial 1986, pp. 430–43). In the Four countries in 1985, 50 (Italy) to 56 per cent (Britain) of the adult population received their main income from the state, against 42 per cent in the United States (Rose 1985). The welfare state was seen as a strength in the boom years and it may even have secured social peace in the current slump. But it has led since 1973 to fears that governments are redistributing too much from the productive to the consuming sectors of society for Europe to earn a rising standard of living in the world.

It may be significant that the one area of social policy where Japan and the

United States lead Western Europe is that most closely related to output: namely, education, especially of technologists and scientists. The European population in higher education, though enormous by pre-war standards, is markedly lower than in the United States (World Bank), and as regards engineers, Japan (Table 2.4), though the differences are not quite as stark as they are sometimes painted.

However, to emphasise the social side of the post-war European system is to gloss over other industrially significant trends with related historic roots. The balances of power inside the countries differ, but in all four countries decision-making structures have become highly corporatist as a result of the growth in the scale of government, manufacturing and labour unions alike.

In the Four, the state has become the biggest producer of manufactures and the largest customer for them. About 9 per cent of the industrial labour force work in state-owned firms in Germany, 12 per cent in Britain and Italy, and (since 1983) as much as 22 per cent in France (Bellon Chevalier 1983, p. 38). More important still, the state buys, directly or indirectly, massive quantities of defence, electrical power generating, communications and other equipment, all of them crucial to manufacturing and often to the national level of 'high' technology.

The average size of firms and plant has grown throughout the past century at least till the early 1970s. Since then the political costs of size, along with the influence of micro-electronics in making smaller-scale production competitive in a number of lines, have halted the trend. Yet many industrial sectors are now characterized in each country by oligopoly or even near-monopoly. In Germany and Britain nearly 45 per cent of the workforce are concentrated in plant with over 500 employees. Italy, with only 13 per cent of the workforce in such plant, comes at the other extreme. Small firms are particularly numerous there and were favoured, for varying reasons, right across the political spectrum, even in the 1950s (see Ch. 5, below) when, in most of Europe, big seemed beautiful and small benighted. Interestingly, the Italian structure in this closely resembles the Japanese, and in both cases is no doubt a reminder of pre-industrial society not deeply buried in the past. Britain, on the other hand, has under 10 per cent of the workforce in plant employing less than 50 people (Samek Lodovici 1986, Tables 25–6).[2]

Finally, labour has also become more organized, though there have been major differences between Britain and Germany, where trade unions have been powerful throughout the post-war period; Italy, where they were weak at first, then strong and militant in the 1970s; and France, where they have gained the initiative only in brief but potent flare-ups as in 1968.

2.5 Economic 'miracles' and integration

Corporatism of this kind tends to underline national separateness because it rests on the institutional traditions and balances between groups specific to each society. Yet the most spectacular development since the war in Western Europe has probably been the movement to regional integration.

The original motives for this were mostly political. The war had destroyed Europe's power and placed it under the tutelage of the superpowers. European integration was partly an attempt to outgrow the Franco-German rivalries which precipitated ruin in 1945, and partly an effort to mobilize the material resources of the region to equal the superpowers. Today's European Community of twelve member states has a larger population than the United States and, like the United States, about a fifth of the world's industrial capacity.

Political motives were reinforced, in the case of the key European achievement, the Common Market, established from 1959 to 1969, by the 'miracles' of economic revival and rapid growth of the 1950s. In themselves these were still primarily national. Economies were still relatively self-sufficient and trade grew no faster than total wealth. Protection and cartelization of domestic markets were frequent. But there was strong growth fed by an apparently insatiable demand and (except in Germany) expansionary macroeconomic policies. As industry took off, controls gradually relaxed. Growth also led to increasing preoccupation with trade and, under US influence, with large markets. If Europe could only integrate her many national markets into one, her manufacturers, benefiting from continental 'economies of scale', might even match the United States. The European Common Market, set up partly for political reasons, was a product also of this economic logic. It seemed the natural extension of the domestic 'miracles', pointing to new achievements on a continuing upward trend.

The Common Market has undoubtedly encouraged economic integration in Western Europe. Its formation has led to industrial trade free of tariff restrictions for all the twenty or so non-Communist countries of the region and their 400 million inhabitants, irrespective of whether they are members of the Community or not. (Even East Germany, Yugoslavia and Israel have virtually free access for manufactures to the Common Market.) Trade between the Community states has grown about twice as fast as trade with the rest of the world. Western Europe's regional market, which accounted for 51 per cent of the exports of ten EC countries in 1958, took as much as 66 per cent by 1984 (*European Economy* 1986, Table 35). This has stimulated a greater division of labour in which the more efficient firms have enlarged their market shares. Tariffs have also been drastically cut towards the rest of the world, partly by the averaging process of the customs union itself, which irons out exceptionally protective duties, and partly as a result of the four major international tariff cutting negotiations since the EEC was mooted (the Geneva, Dillon, Kennedy and Tokyo 'Rounds' from 1956 to 1979). The average level of tariffs of industrial countries has fallen from about 40 per cent in the mid-1930s to between 4 per cent and 8 per cent now (Noguès, Olechowski and Winters 1986, p. 1).

All this has been reflected in great increases in trade, and changes in

Table 2.5.   Trade intensity ratios from 1899 to 1983 (%) for the United Kingdom, France, Germany, Italy*, the United States and Japan

Year	France I/C	France E/P	Germany[†] I/C	Germany[†] E/P	UK I/C	UK E/P	US[‡] I/C	US[‡] E/P	Japan I/C	Japan E/P
1899[§]	12	33	16	31	16	42	3	5	30	25
1913	13	26	10	31	17	42	3	5	34	40
1929	9	25	7	27	16	37	2	6	21	29
1937	7	12	3	15	10	21	2	5	11	40
1950	7	23	4	13	4	23	2	5	3	29
1959	6	18	7	23	6	19	3	4	4	23
1960	(9)	(15)	(12)	(20)	(10)	(15)	(3)	(4)	(6)	(10)
1970	16	17	19	26	16	18	5	6	5	10
1983	26	27	35	43	29	26	10	8	5	14

Notes: I/C = share of imports in consumption (sales + imports − exports) × 100. E/P = share of exports in sales × 100.
   * Italy, *1970:* I/C − 16; E/P − 19. *1983:* I/C − 31; E/P − 38. No other figures available.
   † From 1899 to 1937 the figures refer to West Germany's pre-1939 borders.
   ‡ Figures for North America, i.e. intra-regional trade included.
   § From 1899 to 1959 consumption (C) includes goods consumed at home and in exports.
   ( ) Figures in parentheses are estimates.
Sources: Figures for 1899 to 1959 from Alfred Maizels, *Industrial Growth and World Trade*, Cambridge, Cambridge University Press, 1963, pp. 163, 223. 1970–1983 figures are calculated from the OECD's Comparative Trade and Production Database (see D. Blades and W. Simpson, *The OECD Comparative Trade and Production Database*, Economics and Statistics Department Working Papers No. 18, Paris, OECD, 1985; and A. Brodin and D. Blades, *The OECD Comparative Trade and Production Data Base 1970–1983*, Department of Economics and Statistics Working Papers, No. 31, Paris, OECD, 1986); figures for 1960 are estimated by linking figures from various national sources to the 1970 OECD figures.

trading patterns, since the Common Market was launched. For the three European countries in Table 2.5, import propensities have risen not only against the protectionist years from 1920 to 1959 but even against 1899, and so have those for exports, though not to the peak levels before 1914. The United States shows similar tendencies at a far lower level of intensity. But Japan, once hugely involved in trade relative to her size, now resembles Germany in the inter-war years, with large exports but low imports of manufactures. Compared to that, the European figures suggest some loss of competitiveness, but also a much fuller division of labour than in the past.

This is not due just to the intense trade within Western Europe, which takes up two-thirds of the total. Imports from the rest of the world were equivalent in 1980 to about 14 per cent of the consumption of manufactures of the four big EC countries and Benelux, against 9 per cent for the United States and only 6 per cent for Japan.

Table 2.6. Total spending of public administrations and compensation of employees as percentages of GDP in France, West Germany, Italy and the United Kingdom in 1960 and 1973

Item	Year	France	Germany	Italy	UK
			(% of Gross Domestic Product)		
Spending of public administrations	1960	35	33	30	32
	1973	39	42	38	38
Compensation of employees	1960	47	44	42	60
	1973	55	50	53	60

Sources: Eurostat (1976), *National Accounts ESA 1960–1975*, Statistical Office of the European Communities, Luxembourg, pp. 6 and 10; *European Economy* (1986), Commission of the European Communities, July, Brussels, Table 46.

2.6   Internationalization on the crest of the boom

To the extent that rising trade in the EC has increased specialization, it has implied real economic integration. Yet, even though the 1960s reached the crest of the boom, they did not fulfil the European vision. They failed to generate a European economic union out of the customs union they were creating, or firms for which the Common Market was a true domestic base. European perceptions, tied to domestic power networks and constituencies, remained firmly national.

Paradoxically, this was reinforced by the major new industrial factor of the 1960s: the annunciation of today's world economic and industrial order. It came in the form of US corporations, attracted to investment in the booming Common Market. This produced a perception, strongest in France, of a 'technology gap' between European firms and US 'multi-nationals'—in part in scale and technology, and in part in organization, financial power and global reach. Europeans began to fear for the first time since the 'economic miracles' that far from catching up, they might be falling behind. Though industrial policies had of course been practised before, it was now they entered the centre stage of political awareness. The British, French and German governments all began to subsidize and nuture their own 'high technology' industries (mainly in aerospace, nuclear power and micro-electronics), if necessary by forced mergers to make bigger firms. Outside reluctant cooperation in aerospace, there was precious little 'European' about any of these moves. Italy, possible because of the 'crisis of large organizations' from which she was beginning to suffer, was hardly involved in this phase of nationalism.

The pan-West European trend, if there was one, was to more social democracy, once full employment was achieved even in Germany and Italy around 1960. Rapid growth was used to redistribute incomes to under-privileged social groups and regions (Table 2.6). Public spending and labour incomes rose relative to national product,[3] while corporate profits, for various reasons, began to fall (Hill 1979).

After 1968, the semi-revolutionary year of student riots and factory strikes, the early 1970s were economically turbulent, with inflation rising rapidly in all the Four. It was one of many symptoms of economic and social strains in the long post-war boom approaching a climax and an end. The number of employed in manufacturing now peaked in Britain and Germany —before and not after, the first energy crisis of 1973–4 (CSO, annual; US Department of Commerce, quarterly)—and this added to the difficulties of the subsequent recession.

2.7 Recession breeds mercantilism

The strains of the end of the boom were compounded by the energy crisis of 1973–74 which opened the long and still continuing recession. They were intensified by further progress to a world economy—the rise of competition from Japan and the 'newly industrializing countries' (NICs), not all East Asian. Europe has lost competitive power in electronics, electrical products and motorcars as well as traditional items like steel and clothing, balanced only by gains in aerospace and agro-business (Jacquemin and Sapir, 1987).

The effects have been particularly marked in manufacturing, the sector most exposed to world trade and which has taken the bulk of the loss in employment. Between 1970 and 1984 the four European countries lost 7.6

Table 2.7.　Growth of output and employment, manufacturing, 1970–85*

Country	Output (1)	Employment (2)	Productivity† (3)
France	127	85	190
Germany	127	83	173
Italy	134	91	174
United Kingdom	101	58	156
United States	160	100	168
Japan	189	107	206

* Percentages, 1970 = 100.
† Output per person-hour.
Sources: (1) OECD, *Main Economic Indicators: Historical Statistics 1960–79*, Paris, 1980, and *Indicators of Industrial Activity*, quarterly, Paris, various issues. (2) UK Central Statistical Office, *Annual Abstract of Statistics*, various issues; and US Department of Commerce, *International Economic Indicators*, quarterly, various issues; (3) *National Institute Economic Review* London, various issues.

Table 2.8.   Industrial countries' NTBs, by product category, 1983

Country	Textiles	Steel	Elec. Eng'g	Vehicles	Other mfrs
Coverage ('own imports')					
EEC	52.0	52.6	13.4	15.3	10.3
France	48.4	73.9	41.7	42.9	19.1
Germany	57.0	53.5	6.8	52.0	6.6
Italy	37.2	48.6	7.1	10.2	2.6
United Kingdom	59.6	42.1	12.7	44.3	6.7
United States	57.0	37.7	5.2	34.2	6.1
Japan	11.8	0.0	0.0	0.0	7.7
Frequency					
EEC	45.2	23.4	5.6	9.8	2.6
France	56.0	56.6	31.7	41.2	7.0
Germany	43.9	19.5	0.7	1.4	1.5
Italy	38.4	21.2	1.0	3.6	1.0
United Kingdom	59.8	16.9	1.6	1.7	0.9
United States	30.8	22.8	0.6	1.3	1.6
Japan	14.8	0.0	0.0	0.0	2.8

Source: Noguès, Olechowski and Winters, 1986, pp. 43, 45.

million jobs in manufacturing, or 24 per cent of those at the peak—over half of them in the United Kingdom (Table 2.7). Europe's record has compared poorly for production and employment with the United States and above all Japan.

The response has been a revival of protectionism. It has not been achieved by restoring high tariffs. That approach has been blocked by the General Agreement on Tariffs and Trade (GATT) and by the Common Market itself. In any case, the Europeans have become too dependent on world markets to fall back on purely national ones. Accordingly, states have tried to help their firms expand market shares abroad, while protecting home markets by more covert means. Trade inside the Common Market rose more than twice as fast as exports to the rest of the world till 1973, but between 1973 and 1984 exports to the world rose 10 per cent faster. As for protection, three types of measures have been, and still are, especially significant.

(i)   *Non-tariff barriers* (NTBs—Table 2.8) are protean and virtually impossible to pin down. A World Bank study (Noguès, Olechowski and Winters 1986) has tried to calculate the amount of trade they affect, gauged against countries' own imports and world trade in the relevant categories ('coverage'), and the number of items involved ('frequency'), but without being able to measure the intensity of impact. The authors cover the more formal restraints (like quotas) but not the most covert (such as administrative guidance) and so may well underrate NTBs' force. Clearly, textiles and

Table 2.9. Industrial subsidies as percentages of industrial value added, 1970–85

Year	France A	France B	Germany A	Germany B	Italy	UK A	UK B
1970–4 av.	2.0		1.5	2.9*	3.2	2.4	
1974–9 av.	2.2	3.0†	1.4	4.1†	4.9	3.7	5.7‡
1980		3.0	1.6	4.0	6.8	4.3	7.4
1981		6.0		4.0	6.1	5.3	7.8
1982				3.9	8.3	4.6	
1983				4.0	10.0	2.9	
1984				4.2	8.9	2.4	
1985				4.1			

Notes: For notes and sources, see note 4 at end of chapter.
* 1973–4.
† 1979.
‡ 1976–9.

steel are much protected in Europe and the United States and, to a lesser extent, vehicles in Europe, especially France. France also stands out in electrical engineering. If Japan prevents entry by NTBs, they are not the ones chosen here. Between 1981 and 1983 (the slump after the second energy crisis), NTBs continued to spread.

(ii) All four governments *subsidize* manufacturing in a wide range of ways, including capital funding, R & D support, export credits, regional aid and so on and this seems to have increased with recession since 1973. The figures in Table 2.9 are national, and even where the bases seem to relate to the same categories of expenditure, cross-country comparisons are suspect. The figures should be read mainly for trends within each country. The steep increases in Italian and French, and decreases in British, subsidies in the early 1980s are striking, as is the apparent steadiness of German ones in the past decade. On the whole, the rates seem moderate compared to effective tariff protection, which reached about 9 per cent of value added in Germany in the early 1980s (see Ch. 3, below) and cannot be very different for other European Community countries. But, of course, one set of measures comes on top of the other, and aggregates do not convey the focused impact of selective measures, nor of contrasts such as those between the export credits of Britain, France, Japan (and probably Italy) which applied to between 30 and 40 per cent of exports in 1980 and the 8 per cent of Germany or 13 per cent of the United States (David 1982, p. 141; see Ch. 5, below).

(iii) *Public procurement* is probably the tightest of all forms of protection. Governments tend to reserve public markets to their own 'national champions' carrying the flag in world competition. The basic arguments are that taxpayers' money should not be used to help foreigners undermine national production and employment, and that supporting important indigenous sectors is vital to staying the course with the world's leaders. Whatever the economic wisdom of the case, its political force is obvious. So is that of firms 'at court' profiting from the government-industrial complex, and of labour unions concerned for sheltered employment. The markets involved (armaments, aerospace, telecommunications, electrical, including nuclear, power, rail and sometimes offshore oil equipment, and so on) are often large and of special significance for 'high technology' industries. In 1980 public purchasing amounted to 9 per cent of gross industrial product in France (Bellon and Chevalier 1983, p. 43), which means much more for the sectors primarily affected (p. 93). In Germany it came to some 20 per cent of the production value of the domestic investment goods industries (Horn, Institut für Weltwirtschaft, Kiel, Input–Output Tables). In Britain in 1981 about 13 per cent of engineering output was accounted for by defence orders alone, and the trend has been rising for over a decade.[5] Public procurement has almost certainly been a more pervasive instrument of direction of industry than nationalization. Plausibly, the Common Market is virtually non-existent for a fifth of the engineering and electronic core of manufacturing, including much that is presumed to matter most for the future.

All these forms of trade restriction, which are strictly national, have proved handicaps to European economic integration as well as to imports from outside the region. Quotas on imports from third countries can imply market sharing within the EC. For steel, since 1977, they have turned into a straight EC cartel with national production quotas. State subsidies, public purchases and forced government mergers of firms also imply strong national biases in the long-term strategies of firms and entire sectors of manufacturing.[6]

The main aim of these mercantilist manoeuvres has, of course, been to correct Europe's gradual loss of competitive power on world markets (see Table 2.3). The main fear has been Japan's rapid rise as an exporter of high technology. Even Germany has been losing ground (Tables 2.10–11). In 1984, however, the Four together still had larger world market shares in high technology exports than the United States or Japan.

After the second energy crisis of 1979–80, which Germany weathered less well than Japan, the universal talk of 'restructuring' industry to adjust to new technologies and world markets took on a special tone in Europe. 'Europessimism' expressed fears that societal obstacles to adjustment and innovation raised too many handicaps to competition with both the United States and Japan ahead, and with the NICs surging forward from the rear. There was a major debate on how to restructure industry. Some argued that output must be sustained by macro-economic policies boosting demand. Without that, there would be too few markets for new industrial branches to grow, and unemployment would make the labour unions resist change.

Table 2.10. Comparative changes in world export shares of technology-intensive products*

Country	1965	1975	1984
United States	27.5	24.5	25.2
Japan	7.3	11.6	20.2
France	7.3	8.4	7.7
Germany	16.9	16.8	14.5
United Kingdom	12.0	9.6	8.5
Italy			3.6

* Technology-intensive products are defined as those for which R & D expenditures exceed 2.36 per cent of value added.
Sources: Except for Italy, National Science Foundation, US, *International Science and Technology Update*, 1986, quoted in Kaldor, Sharp and Walker 1986. For Italy, OECD, *Statistical Bulletins of Foreign Trade. Series C, Trade by Commodities, 1984*, Paris, 1985, on basis of list of 'high technology' sectors (except cars and lorries) in Annex 6 of Commission of the EC, *The Competitiveness of European Community Industry*, III/387/82, Brussels, 1982. Corresponding OECD market shares on this basis were for Germany 13.8 per cent, UK 7.7 per cent and France 6.4 per cent.

Table 2.11. World trade in electronic products, 1979–84 (billion US $)*

Country	Exports		Imports		Balance +/–[†]	
	1979	1984	1979	1984	1979	1984
Japan	13.77	35.50	2.17	3.74	+11.60	+31.76
Asian Four[‡]	7.16	15.29	5.38	11.82[§]	+1.78	+3.47
EC (10)‖	11.20	14.67	13.73	21.95	−2.53	−7.28
Germany	7.60	9.25	7.20	9.93	+0.40	−0.68
North America‖	13.24	24.69	11.80	36.43	+1.44	−11.74

* Including automatic data processing machines, telecommunication equipment, business electronics, consumer electronics and electronic parts.
† + = export surplus; − = import surplus.
‡ Taiwan, S. Korea, Hong Kong, Singapore.
§ Taiwan 1983.
‖ Excluding intra-trade.
Source: GATT 1985, Tables A23–5.

Others responded that problems lay primarily with rigidities that hampered supply. Wages and consumption, public and private, were eating too much into profits and 'crowding out' investment. Excessive emphasis on distribution had led to neglect of the foundations of industrial production, like profits and vocational training.

In the 1980s there was a proliferation of governments which, whatever their supposed colour, left or right, pursued policies designed to reassert production priorities against those of income distribution. Disinflation, shading into deflation; cuts in public budgets and taxes; the elimination of the financial deficits of nationalized industries even at the cost of jobs; the encouragement of innovation and better manpower training—by 1983 these had become the declaratory purposes of all. The price was high unemployment and low growth. No state seemed to escape the contradiction between high demand policies falling foul of supply rigidities and low demand policies which reduced incentives to industrial renewal.

2.8 Germany and Europe

All the same, there may be an element of exaggeration in Europessimism. On several occasions since the war, anxiety has been voiced about the United States' economic decline, as expressed by low apparent levels of investment and growth in productivity per worker. In the 1960s Western Europe was regarded as one of the boom regions of the world. Countries like Germany, Sweden and Switzerland are not lagging in innovation in all sectors by any means, and others, such as Belgium, France and Italy, seem to be moving up the scale in some (Patel and Pavitt 1986). The United States has grown faster because she has pursued more expansionary policies than Germany; but she has suffered more from Japanese competition and in the Reagan Presidency built up a huge trade deficit. Europe's sluggishness may have been less extreme than Japan's growth, and even that seemed to be slowing down sharply after the revaluation of the Yen of 1986.

Much will depend on the choices and performance of Germany. The European system has come increasingly to depend on her economic leadership. She is much the largest export market (and supplier) of most of her neighbours. In ascending order, France, Italy, Denmark, Norway, Greece, Switzerland, Benelux and Austria all, in 1984, counted on West Germany for 15 to more than 30 per cent respectively of their world exports. Germany and these economies specially close to her, in their turn account for over two-fifths of the rest of Western Europe's exports (UN 1983). Directly and indirectly, Western Germany has tended increasingly to determine the rate of activity of the region. This has been virtually institutionalized in the European Monetary System (EMS). Whether Germany speeds up or slows down, the ripples tend to spread across Western Europe.

In sum, despite national differences, one can detect an increasingly common European predicament in relations with the rest of the world; to a lesser but still significant extent, converging responses; and a growing tendency for Germany to act as economic bell-wether to the region. One of the questions for the future is whether Germany's leadership cements integration in Europe or perpetuates the national patterns and shortcomings of the region in the past.

Notes

1. Deaglio (1985) estimates the Italian black economy in 1982, as an order of magnitude, at 20 per cent of the official one. Sectoral estimates are also made which put 'black' income at 30 per cent over official in retail trading, 25 per cent in rents, 20 per cent in textiles, clothing, shoes and transport and 15 per cent in engineering, food, wood and furniture. The 'criminal', as distinct from 'black' economy (i.e. the income of the Mafia, Camorra, etc.) is estimated at 4 per cent of GDP. Revised official national income calculations for 1987 will significantly raise GDP.

2. A survey of enterprises with 20 or more employees in 1981 by the European Commission found that 23 per cent of manufacturing gross value added (GVA) in Italy was generated by those with 20–99 employees (12 per cent in Britain and Germany; 17 per cent in France). Only 47 per cent of GVA was generated in firms with 500 employees or over in Italy against 60–65 per cent in the other Three (Eurostat, 1986c). The sectoral breakdown of employment in 1983 in manufacturing in France, Germany and Italy (Eurostat, 1986b) gave the following results (Britain not available):

Sectors	France	Germany	Italy
Textiles*	23	18	40
Engineering†	48	55	35

    * NACE 42 Textiles, clothing, leather and footwear.
    † NACE 19 Metal products: 21 Agricultural–industrial machinery: 23 Office machines: 25 Electrical goods: 28 Transport equipment.

3. Horn (1982), p. 89, Table A2, shows that gross labour income in West Germany rose from 60.4 per cent of national income in 1960 to 72.2 per cent in 1980, while non-distributed profits fell from 14.3 per cent in 1960 to 2.9 per cent in 1980.

4. Because of different coverage and definitions of subsidies (in the numerators) and value added (in the denominators) for each of the series, it is difficult to compare one series with another. The main use of the table is to track the evolution of subsidies for each country over time. The most complete and reliable estimates are probably those in Germany Series B. All GDP data are from OECD, *National Accounts of OECD Countries*, Paris, various years.
    Germany Series A: Federal government subsidies to business enterprises as a percentage of GDP in industry (mining and manufacturing). Included are subsidies to coal mining, energy and raw materials production, promotion of technology and innovation, specific sectoral aids, regional aid, interest rate subsidies and other general measures. Subsidies to transport are excluded. Data are from Bundesregierung (1983).
    Germany Series B: federal, state (*Land*) and local government subsidies (including direct subsidies and tax concessions) as a percentage of net product (net of subsidies) in industry; from Table 7 of Gerken *et al.* (1985).
    France Series A: industrial subsidies as a percentage of industrial value added; subsidies include specific sectoral aid, regional aid, R & D support, industrial policy credits, interest rate subsidies, export credit insurance and subsidies and miscellaneous aids, from Table IV.4 of Messerlin (1984).
    France Series B: all public subsidies (central and local government, EEC, social security) to industry as a percentage of industrial value added, from Table 3 of Dutailly (1984).
    Italy: regional, sectoral, public enterprise, trade and R & D subsidies as a

percentage of industrial value added (Ch. 5), calculated from Table 2.1 of Brosio and Silvestri in Ranci (1983) and Table 5 of Artoni and Ravazza in Artoni and Pontarollo (1986).

UK Series A: direct central government support to industry (manufacturing and mining *less* North Sea oil) as a percentage of industrial GDP; direct support includes regional, selective trade (exports) and R & D support and excludes support to employment and public enterprises; figures are for financial, not calendar, years (1970/1 is given as 1970, and so on); ratios for 1982–4 are estimates; from Tables 35 and 36 of Sharp and Shepherd (forthcoming).

UK Series B: this is the same ratio as Series A except that support to public enterprises has been added in the numerator.

5. This percentage is derived from Kaldor, Sharp and Walker (1984), Table 2, after correction, from data in Eurostat, 1986a, pp. 38–41, to allow for differences between production value and value added. These figures exclude the purchases of the nationalized industries, which also pursue a Buy British policy when it is open to them and in particular the National Health Service for pharmaceuticals, British Telecom for telecommunications, the Central Electricity Generating Board, the National Coal Board, and so on. Estimates for Italy suggest public procurement is of major importance there too (see Ch. 5).

6. The 'White Paper from the Commission of the European Communities to the European Council' on 'Completing the Internal Market' of June 1985 listed more than 300 measures necessary to eliminate the barriers to a full Common Market, such as frontier formalities and health controls; divergent industrial standards; obstacles to the establishment of persons, freedom of services, patents, transport and capital movements; as well as legal and fiscal differences.

References

Artoni, R. and Pontarollo, E., eds. (1986), *Trasferimenti, Domanda Pubblica e Sistema Industriale*, Bologna, Il Mulino.

Bellon, B. and Chevalier, J.-M., eds. (1983), *L'Industrie en France*, Paris, Centre de Recherche en Economie Industrielle.

Best G. (1971), *Mid-Victorian Britain 1985–75*, London, Weidenfeld (new edn., Panther, 1973).

Bundesregierung (1983), *Bericht der Bundesregierung über des Finanzhilfen und Steuervergünstigungen für die Jahre 1977 bis 1980 gemäss # 12 des Gesetzes für Förderung der Stabilität (10ter Subventionsbericht)*, Bundestagdrucksache 10/352, Bonn.

CSO—UK Central Statistical Office (annual), *Annual Abstract of Statistics*, London.

David, F. (1982), *Le Commerce International à la Dérive*, Paris.

Deaglio, M. (1985), *Economia Sommersa e Analisi Economica*, Turin, Giappichelli.

Dutailly, J.-C. (1984), 'Aide aux Entreprises: 134 milliards de francs en 1982', *Economie et Statistique*, September, Paris.

European Economy (1986), July, Commission of the European Communities, Brussels.

Eurostat—Statistical Office of the European Communities (1986a), *Yearbook of Industrial Statistics 1985*, Brussels.

——— (1986b), *National Accounts ESA, Detailed Tables by Branch 1986*, Brussels.

——— (1986c), *Structure and Activity of Industry 1981: Data by Size of Enterprises*, Brussels.

Financial Times, 10 February 1987, 'US still living better than most' (from OECD and Eurostat calculations of real per capita GDP in OECD countries for 1985).

GATT (1985), *International Trade 1984/5*, General Agreement on Tariffs and Trade, Geneva.

Gerken, E., Juttermeier, K.H., Schatz, K.-W. and Schmidt, K.-D. (1985), *Mehr Arbeitsplätze durch Subventionsabbau*, Kiel Discussion Papers 113/4, Institut für Weltwirtschaft, Kiel.

Hill, T.P. (1979), *Profits and Rates of Return*, Paris, OECD.

Horn, E.-J. (1982), *Management of Industrial Change in Germany*, Sussex European Papers No. 13, Brighton, Sussex European Research Centre, Sussex University.

Jacquemin, A. and Sapir, A. (1987), 'European Integration or World Integration', Centre for European Policy Studies, Brussels, mimeo.

Kaldor, M., Sharp, M., and Walker, W. (1984), *Industrial Competitiveness and Britain's Defence*, Lloyds Bank Review, October.

Messerlin, P. (1984), *Managing Industrial Change in France*, Brighton, Sussex European Research Centre, Sussex University.

Montbrial, T. de, ed. (1986), *Rapport Annuel Mondial sur le Système Economique et les Stratégies (Ramsès)*, Paris, Institut Français des Relations Internationales.

Musson, A.E. (1978), *The Growth of British Industry*, London, Batsford.

NEDO—National Economic Development Office (1977), *International Price Competitiveness, Non-Price Factors and Export Performance*, London.

Noguès, J., Olechowski, A. and Winters, L. (1986), *The Extent of Nontariff Barriers to Imports of Industrial Countries*, Staff Working Paper 789, World Bank, Washington DC.

OEEC—Organization for European Economic Cooperation (1960), *Industrial Statistics 1900-1959*, Paris.

OECD—Organization for Economic Cooperation and Development (1966), *Main Economic Indicators, Historical Series 1955-1964*, Paris.

——— (1984), *Main Economic Indicators, Historical Series 1964-1983*, Paris.

——— (1985), *Statistical Bulletins of Foreign Trade, Series C, Trade by Commodities, 1984*, Paris.

Patel, P. and Pavitt, K. (1986), 'Is Western Europe Losing the Technological Race?', Science Policy Research Unit, Sussex University, mimeo.

Ranci, P., ed. (1983), *I Trasferimenti dello Stato alle Imprese Industriali negli Anni Settanta*, Bologna, Il mulino.

Rose, R., ed. (1985), *Public Employment in Western Nations*, Cambridge, Cambridge University Press.

Samek Lodovici, M. (1986), 'Le piccole imprese manifatturiere in Italia e negli altri maggiori paesi industriali, in I. Cipoletta, ed., *Struttura industriale e politiche macroeconomiche in Italia*, Bologna, Il Mulino.

Sharp, M. and Shepherd, G. (forthcoming), *Managing Change in British Industry*, ILO, Geneva.

UN—United Nations (1983), *Yearbook of International Trade Statistics*, New York.

US Department of Commerce (quarterly), *International Economic Indicators*, Washington, DC, various issues.

World Bank (annual), *World Development Report*, Washington, DC.

Woytinski, W.S. and Woytinski, E.S. (1955), *World Commerce and Governments*, New York, Twentieth Century Fund.

3 Germany: a market-led process

Ernst-Jürgen Horn*

Industrial policy is concerned with promoting industrial growth and efficiency, and adapting industrial structures to economic, technological and
social change. It deals with the supply side of the economy, and its major
instruments are subsidies (including preferential tax treatment), public
procurement, nationalization of firms, trade protection, competition policy
and regulation of markets.

Though the term has come into widespread use only recently, industrial
policy is by no means new. After World War II Western European governments coping with economic reconstruction were inevitably confronted
with supply policy issues but, once full employment had been achieved,
became preoccupied with demand management. An implicit industrial
policy, however, persisted especially in relations between governments and
large firms (for instance through protection, regulation of competition,
technology development, assistance to declining sectors or regions). Over
the past two decades, this implicit policy has developed into an explicit and
more comprehensive approach which recognizes that the elasticity of supply
response sets a limit to overall economic performance and that restructuring
industry is crucial to improving both.

A comprehensive analysis of industrial policy would encompass a very
large variety of measures. For practical reasons, this analysis is confined to
the development of the most important features. The first section sets out
the perception of problems, stated objectives, measures taken and priorities
applied in the Federal Republic of Germany since World War II. The second
discusses the implications of the environment in which industrial policies
operate, concentrating on decision-making in government, business and
labour, resource bottlenecks and social and political resistance to change.
The third evaluates the effects of industrial policy, and the fourth discusses
the options for the future.

---

* This chapter is an updated version of Horn (1982).

3.1 Perceived policy problems since World War II

Three phases in West Germany's post-war economic development can be distinguished:

(i)   reconstruction of the national economy and intenational economic relations (post-war to the late 1950s);
(ii) full employment and sustained economic growth (up to the breakdown of the Bretton Woods system and the first oil price crisis in the early 1970s);
(iii) slow growth, high unemployment and major structural adjustments (the current phase).

From reconstruction to full employment

In 1946 industrial production was one-third of that pre-war, indigenous food supply well under 1,000 calories per head per day and the labour force reduced by several million men held as prisoners of war. The Yalta and Potsdam agreements of the Allied powers envisaged a primarily agricultural economy with restriction of industry in general, destruction of the arms industry, break up of cartels and payment of reparations. But soon the developing East–West conflict changed the priorities of the western occupying powers and, in reality, the new federal and state (*Länder*) governments have been free to shape economic policy since about 1949.

The debate on the economic order

The central feature of the policy that emerged was the concept of a social market economy comprising reliance on free markets, promotion of competition and prevention of monopolies, with social provision for the economically weak. The foundations of the policy were laid in 1948 when the key regulations of the formerly centrally planned system were removed. The West German 'economic miracle' which ensued was unforeseen by most economic experts.

As early as the 1930s a group of liberal economists (the Freiburg School) had begun to design a liberal alternative in economic policy to the increasing market intervention of the Third Reich. They believed that the state should not refrain completely from intervention but that intervention should concentrate on defending the liberal order and securing freedom of markets in particular. Müller-Armack and others developed the concept of the social market economy, laying stronger emphasis on social policy. They argued that while a market economy inherently has a social element in providing a basis for increasing the wealth of all citizens, government should redistribute the results of market processes if these prove socially unacceptable. The aims of the social market economy can be summarized as follows:

(i) the highest possible economic welfare through competition, steady economic growth, full employment and free international economic relations;

(ii) an efficient monetary framework—and in particular a stable average price level achieved through an independent central bank, stable budgets and balanced foreign accounts;

(iii) social security and progress through maximization of the national product, effective competition and adequate redistribution of income and wealth.

It was a natural reaction, following the years of total control, for many German economists to favour a relatively free market economy. For more than a decade, intensified during the war, the German economy had been centrally planned, a system which the Allied military governments extended in view of the chaos after the war. Until 1948, food and essential commodities were rationed, prices and wages frozen, production and distribution regulated and foreign trade and exchange controlled. The monetary system was in ruins: British and American cigarettes were an important medium of exchange.

The military governments introduced monetary reform in the Western occupation zones on 20 June 1948, creating the Deutsche mark. Overnight, the black market vanished and the preconditions for economic recovery were established. Six days later, the law on the liberalization of markets and the removal of central planning came into force. This was nominally an act of the military government. In fact, liberalization was pushed through by German economists and civil servants, led by Ludwig Erhard, director of the economic 'self-administration' in the American and British zones. He took the responsibility for dismantling controls on output and consumption, against the wishes of the military government, the Social Democrats, the newly established unions and many Christian Democrats.

Industrial production now took off dramatically (by 50 per cent during the second half of 1948), but so did demand, fed by the massive expansion in volume of new money. Prices rose rapidly while a wage freeze was still in force. The blame was widely laid at the door of premature liberalization or of liberalization as such. The unions proclaimed a general strike on 12 November 1948. they succeeded to the extent that the wage freeze, the most important remnant of central planning, was removed. Otherwise, the course of economic policy remained unchanged.

In November 1948 the new central bank (the Bank Deutscher Länder, later to become the Deutsche Bundesbank) introduced a tight monetary policy. The price level fell considerably, but unemployment grew. The Korean crisis brought a further challenge, but policy held firm in the face of criticism. By 1953 the social market economy was successfully established and by 1959 accepted even by the Social Democratic Party, in its Godesberg Programme.

Industrial policy during reconstruction

On 22 June 1948 tax reform was introduced. The highest marginal tax rates on personal and corporate income (fixed by the Allied Control Council) were reduced and depreciation allowances on investment were extended particularly to 'key sectors' for reconstruction: mining, agriculture, public utilities, shipbuilding, shipping and housing construction.

At a time of acute capital shortage, this tax system encouraged capital accumulation in the firm, with a bias towards key sectors, and led to a relatively unequal distribution of wealth. Though, as more normal conditions returned in the 1950s, depreciation allowances were curtailed and tax rates reduced, preferential tax treatment for specific sectors of industry or regions has been a continuing feature of economic policy.

Marshall Aid contributed significantly to investment in the 'key sectors' by way of credits for scarce imported equipment. By 1952 the European Recovery Programme Fund which administered Marshall Plan aid had accumulated 5 billion marks from repayment of these credits (10 billion marks by 1970) and this fund still operates today with emphasis on regional and medium and small business development. But Marshall Aid, corresponding to 7.1 per cent of fixed capital formation between 1948 and 1952 was not the main driving force in recovery.

Banking (together with some important sectors such as agriculture, energy, communications, insurance, transport and housing) had been excluded from the liberalization of 1948, and interest rates for loans and deposits and foreign exchange were controlled. (The Deutsche mark became freely convertible in 1958. The control of interest rates on loans and deposits was removed in 1967.) The resultant credit rationing tended to discriminate against smaller firms, and a special programme for such firms was introduced into the European Recovery Programme. In 1952 a forced loan of one billion marks was distributed in financial aid for the basic products industries, involving some transfer of resources from small to big business.

Trade liberalization and European integration

The Marshall Plan recognized that the West German economy was crucial to the economic recovery of Western Europe, and the OEEC, founded in 1948, was charged with the liberalization of European trade and the reintegration of Western European economies, including West Germany.

During the early reconstruction period, increasing domestic demand coupled with a shortage of capacity for the production of export goods induced severe balance-of-payments constraints. Until devaluation in 1949 (by about one-third in line with the pound and other European currencies), the Deutsche mark was clearly overvalued. Following devaluation, the balance of payments improved, import controls were removed, and in 1951 the balance of payments went into surplus. Thereafter, aided no doubt by the expansion of world trade during the Korean crisis, West

Germany began to enjoy a 'structural' trade surplus which persisted for three decades.

The treaty on the European Coal and Steel Community in April 1951, foreshadowed the wider integration of the EEC customs union from 1959 onwards, while GATT liberalization rounds and EFTA further influenced the direction and growth of international trade.

Deconcentration and competition policy

Germany has always been regarded as a classic case of cartelization and there is some truth in this. Up to 1923, for instance, firms were permitted to form cartels, and later the Third Reich enforced cartelization as an instrument of central planning and economic power politics. Accordingly, decartelization and deconcentration to some extent became a common cause for Western Allied governments and German social market economists after the war.

Deconcentration policy was principally aimed at all firms with more than 10,000 employees, in particular, with IG Farben (chemicals), coal, steel and the large banks. Decartelization was originally imposed by the Allied governments. A specifically German Cartel Act was not introduced until 1957. By this time, with the exception of IG Farben, the large firms and banks split up by the military government were already largely reintegrated. It was a weak Act exempting wide areas of the economy regulated by government and concentrating on industry and trade. For these, however, and with regard to private market power and mergers in general, it was not, at least by Western European standards, a weak cartel Act.

Research and public procurement

Immediately after the war the prohibition of research in many important areas, the dispossession of all German patents by the Allied governments and the emigration of highly qualified scientists and engineers led to substantial lags in technological development. Once the federal government had achieved sovereignty by joining NATO in 1955, it was possible to start correcting this. It was widely agreed that the reconstructed West German economy was entering a new phase in which the major task would be to catch up on the leading industrial countries, and that the state was to play an active role in this process. From the beginning, research policy in the non-university area concentrated on 'big' research. The main programmes developed over time showed a similar pattern to that observed in the leading Western industrial countries. Thus research policy essentially pursued a strategy of imitation. But, for obvious reasons, a relatively small effort went into the military field so that, in comparison with other countries, conditions for development in the civilian field were relatively favourable.

Reconstruction of an aircraft industry and the development of nuclear energy were the first priorities. The production of US military aircraft under licence provided an opportunity for the government, the main customer, to restructure the industry. Initially comprising some twenty firms, it was largely concentrated by 1977 in three large units employing 52,000 persons. Until Airbus, production was almost entirely military. In 1973 subsidies to, and public purchases from, the industry amounted to 3.3 billion marks (63,000 marks per employee), while civilian sales were worth only 0.5 billion marks.

Nuclear energy was so high a priority that a separate federal ministry was established, and several large public research laboratories were founded (beginning in 1956), very much in the German historical tradition. Research in private firms was substantially subsidized, and the government co-ordinated the overall effort.

Programmes for data processing and civilian space and aircraft technology were introduced during the 1960s, and the Ministry for Nuclear Research proliferated into a Ministry for Scientific Research and then into a Ministry for Education and Science and a Ministry for Research and Technology (at the beginning of the 1970s). This reflected an initially gradual and then, in the 1970s, massive shift of non-nuclear policy towards direct, project-orientated research subsidies for private firms. The traditional tax rebates for investment goods used in R & D had hardly discriminated among sectors and firms of different size. The new emphasis clearly indicated growing interventionism.

Economic performance during the 1950s

By the end of the 1950s, full employment had been achieved. Between 1950 and 1960 total employment increased by more than 5 million, that is by one-quarter. Agriculture fell from 23 per cent to 14 per cent of employment, by more than 1.5 million persons. Real product more than doubled. The most dynamic expansion of output and employment was in manufacturing, whose share of total employment went up from 32 to 37 per cent between 1950 and 1960.

The main characteristics of the growth process can be summarized as follows (Kommission für Wirtschaftlichen und Sozialen Wandel 1977, especially Ch. 2):

(i) Returns in output to capital invested were very high, with emphasis on bottlenecks.
(ii) Productivity rose faster than wages, reflecting an abundant labour supply fed notably by refugees from the East, and a non-aggressive union stance on wages.
(iii) After the Korean War, inflation was practically non-existent.
(iv) Economic expansion spread across all sectors.

The state intervened heavily in markets during the early phase of reconstruction and greatly reduced intervention afterwards. State interventions were then almost exclusively orientated towards the supply side of the economy. There was hardly any need to stimulate private demand. On the contrary, the major task was to hold it down to the capacity of production.

Apart from tax incentives for private investment, public expenditure policy concentrated on social issues and on the reconstruction of public infrastructure. Tax revenues and the public debt ratio as a percentage of national income hardly increased. Till rearmament began, the federal government actually managed to achieve a substantial budget surplus. Private investors faced only moderate competition from the state in capital markets.

Changing priorities of economic policy during the 1960s

From the beginning of the 1960s, with full employment achieved and business cycles and price stability becoming the major issues, the concept of the social market economy was increasingly called into question by demands for more active demand management and for a more active role of the state in general. Reflecting these changes in perceptions, an independent Council of Economic Experts was established in 1963 under a law which defined four key macro-economic aims: price stability, high employment, balance-of-payments stability and appropriate economic growth.

Following the recession of 1966–7, largely induced by anti-inflationary measures in the aftermath of the federal election of 1965, Ludwig Erhard's coalition government (of Christian and Free Democrats) was replaced by the 'Great Coalition' of Christian and Social Democrats. The Stability and Growth Act of 1967 established a 'Concerted Action' (*Konzertierte Aktion*) which was to function as an organized clearing house between government and major interests, particularly employers' associations and the unions. This 'new economic policy' closely connected with Karl Schiller, the Socialist Economics Minister, seemed to achieve economic recovery following the recession, and the pre-eminence of demand management policy was not questioned until after the world recession of 1974–5.

The revaluation debate

The extent to which the dramatic rise of the German share in world exports (from 5.7 per cent in 1953 to 11.3 per cent by 1973) was due to an undervaluation of the Deutsche mark remains an open question. There was an export boom following the 1949 devaluation, but German export prices rose comparatively faster than those of other industrial countries in 1951 and 1952, and largely approached foreign prices during the Korean boom, afterwards developing in parallel. Revaluation by 5 per'cent in 1961 to 4 marks to the dollar was intended to remove the 'structural' disequilibrium in the current-account balance, but had little practical effect.

The question at issue in the revaluation debate was how to achieve price stability at home in the face of inflation abroad under a regime of fixed exchange rates. The Council of Economic Experts maintained that an open economy could not, in the long run, escape world inflationary trends without more flexible exchange rate adjustments (upwards). This argument was attacked by both the federal government and private business, and the issue figured large in the 1969 federal election campaign when Schiller and his party championed the cause of more flexible exchange rates. It proved a major factor in the election victory of the new coalition of Social and Free Democrats.

Strong appreciation of the mark after the breakdown of Bretton Woods in the early 1970s indicated that it had been considerably undervalued in the past. Germany industry had had an artificial advantage in international competition, with the export sector of the economy favoured at the expense of the domestic one. Past measures against imported inflation had been more efficient than expected, and it was this which enhanced the magnitude of adjustment problems after the realignment of exchange rates.

Immigration of labour

Throughout the 1950s the west German labour force had continued to grow through a steady inflow of refugees from East Germany and of ethnic Germans from Eastern Europe. The East German government stopped the refugee movement by the erection of the wall between East and West Berlin in 1961. The strong demand for labour prevailing in the booming economy increasingly attracted foreign labour, especially from Southern Europe. This immigration started during the late 1950s, when shortages emerged in some segments of the labour market, mainly for 'dirty' and seasonal jobs. As the German labour force was shrinking for demographic reasons during the 1960s, immigration was widely regarded as necessary to keep the economy moving. As early as 1963 there were more than one million foreign workers (5 per cent of all domestic employees). The recession of 1966–7 temporarily checked immigration. But in the subsequent boom, it rose again on an unprecedented scale, to over 2.3 million (10 per cent of all domestic employees) in 1973.

The social cost of immigration became a public issue. It was not till 1973 that the government put a stop to the (legal) recruitment of foreign labour. By 1978 the number of employed foreigners had decreased by over 450,000; it then recovered slightly in the relatively good years of 1978 and 1979, but fell again in the steep recession after the second oil price shock to 1.6 million in 1984. The unemployment rate of foreign workers had been distinctly above average for years. Most foreign workers with more than five years residence gained an unlimited permit to stay and a second generation of foreigners has grown up and increasingly entered the labour market.

Economic policy and European integration in the 1960s

The emerging Common Market induced the reformulation of priorities in domestic economic policy. At the same time, competition from the American multinationals was regarded as a challenge to domestic firms calling for policy responses. The concept of the social market economy had originally placed strong emphasis on economic freedom and resistance to concentration, but this began to be questioned during the 1960s. It was argued that large European firms were needed to compete on a continental European market with the American 'multinational' challenge. The growing interest in economies of scale and technical development reinforced this view. The federal government became concerned to remove obstacles to concentration and the promotion of cooperation among smaller firms. Concentration accelerated after the mid-1960s and there was a wave of mergers so that, by the 1970s, the domination of large firms in key sectors was again causing concern. The Cartel Act was amended to curtail concentration, and during the 1970s the share of large firms in industrial employment decreased significantly while the performance of small and medium firms, in the face of declining industrial employment, was relatively good.

Increasing state intervention emerged during the 1960s by way of subsidies. According to the rather narrow national accounts definition, which covers only part of financial aid to firms and does not cover tax rebates at all, subsidies increased from 5.8 billion marks in 1960 to 21.4 billion marks in 1970 (equivalent to 8 per cent and 13 per cent of tax revenues, respectively). The figures clearly indicate the growing importance of what is called structural policy in West Germany.

Structural policy has three components: sectoral, regional and technology policy. Sectoral structural policy emerged—from the late 1950s onwards—from rescue operations in hard-coal mining and shipbuilding and from the attempt to build up the aircraft and nuclear power industries. During the 1960s the aircraft programme was extended to aerospace, data processing, iron ore mining, crude-oil exploration and raw materials other than fuels. Three areas of sectoral intervention can be distinguished: adjustment assistance to shrinking sectors, supply of important raw materials and the development of high-technology sectors.

Regional structural policy emerged after the war because the new intra-German border created major adjustment difficulties in the adjoining regions, and because of the isolation of West Berlin. Over time, regional policy was extended, and roughly two-thirds of the total area of the Federal Republic now receive some regional preferences, mainly tax rebates and preferential loans for investors. Along with agriculture and universities, regional policy constitutes one of the only three areas jointly administered and financed by the federal government and the states. These three 'common tasks' (*Gemeinschaftsaufgaben*) have been increasingly criticized in recent years for inefficiency and lack of focus and of clear lines of responsibility.

At the federal level, the responsibility for the structural policy measures so far discussed (as well as miscellaneous measures to encourage R & D, small- and medium-sized firms, and labour mobility and retraining) lay largely with the Ministry of Economics. During the second half of the 1960s, the federal government tried to achieve a better coordination of its many structural policies. The Federal Minister of Economics, Schiller, developed a set of principles for sectoral policy (1966) and regional policy (1968). These principles were designed to limit the criteria for, and extent of, intervention and to maintain the role of markets. Structural interventions should, for instance:

(i)   deal only with sectors and not with single firms;
(ii) be temporary;
(iii) be taken only in cases where adjustment caused major social hardship;
(iv) help firms to help themselves;
(v)   not suspend the functioning of markets.

These principles were never backed up by federal law and it is hard to detect any major impact of their liberal spirit on the course of 'structural' intervention. On the contrary, depression after 1973/4 increased the demand for it.

On technology policy there has never been a clear-cut separation between the roles of the Federal Ministry of Economics and Ministry of Research and Technology. In practice, the latter dealt more directly with project-orientated funding of industrial R & D (where the Defence Ministry also played a substantial though hidden role), while the former mainly administered general support schemes for R & D in industry.

During the 1960s West German industry's own funds devoted to R & D started to catch up with leading industrial countries, overtaking them in the 1970s (Breithaupt et al. 1979; Pavitt and Walker 1976; Keck 1976). Government funds for R & D grew more rapidly than abroad, though the relative level of government contribution to industry, like military R & D, was lower than in other leading Western countries throughout the 1960s and 1970s. On the other hand, government laboratories and research institutions outside the universities made a major contribution.

The funds of the technology ministry either supported 'institutional research' inside and outside the universities or were devoted to R & D programmes defined by the ministry and carried out by industry and public research institutions. The ratio of institutional to non-institutional R & D support declined through the 1960s and 1970s (from 8 : 2 in 1962 to 5 : 4 in 1970 and 4 : 5 at the end of the 1970s). The increasing share of non-institutional R & D support indicated the rising project orientation and sectoral bias of R & D policy. The sectors most favoured were (in 1972) nuclear energy (42 per cent of project-orientated R & D support), data processing (21 per cent), aircraft and space (21 per cent), and other new technologies (12 per cent). There was—and continues to be—a concentration on a relatively small number of firms.

State-owned enterprises

Another point worth noting is the fact that, despite the prevalent private enterprise philosophy, state-owned enterprises (inherited mostly from past regimes) accounted for 7.5 per cent of total employment and 10 per cent of value added during the 1970s. In the utilities, transport and communications they often enjoy a monopoly, while in industry—except for coal—they tend to face competition. State governments and local authorities are almost exclusively engaged in non-manufacturing sectors, while the federal government, which controls two-thirds of all public enterprise activities (measured by employment), has a substantial stake in manufacturing (steel, shipbuilding, railway equipment, aluminium, automobiles). The more profitable firms, like Volkswagen and VEBA, have been largely privatized.

In general, however, public firms are not highly profitable, particularly as they are often required to fulfil social and political government objectives. The Federal Railway, for example, absorbed subsidies amounting at the peak some years ago to one per cent of GNP per annum. Where public enterprises enjoy a monopoly in an area of expanding demand, they tend to extend the field of their operations. The Federal Post Office (the largest European service enterprise) has been trying to extend its network monopoly in telecommunications towards terminal equipment, thus discouraging private initiative for the development of new products and techniques.

The West German economy responded well to the challenges of the 1960s. Following European integration there was a swing towards intra-EEC trade with remarkable differences as between product groups. In production goods, integration had a stronger impact on imports than on exports, in consumption goods the reverse. The greatest trade growth was in processed food, reflecting the move from the highly protective national agricultural policy to the equally protective European one. Industry was also partly protected by an undervalued currency so that, until the early 1970s, performance appeared more impressive than it was in reality.

Structural adjustment and slow economic growth since the early 1970s

The programme of the new Social–Liberal coalition government, formed in 1969 with Willy Brandt as Chancellor, comprised improvement of the public infrastructure, enlargement of university education, social justice through income redistribution to weaker groups, a guarantee of full employment, and increased control of private investment through the vast R & D subsidies operated by the Ministry for Research and Technology. The ambitious task of this ministry was to ensure the development of key technologies and help restructure and modernize the economy.

This programme was seriously inhibited by rising inflation, revaluation of the Deutsche mark (affecting competitiveness in world markets) and, from 1973, the restrictive monetary policy of the Bundesbank against the background of flexible exchange rates and the effects of the first oil price shock. A downswing in the economy was reinforced by very high wage settlements in 1974. The economy fell into the deepest recession since the war. Brandt resigned in May 1974, and Helmut Schmidt took over.

The government responded to the crisis with a policy of massive demand expansion but the resulting upswing was shortlived and, afterwards policy-making was locked in the dilemma of unemployment coinciding with inflation.

As to the cause and cures of the recession two conflicting schools developed. One school attributed poor performance to lack of effective private demand but was divided on how to stimulate it (public expenditure or wage increases?). Another school (including the Council of Economic Experts) concentrated on the supply side and proposed that the greater investment risks resulting from accelerated structural change and increasing international competition be met by improving the profitability of investment to create new jobs. This could be done either by reducing costs (through incomes policy or tax incentives) or by raising productivity.

Though the debate continues, developments since 1975 have reflected the arguments of the supply-side school. Several attempts at demand stimulation failed to induce a sustained upswing while the massive public borrowing to finance it tended to 'crowd out' private demand for capital finance. The supply-side argument was further reinforced by the diversity of growth patterns: some industries were at full capacity while others suffered from declining demand and obsolescence.

Slow growth seemed attributable mainly to the appreciation of the Deutsche mark, rising energy costs and increasing competition from developing countries. There was a dramatic decline of one million (or 11 per cent) in manufacturing employment from 1973 to 1977, which barely rose again subsequently. The environment had fundamentally changed since the 'golden' 1950s. It has been argued that the new phase is a sort of 'normalization' since manufacturing had previously been artificially favoured at the expense of the service sector (Fels *et al.* 1981).

Following the limited success of public expenditure policy in stimulating growth after the first oil price shock, belief in the possibility of a trade-off between inflation and employment declined and the government turned to new policies: high priority for reducing inflation, support of private investment, cutting of corporate taxation, extension of depreciation allowances, support of R & D in small firms, and energy conservation encouraged by financial premiums and tax incentives. The only major new measure in demand management, the *Zukunftsinvestitionsprogramm* (Investing-in-the-Future Programme) of the late 1970s, was initiated in response to pressure, especially from the United States, for West Germany to act as a 'locomotive' for the world economy. This proved counter-productive, since it caused an inflationary economic boom and achieved little at high cost for the economy as a whole.

On balance, over the second half of the 1970s a substantial shift towards supply policy took place. Investment, favoured by relatively moderate wage settlements in the preceding years, started to recover in 1978 and profits improved. Employment, which had decreased by more than 1.4 million persons from 1973 to 1976, increased from 1978 to 1980 by almost 800,000 but mainly in services and in the public sector (300,000 each). In manu-facturing, employment recovered by less than 100,000. Nevertheless, the decline in the number of firms was reversed, even in industry. Business equipment expenditure boomed. The period just before the second oil price explosion was a time of renewed optimism. Unemployment rates declined to 3.7 per cent in 1979–80.

The second oil crisis after 1979–80 abruptly halted the recovery. In the recession of 1981–2 and during the two following years of moderate recovery, the number of employed persons fell by another one million, and in manufacturing alone by 900,000. The unemployment rate reached a peak, in the first half of 1985, of almost 10 per cent (or 2.4 million unemployed).

The international competitiveness of industry became an issue in the economic policy debate. The current account had switched into deficit in 1979 and ran deeper into the red in 1980. This reflected not only the increase in the oil bill but also a slight and steady erosion of the manufacturing trade balance in the previous years. This was due to the appreciation of the currency, which peaked in 1979. The main issue of the debate was the new technological gap said to have emerged *vis-à-vis* the United States and Japan (Börnsen, Glismann and Horn 1985). More recently, immediate concern with this issue has faded again due to rising trade surpluses associated with the strong appreciation of the dollar (1980 to 1985). Policy discussion has continued, however, on the extent to which institutional rigidities in West Germany cause weak innovation performance and call for deregulation.

Economic policy ran into strong turbulence after the second oil price jump of 1979–80. The deficits in public budgets had already been high in the relatively good years before the recession. Now they reached unprecedented levels (about 5 per cent of GDP in 1981) that seemed to require a cutback in public budgets. The Free Democrats preferred cuts of expenditures (not least in social expenditures and subsidies) and market deregulation; the Social Democrats, though acknowledging the necessity of expenditure cuts in principle, insisted on income tax increases for upper-income ranks as com-pensation. The Social and Free Democrats could not agree on how to handle these. Their coalition fell apart under the strain and in October 1982 it was replaced by a Christian and Free Democrat coalition under Helmut Kohl as Federal Chancellor.

The declared aim of the new federal government was to achieve a funda-mental turn away from what was perceived as Social Democratic policy. This meant mainly cuts in subsidies, social expenditure and taxes, the privat-ization of state-owned firms and deregulation of markets. The main effort has borne on budget cuts. Only small steps at best had been taken towards the other aims up till the elections of January 1987.

3.2 The environment for industrial policy

The structure of political decision-making

The federal structure of West Germany distributes economic power between the federal, the state (provincial) and local authorities. In principle, state governments and local authorities are fiscally independent from the federal government, though a grey area of mixed financing has emerged, reflecting a degree of central budget imperialism. They receive directly about one-half of tax revenues (from their own sources or their share of federal income and value added taxes). They account for more than four-fifths of public investment (local authorities alone for more than two-thirds), so that the capacity of the federal government to exercise overall economic control is somewhat limited. Furthermore, the economic power of the state governments is reinforced by the rule that the Bundesrat, the second house of the West German parliament, which is made up of representatives of the state governments, has to agree to virtually all major steps of federal economic policy.

Federal government measures (including federal agencies and banks) account for only slightly more than half of total public aid to the business enterprise sector (Jüttemeier 1984, p. 48). For industry (mining and manufacturing), federal funds are more important, reflecting the fact that a major portion of high-technology and regional support goes to industry. However, industry is on average far less subsidized than the service sectors. In relation to net value added (excluding subsidies), in 1973 — the first year for which comprehensive information on public aid was made available (Jüttemeier and Lammers 1979; Jüttemeier 1984; Gerken *et al.* 1985) — total subsidies amounted to about 9 per cent in the business enterprise sector and less than 3 per cent in manufacturing (rising to 4.2 per cent in 1984, due to a wave of subsidies for steel and shipbuilding). For the business enterprise sector as a whole, the ratio peaked at 11 per cent in 1979 and has remained around 10.5 per cent since (Gerken *et al.* 1985).

As the state governments enjoy considerable bargaining power in relation to the centre, intervention by the federal government substantially reflects their interests (coal-mining, steel, shipbuilding), and they also are well equipped to pursue autonomous policies outside the three 'common tasks' already mentioned.

A fairly consistent pattern of intervention has, however, become apparent. Federal action mainly covers sectoral structural policy (energy, coal, steel, shipyards, shipping and aerospace), technology policy, and public shareholding in industry. Federal funds are provided mainly for large firms, though programmes for small and medium-sized firms have been considerably extended since the mid-1970s. State governments also provide substantial aid to small- and medium-sized businesses and incentives for new ventures, and occasionally come to the rescue of local firms. State governments, depending on local electorates, are of course particularly sensitive to the problems of local firms. Their main measure has been the provision of loan guarantees to banks controlled by the state or local authorities, and even to private commercial banks. Given the large number of rescue operations and the inevitability of some failures, this kind of intervention has led to various subsidization scandals.

In recent years, state governments have tried to stimulate new firms and industries, preferably in high technology. In line with international fashion, so-called technology parks have been established in many university towns. The state government provides infrastructure and advice for new entrepreneurs, the hope being that technology transfers from the universities will stimulate innovative activities. The federal government has been notably more reluctant to intervene at the firm level (at least directly), and has often left the big banks to rescue giant firms (Krupp, Volkswagen, AEG), presumably at the expense of the bank shareholders and customers. Nevertheless, the federal government was also involved in most cases in one way or another, if only in the background.

The role of the banks

The West German banking system is said to have an extraordinarily intimate relationship with the big industrial groups. The three big banks in particular (Deutsche Bank, Dresdner Bank, Commerzbank) are often regarded as the supervisory board of the supervisory boards of industrial concerns. Criticism of their allegedly excessive economic power raises questions about a 'universal' system which allows the banks to act as brokers, investment analysts, dealers and much else besides. Major changes have been proposed (Eckstein 1980, pp. 465–82), in particular with regard to:

(i) participation of banks in non-bank corporations (only West Germany and Luxembourg lack all restrictions on the participation of banks in non-bank corporations);
(ii) the *Depotstimmrecht*, that is the proxy votes by banks on behalf of shares deposited with them by clients;
(iii) the representation of banks on the supervisory boards of non-bank corporations.

Two recent investigations have shed light on the penetration of the corporate sector of the economy by the banks (Monopolkommission 1978; Studienkommission 1979). Their findings refer to the voting power of the banks in the 100 largest corporations (*Aktiengesellschaften*) in industry and trade in 1974–5. These are not necessarily identical with the 100 largest firms, since the total includes a number of (mainly limited liability) companies with a different legal structure.

(i) At the annual general meeting of sixteen corporations, the bank-owned shares came to over 25 per cent of shares represented. Counting proxies, the banks represented over 25 per cent of the votes in forty-one corporations, and over 50 per cent in thirty. (A holding of equity in any corporation of 25 per cent plus one share represents the legal minimum to block a change in the statutes and provides certain tax advantages.) Through proxies alone, the banks could vote for more than 10 per cent of the shares in fifty cases and for more than 25 per cent in twenty-nine cases.

(ii) The banks had no vote at all at the annual general meeting of forty-four corporations. In fifteen cases, they represented (including proxies) shares of less than 25 per cent. These are largely corporations majority-owned by foreign companies, by (founder) families and by foundations and, in some cases, by the state.

(iii) The representation of the banks on the supervisory boards of corporations goes far beyond what could be inferred from their voting shares. There is hardly a corporation where the banks do not have at least one member on the supervisory board.

(iv) The three large banks are pre-eminent as far as holdings of equity in non-bank corporations and proxy voting in annual general meetings are concerned. With the three large banks are 41 per cent of the banks' holdings of equity in non-bank corporations. In fifteen cases these banks voted for more than 25 per cent of the shares as proxy holders. The value of their participation in non-bank corporations exceeded the value of their own shares (at current rates of exchange).

(v) The influence of the banks is particularly strong in iron and steel, engineering, vehicle manufacture and department stores.

It is hard to assess how far the close relationship between the banks and the big corporations contributes to overall industrial performance. It has been argued that the banks are well equipped to provide strategic advice and that, wanting good returns, they are vitally concerned with the efficiency of their clients. Others counter that they are preoccupied with big firms and that, if their loans can be considered as venture capital, this implies a major distortion of capital markets. The system also fosters economic concentration, and fear of banks' misuse of their power has led to demands to limit the bank–industry connection. To put all this in perspective, it should be remembered that firms with under 1,000 employees provide half the jobs in industry and two-thirds in the economy as a whole. Moreover, a study comparing the British and German banking systems found little evidence that German banks could, or tried to, influence day-to-day management (Economists Advisory Group Ltd 1981, Ch. 5).

Industrial relations

The remarkable stability of industrial relations in West Germany is often regarded as a key factor in the performance of industry. Though this stability may be as much effect as cause, there are some characteristics peculiar to German unions and to German institutional regulations which seem to have been essential to the successful functioning of industrial relations (Jacobs *et al.* 1978). The incidence of strikes in Germany has been considerably lower than in other industrial countries. This reflects the lessons drawn by the unions from the consequences of confrontation during the Weimar Republic. After 1948 they opted for cooperation, tailored their wage demands to overall economic conditions and the need for growth, and welcomed technological change and innovation. There was full employment from the mid-1950s to the 1970s so that the unions were not generally concerned about job opportunities. In some cases they acted to protect jobs in declining sectors (coal-mining, shipbuilding and textiles), sometimes in cooperation with the employers. Such actions have become more frequent since the economic crisis of the 1970s. The unions have also become much more sceptical about the effects of rationalization.

The unions have organized on the principle of one union for each industry, with the exception of a special union for white-collar workers. This has avoided the complications of inter-union competition. Interestingly, this was largely due to the influence of the British government after the war. The legal-institutional framework guarantees autonomous collective bargaining and ensures a controlled framework for managing disputes. For example, strikes are prohibited until the period of the last wage settlement ends, and there is provision for conciliation if agreement cannot be reached in direct negotiations.

Labour has been integrated into the decision-making process in industry in several ways. First, a 1952 Act (modified in 1972) established works councils directly elected by employees independently of the unions. The works councils have rights of information and consultation on working conditions and manpower organization in the firm. For large firms, a so-called 'simple co-determination' (minority representation) of labour on the supervisory boards was established. Second, in the coal and steel industry 50 per cent numerical and voting participation for labour in the supervisory boards (except the vote of one neutral member) was introduced in 1951. Provision was also made for a labour director nominated by the unions. In 1976 co-determination on supervisory boards was extended to all large firms, with labour parity less one vote and some of labour's seats going to managerial employees. Third, the Concerted Action of the Stability and Growth Act of 1967 was intended to improve coordination among major interest groups—especially unions and employer associations. But when the employers sued in the Federal Constitutional Court to block the Co-determination Act of 1976, the unions withdrew and brought Concerted

Action to an end. Since the early 1970s, organized labour has become somewhat less cooperative. The great metal-workers strike of 1984 showed that stable industrial relations cannot be taken for granted. A new generation of labour leaders seems to be more ideologically orientated and less concerned to take responsibility for the overall state of the economy.

Other major institutional influences

Under West Germany's proportional representation system, the number of seats each party obtains in the federal parliament (Bundestag) depends on its share of votes, so long as it has a minimum of 5 per cent of the total. The result is a party system based on two big parties (Christian and Social Democrats) and traditionally one, and more recently two, small parties (Free Democrats and the Greens). Only once in 1957, has a party (the Christian Democrats) obtained an absolute majority in a federal election. Coalition government has therefore been the norm. This has diminished the differences between the policies of ideologically different administrations, in contrast to Britain where the pendulum swings much more widely. In the years preceding the change from the coalition of Free and Social Democrats to that of Christian and Free Democrats in October 1982, even Social Democrats increasingly stressed the role of private investment in economic recovery, while the Christian Democrats were careful to avoid excessively radical proposals for 'cutting government back to size'. Since then, with the Social Democrats in Opposition and the Greens represented in the Bundestag, verbal divergences on economic policy issues have increased again. But apart from the Greens, there still seems to be a broad area of tacit consensus, notwithstanding strong Opposition rhetoric, especially on nuclear power and social issues.

The involvement of the *European Community*, in the coal and steel industry, in foreign trade policy, regional policy and competition policies has influenced intervention in industry. True, the major instruments of intervention remain under national control. The EEC has only recently acquired wider competence (the amendment to the EEC treaty that became effective on 1 January 1987) and funds for industrial intervention. The Commission also lacks efficient sanctions against governments violating EEC principles. Nevertheless, the Community influences intervention in industry in two ways. First, the need for coordination among member countries has shifted parts of the decision-making process to the European centre. Second, industries demanding protection can complain directly to the Commission. In West Germany, a substantial part of increasing industrial intervention is the consequence of European initiatives. The European Community has primarily been concerned with declining industries (textiles, clothing, coal, steel, shipbuilding), though there have been growing Community efforts to promote high-technology and innovative activities in recent years.

The environment for decision-making in industry and economic policy has latterly been affected by the rise of *public-interest groups*, directed not only at the nuclear industry but at all large-scale investment. The judicial system, which has a special branch for dealing with public administration issues, makes it relatively easy to block or significantly postpone state approval of private investment. Minority groups seem less willing than in the past to accept majority decisions, particularly on environmental questions. Political parties cannot afford to disregard these changing social attitudes to economic development.

The distinguishing feature of reform in the *educational system* since the mid-1960s has been the rapid expansion of higher and university education. Post-school training on the job, combining training in the plant with theoretical education at special state schools, has become less attractive for the more talented pupils. Even with high unemployment, skilled production workers have become scarce. This has effectively reduced the elasticity with which the supply side of the economy can respond to changing conditions.

3.3 The interaction of public and private strategies

Industrial adjustment problems since the early 1970s

The main structural economic change in West Germany since the early 1970s has been the loss of over 2 million jobs in manufacturing (20 per cent). It was not until the second half of 1985 that manufacturing jobs increased again significantly. The decline in manufacturing reflected only in part the two oil shocks and ensuing recessions. It was also, to a considerable extent, the consequence of structural adjustment pressures. These included: (i) the breakdown of the Bretton Woods system and a currency appreciation cancelling previous artificial competitive advantages, to the point of creating artificial disadvantages by over-shooting; (ii) high wage settlements (excessive in 1974) squeezing profit margins; (iii) rising real energy costs, causing difficulties for a technological system based on cheap energy, and for wage bargaining; (iv) increased competition from new sources of supply, in particular from Japan and newly industrializing countries (NICs).

After the first oil price rise, economic depression hampered rapid adjustment. In the longer run, however, the relatively weak response itself seems to have contributed to poor macro-economic performance. Capital formation remained sluggish for years; it only temporarily gained momentum at the end of the 1970s and soon weakened again in the course of the second oil price crisis. Unemployment, although declining from 4.7 per cent of the labour force in 1975 to 3.7 per cent in 1979–80, remained high by past standards, and in part reflected a growing labour supply because of rising numbers of school leavers.

Nevertheless, prospects for the overall economy did not look bad on the eve of the second oil price shock. Inflation fell from 6.9 per cent in 1973–4 to 2.7 per cent by 1978. Real GDP increased by 3 per cent in 1978 and by 4 per cent in 1979 to 15 per cent over the 1973 level and employment increased, too, though at modest rates. It could appear that the economy was moving back to pre-1973 patterns of development. But brighter prospects were largely confined to service sectors. Manufacturing did not fit into the picture. Employment remained below the level of the recession year 1975 throughout the second half of the 1970s; real value added was just 11 per cent higher in 1979–80 than in 1973.

Manufacturing was the sector most exposed to the adjustment challenges of the 1970s. An appreciating currency and reinforced foreign competition from new sources of supply mainly affected export and import substitution industries. To maintain market positions at home and abroad, industry would have had to lower prices in US dollar terms. Rising labour costs at home could not be passed on to customers, given the competitive conditions. Though much marginal supply was wiped from the market, industrial profitability and productivity (at current prices) worsened considerably relative to domestic sectors (Fels *et al.* 1981). Standardized labour-intensive or raw-material-intensive lines of production were hardest hit. The transition process in industry towards skill-intensive, research-intensive and more sophisticated products (including complementary software and other services) which had been proceeding for a long time, was dramatically accelerated. but much of this restructuring took place in the form of lower rates of employment decline rather than of real expansion in 'growth' activities.

The West German international trade position (excluding trade in petroleum and petroleum products) steadily deteriorated in the second half of the 1970s (Fig. 3.1), almost exclusively due to changes in manufacturing. The decline of net merchandise exports was a major component underlying the shift of the current account into deficit which eventually occurred in 1979, coinciding with a renewed boost of the bill for oil imports. This is not to deny that the second oil price rise would have brought the current account into deficit in any case. The real appreciation of the Deutsche mark, particularly after 1977, adversely affected the foreign-trade balance. West German shares in world exports fell (Fig. 3.2). The drawbacks of such an indicator — affected by the impact of rising oil prices (the share of fuels in world exports peaked at 24 per cent in 1981, up from 11 per cent in 1973), exchange rate fluctuations and diverging business cycles — cannot explain away the marked drop in the West German export share trend relative to the performance of industrial countries as a group.

In the 1980s, adjustment challenges changed. The slump after the second oil price shock hit West German industry hard and proved long-lasting. Real value added did not recover above the 1980 level before the second half of 1984. Profit rates in manufacturing, which had stabilized from 1976 to 1979, fell to an all time low in 1982. Real interest rates on financial assets which

Figure 3.1.   Net merchandise exports, oil imports, terms of trade and real exchange rate of the Deutsche mark, 1970–85

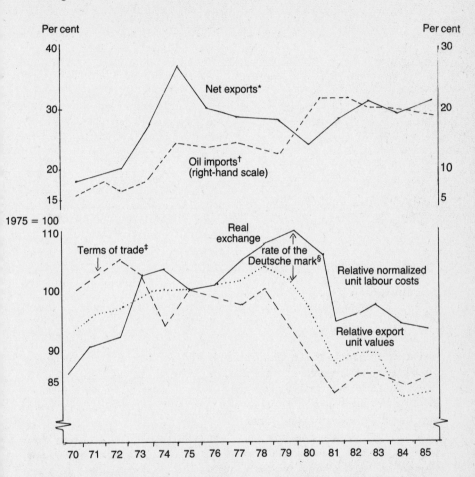

* Net merchandise exports (excluding imports of crude petroleum and petroleum products) in per cent of merchandise exports.

† Imports of crude petroleum and petroleum products in per cent of merchandise exports.

‡ Index of export unit values related to index of import unit values; from 1980 onward, based on original data with new base year 1980 = 100.

§ In relation to currencies of the thirteen most important other Western trading nations (sixteen reference countries from 1980 onward).

Source: International Monetary Fund, *International Financial Statistics*, current issues, own calculations.

Figure 3.2.   Share of West German exports in world merchandise exports, 1970–85*

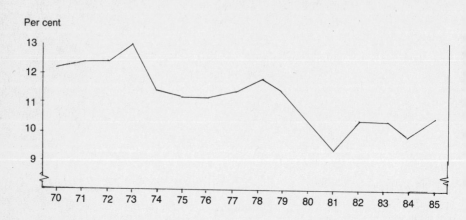

* Based on data in US dollars at current prices and exchange rates.
Source: International Monetary Fund, *International Financial Statistics,* current issues, own calculations.

had sharply risen before, were considerably higher than real rates of return on fixed-capital investment from 1981 to 1984 (Dicke and Trapp 1985). Fixed-capital formation declined, many industrial corporations preferred to invest in financial assets (mainly government bonds) or abroad. There were high net direct investment outflows.

Relief came from a depreciating Deutsche mark and from modest wage settlements. The devaluation of the currency occurred in a major slide in 1980 and 1981. Considered against the US dollar alone, devaluation continued until spring 1985 towards a level implying a strong over-shooting downward. The net trade position in manufactures started to improve markedly as early as 1981, and the current-account surplus re-emerged with increasing strength. The terms-of-trade deterioration from 1979 to 1981 implied a major pressure on production costs, much stronger than in 1973–4. Again, initially, real-wage restraint did not offset the rise of other real costs, although in absolute terms hourly real-wage rates in industry slightly declined. The 'real-wage position' of labour increased substantially (Sachverständigenrat 1985), resulting in squeezed profit margins. In the following years, however, the real-wage position fell by considerably more than it had risen before. Hourly real-wage rates did not surpass 1980 levels again before 1985, the third year of the cyclical upswing. Hence the recent strong recovery of industry has only in part been led by exports and devaluation. It has also been backed by cuts in domestic costs. Along with rising capital formation and employment, this suggests that restored profit margins may in 1986 have a solid base.

A remarkable feature of industry's performance since the second oil price shock is that expenditures on R & D were hardly affected by the recession. The ratio of R & D expenditures to value added in industry (or to GDP in the overall economy) increased between 1979 and 1985, although the contribution of government funds decreased in relative terms. The private sector correspondingly reinforced R & D efforts (Bundesminister für Forschung und Technologie 1986). This points to a potential success in restructuring industry. The debate on the new and allegedly widening technology gap *vis-à-vis* with the United States and Japan (Horn 1983; Bundesminister für Wirtschaft 1984; Schmidt *et al.* 1984; Börnsen, Glismann and Horn 1985) which had stirred the public in the early 1980s, soon faded in the upswing after the second oil crisis. It fits into the picture that the loss of export market shares (in US dollar terms), which occured in the 1978–81 period, was not particularly strong in high-technology products; in the recovery of export shares since, high-technology exports have performed above average. The revival of confidence also indicates that it seems to have paid off for West German companies not to cut back innovative activities in recession and to stick to longer-term technological strategies.

On balance, West German industry seems to have coped rather well with adjustment pressures over the past one and a half decades. But the costs of adjustment have been heavy. There has been a huge loss of jobs and a high number of bankruptcies in manufacturing. From this angle the performance appears less persuasive. The adjustment pressures and the ability of industry to meet them should be looked at in a broader perspective.

Adjustment problems since the first oil price shock have been minor in size (though not necessarily in importance) compared with the post-war period. By 1959, when full employment was achieved, West Germany had absorbed more than 12 million refugees and displaced persons from the East. The labour force rose by almost 4 million to 25.3 million between 1950 and 1957. Most of these people did not, initially, find good starting conditions: the capital stock with which to employ them had still to be formed. The government's capacity to assist was limited. The resources at its command in public infrastructure and social services were ridiculously inadequate to the problems to be overcome. On the other hand, the newcomers had the same language and culture as the West Germans and were similarly well educated, highly adaptable and mobile. Abundant labour supply kept wages low. Presumably, wages were initially below the marginal product of labour in overcrowded agriculture. As regards entrepreneurs, it seems that the war had created an activity gap in economic matters which was going to be closed. The supply of entrepreneurs proved to be rather elastic, indicating confidence in the future, once the foundations of the new economic order had been laid.

In the reconstruction period, rapid structural adjustment took place almost by itself. It is in comparison with this 'miracle' that the fundamental causes of slow structural adjustment after the first oil crisis show up clearly. West German industry, having by the late 1960s exhausted most of the potential for catching up with US technology, seems to have entered a critical stage of transition characterized by declining 'supply elasticities'. These constraints on the dynamics of industry include institutional constraints (government intervention and public-interest group rivalries); a shortage of entrepreneurship (a shift in social behaviour towards risk avoidance); a shortage of factors complementary to investment and innovation; distortions in relative prices (in particular, excessive real wages and depressed profits); welfare state regulations diminishing structural adaptability (Giersch 1979). In sum, industry's ability to adjust appropriately, and in time, was limited after the first oil shock in comparison with the reconstruction period. One has to take into account, however, that the structural adjustment pressures after the first oil price shock were of a different nature. They demanded innovation, while in the 1950s much of the adjustment was merely catching-up.

Patterns of government interventions

A coherent and comprehensive concept of industrial policy has never been developed in West Germany. The principles of structural policy came nearest to defining such a framework for government intervention in industry. But they were merely a declaration of intent by the federal government and have not decisively influenced decision-making. There has instead been a cumulation of selective measures over time. Today industrial policy represents a conglomerate of measures for a variety of (sometimes contradictory) aims. In some cases, for instance, the interventions are defended as a remedy for (supposed) market failure in allocating resources efficiently and in promoting economic growth; in other cases they are designed to preserve traditional structures of production and employment or to smoothen adjustment processes. The principles of structural policy once designed to limit and to guide government intervention, hardly show up in this pattern. It is precisely since the early 1970s that industrial policy measures have become most selective and distorting.

In West Germany, as elsewhere, the typical main branches of industrial policy are international trade protection (import barriers, export promotion, preferential treatment of domestic suppliers) and assistance to domestic firms or industries. Both discriminate by their very nature, as between foreign and domestic suppliers, as between domestic industries and sometimes as between firms in the same industry. The importance of trade protectionism declined over the post-war period, at least until the 'new' protectionism of the 1970s. 'Domestic' assistance (mainly subsidies and public procurement) has been of growing importance, particularly since the first oil crisis.

In theory, the political responsibility for commercial policy has shifted to the European Community. The common external tariff system and a common trade policy distinguish the Community from a mere free-trade association. The structure of tariff protection has always favoured low-skill labour-intensive and raw-material-intensive production and discriminated against human capital and R-&-D-intensive manufactures (Donges *et al.* 1973; Breithaupt *et al.* 1979). Tariff policy therefore tends to contradict R & D policy. But tariff protection has substantially decreased. In 1972, following the Kennedy Round, the average nominal tariff rate for industrial products amounted to 9 per cent (unweighted average) and fell to about 6 per cent when the Tokyo round cuts were completed prematurely in 1985.

During the past decade non-tariff barriers (quantitative restrictions, price-raising measures at the frontiers, anti-dumping procedures, import surveillance, etc.) have increased in importance both absolutely and in relation to tariff protection, mainly discriminating against low-wage countries and Japan. Considerable autonomy is also left to each EC member state. The federal government has shown little activity in this field in comparison to other member countries. It has hardly ever resorted to Article 115 of the EC treaty, which makes it possible to exempt third-country imports from Community treatment; and only a few cases of bilateral restrictions have become known, such as the suspected but not officially confirmed 'voluntary' agreements to restrict Japanese car exports into Germany in the early 1980s. The federal government has not actively promoted protection at the EC level. Nevertheless, 18 per cent of German imports from developing countries and 12 per cent of German imports from third industrial countries were affected by non-tariff barriers in the year 1983 (Donges and Schatz 1986). Corresponding figures for most other member countries are distinctly higher (with an EC–ten average of 25 and 19 per cent, respectively). But the liberal trade rhetoric of the federal government seems to be a more adequate yardstick. Moreover, it could be argued that the federal government should have been less reluctant to resist protectionist tendencies in the Community. There is a suspicion that the attraction of increased opportunities for West German suppliers in the Common Market may have influenced this attitude at least as much as Community solidarity.

Quantitative import restrictions have always been rather frequent against socialist countries of Central and Eastern Europe which are not members of GATT or which are discriminated against despite GATT membership (Hungary, Poland, Romania). Other prominent instances of non-tariff barriers are:

(i) The restriction of textile and clothing imports under the Multi-Fibre Agreement and through a comprehensive system of bilateral 'agreements'.

(ii) The crisis management in iron and steel under the regime of the European Community for Coal and Steel, beginning with the Davignon plan in 1977 (Dicke and Glismann forthcoming). The EC-negotiated bilateral 'voluntary export restrictions' (VERs) covered 70–80 per cent of EC imports in 1984.

(iii) Cases of exemption from Community treatment by other member countries. These were particularly frequent during the 1981–4 recession.

(iv) VERs between Japan and the EC. Since 1983, temporary VERs have been negotiated for video cassette recorders (VCRs), colour TVs, cathode ray tubes, numerically controlled machine tools, radio receiving and transmission equipment, quartz watches and, presumably, cars.

(v) Many anti-dumping and import surveillance procedures directed primarily against NICs. These often result in 'orderly marketing agreements'.

For West Germany non-tariff barriers (NTBs) have been most relevant in textiles and clothing, steel, coal, ceramics, wood and wood products, leather and glass.

For the EC, non-tariff protection has shown marked cyclical ups and downs. It has duly declined recently in response to economic conditions. In any event, it can be expected to remain an important trade policy instrument. First, the philosophy underlying EC commercial policy incorporates safeguards, countervailing duties, and the like, as essential measures of last resort. During the Tokyo round, the EC rejected any major international rules to constrain them. Second, the efforts to complete the internal market (Commission of the European Communities 1985) tend to induce claims to more external protection. This has become most obvious regarding high-technology products where France has explicitly advanced proposals for such a trade-off. Precedents already exist; for instance, the EC unilaterally raised the tariff on VCRs from 8 per cent to 14 per cent effective 1 January 1986. Third, the New Trade Policy Instrument introduced in 1984 made it easier for private firms to petition for import relief and strengthened the competence of the Commission to initiate safeguard clause procedures. In such cases the Council can overrule decisions of the Commission only by qualified majority. This has made it all the more attractive for West German firms to bypass the federal government and direct claims for protection to the European centre.

As concerns domestic intervention (e.g. subsidies, regulations, public procurement), the national autonomy of EC member states is hardly restricted, except where national measures conflict with EC competition rules or with the explicit institutional competence of the EC (as for coal and steel). This can be expected gradually to constrain national freedom as the internal market is being pushed forward in accord with the far-reaching aims of the EC treaty. The EC-centre (the Commission) is also gaining a foothold in technology and industrial policies, where it has not hitherto been relevant. The international trading order (the GATT) does not provide effective restrictions on domestic measures either. The subsidy codes agreed in the Tokyo round have proved irrelevant in practice. Technology policy measures were largely excluded in any case. These are precisely the key areas of international dispute on industrial policy.

It is hard to assess the activity of domestic market interventions, not to speak of their effects. Access, price, quantity and quality regulations in the West German economy require detailed study, industry by industry, product by product. Systematic statistical information on discriminatory practices in public procurement is hard to come by. Transparency is much higher on direct financial assistance to industry, and in the last resort government aid to industry makes up the core of industrial policy. Comprehensive studies carried out at the Kiel Institute for World Economics (Jüttemeier and Lammers 1979; Jüttemeier 1984; Gerken *et al.* 1985; Donges and Schatz 1986) provide detailed information for the 1973–85 period. For industry as a whole (mining plus manufacturing) subsidies increased much more rapidly than value added. The subsidy rate (subsidies as a percentage of net value added excluding subsidies) rose from 2.9 per cent in 1973 to a peak of 4.2 per cent in 1984. It has been inferred from this that direct financial assistance has been increasingly used to compensate for the loss of autonomy in commercial policy (Donges 1980). At least, interference through fiscal measures allows federal and state governments to broach their various structural policy objectives more directly, and more selectively. Interestingly, the effective fiscal protection rate of industry proper (mining and manufacturing) is much lower than the effective tariff protection rate (about 9 per cent of value added in manufacturing in the early 1980s). But in reality tariff protection has become a paper tiger: regular MFN tariff rates only apply to non-preferential imports, that is to imports from Australia, New Zealand, the United States, Canada, South Africa, Japan and Taiwan, and to imports from developing countries in excess of their tariff-free quotas. Tariff protection for most trade has become low to non-existent.

Apart from *ad hoc* rescue operations, most government aid to industry is in the framework of technology policy and 'structural' policy. The sectoral aspect of structural policy tends to be underestimated because state governments' actions, though important, are poorly documented. Regional subsidies tend to be overestimated because the preferential treatment of West Berlin is included, and in this case it is not clear what should be regarded as genuine subsidy. In its regional policy, the Federal government has repeatedly claimed to have generated large numbers of new jobs and achieved some convergence of regional income and productivity levels. Of course, no one knows what would have happened without regional policy, and funds have been dispersed over wide areas. Regional disparities do not seem to have become smaller over the last two decades.

As to sectoral structural policy, the highly selective distribution of government aid has concentrated on industries in trouble at one end of the spectrum (coal, steel, shipbuilding) and at the other on high-technology sectors.

Declining industries:

(i) *Hard-coal mining* has been under the tutelage of government since its first major crisis in the late 1950s. Subsidy rates increased to a peak of 159 per cent of net value added (excluding subsidies) in 1979, and were still above 80 per cent before the recent fall of oil prices, which together with the appreciation of the Deutsche mark, has put the industry under renewed strain. The stated objective of coal policy has always been to guarantee a certain degree of self-reliance in energy supply. As production conditions have steadily worsened in comparison to foreign supply (due mainly to the increasing depth of exploitable coal deposits), subsidies can be expected to continue to rise further.

(ii) As with agriculture and coal, competence for the *iron and steel* market is largely with the Community. In the temporary steel crises of the past, import protection against third countries was the remedy. In the recent and much deeper and longer-lasting slump, the Commission introduced—in addition to stringent import restrictions—comprehensive regulation of the internal market, including floor prices and production quotas by product and by company. This European super-cartel has not prevented a subsidization race among European governments in the attempt to restructure the industry. The federal government has proved relatively reluctant to subsidize. Nevertheless, the subsidization rate exceeded 9 per cent in 1982. An efficient newcomer, the Korff Stahl AG, was forced into bankruptcy by the quota regime and by subsidized competition. In the 1980–5 period West German subsidies (56 marks per ton rolling mill steel) were only one-quarter of those in other European steel-producing countries (Herdmann and Weiss 1985). That measure reveals a substantial distortion, but in the last resort West German steel needs to face up to subsidized competition from third countries.

(iii) In 1973–4 *shipbuilding* was subsidized at 12 per cent of net value added. This has approached levels betwen 20 and 40 per cent since 1979. The shares of West Germany in world shipbuilding exports and employment have been declining since the late 1950s. The federal government started the first aid programme in 1962. By the end of the eighth aid programme (1976–83) shipbuilding had received 2.5 billion marks. Despite this, it has sunk into the deepest crisis ever experienced.

High technology:

(i) Defence policy and the alleged need to close a technological gap have favoured subsidization of the *aircraft industry* since the mid-1950s. For the foreseeable future the industry is not likely to be able to stand on its own feet. Even the allegedly successful Airbus programme has been absorbing increasing subsidies. Public grants have already reached 2.4 billion marks; further grants of 0.9 billion marks and loan guarantees of 4 billion marks are under discussion. The aerospace industry benefits from military procurement and from public policy to promote civilian technology (e.g. commercial satellites, cooperation in the European Space Agency and cooperation with the NASA space shuttle programme). It has performed relatively well, recently, in terms of employment and value added, but largely at the expense of the taxpayer. The subsidization rate has remained fairly high (20 per cent in 1982), though it came down from over 60 per cent in the early 1970s. New programmes, in particular the diversification of the Airbus family (including a four-engine long-distance aircraft) and the development of a new European fighter aircraft can be expected to drive up subsidization again.

(ii) In the late 1960s and early 1970s, with the construction of a number of plants at home and successful exports, the development of *nuclear energy* looked like a success story. A highly developed technology and safety standards superior to the international norm were expected to result in rapid expansion. But growing public anxiety about nuclear power and the activity of environmentalist groups has steadily raised the barriers to the construction of nuclear power plants in West Germany. Given the 25 billion marks of public money already spent on R & D in nuclear energy between 1956 and 1979, this could prove the most important failure of industrial policy. All the same, nuclear energy now contributes over three-tenths of electricity generation. After Chernobyl one can question whether the current federal government (at the outset, unlike its Socialist–Liberal predecessor, strongly pro-nuclear energy) will approve the construction of any new reactors.

(iii) In *telecommunications* the procurement policy of the federal Post Office has always been an outstanding example of comprehensive market regulation. Though the Federal Post Office claims that it is not discriminating against foreign supplies, factual evidence for market segments where the information is available often reveals the opposite. Regarding switching devices, for instance, the market is reserved to four domestic (though not all domestically owned) firms, with fairly constant market shares over time. The leading supplier is Siemens with about 50 per cent of the market in the 1975–82 period.

In general, federal technology policy shifted towards selective intervention by expanding project-tied R & D funding during the 1970s. Critics have raised a number of objections. Funds are concentrated on a small number of large corporations: in 1979, six firms received 44 per cent of the funds distributed by the Federal Research and Technology Ministry. There is excessive bureaucratic influence on firms' R & D priorities. Policy discriminates against small businesses not powerful enough to surmount bureaucratic barriers. And R & D lacks awareness of market needs and possibilities. In response to these criticisms support to R & D in small- and medium-sized firms has been significantly increased by public grants to R & D wage costs, investment premiums, provision of risk venture capital for innovation, and improved information services on technological developments and opportunities. The pendulum has swung back to non-selective, non-discriminatory measures since the late 1970s. The present federal government confirmed the shift after 1982, though it has maintained virtually all inherited programmes and even created some new ones.

The 'national champion' approach has never been highly regarded in policymaking except in the aircraft industry, coal and energy (though the state governments are more inclined to back their favourite regional industries). There have been, nevertheless, elements of such an approach. The regulation of mergers has been used, in effect, to discriminate against foreign investment (e.g. when GKN tried to take over Fichtel & Sachs or BP tried to acquire a major share in Preussag), and the Deutsche Bank was applauded for taking over 25 per cent of the equity capital of Daimler Benz to prevent the shares falling into the hands of newly oil-rich countries. In public procurement (civilian and military hardware, the railways, the post office, state-owned public utilities) there is a strong preference for the domestic product, particularly in cases where technology policy wishes to demonstrate its success in the market-place.

The federal government has proclaimed a fundamental turn in industrial policy towards cutting back selective intervention, including deregulation, privatization and reducing subsidies. Such policy changes can be only achieved gradually. So, in the case of the regionally concentrated industries in crisis (shipyards and iron and steel), the federal government has not resisted the pressure for protection and has granted new subsidies. But in other areas, significant policy changes are under way or to be expected:

(i)   the reform of capital market regulations in order to improve the supply of venture capital;
(ii) the removal of barriers to the introduction of new electronic media;
(iii) measures favouring the foundation of new technology-based firms.

Favouring new technology-based firms has become a fashionable theme of industrial policy all over Western Europe (Commission of the European Communities 1983). Such firms, which have been rare so far, are supposed to stimulate substantially innovation in industry, as they have apparently done in the United States.

The results of government intervention

The central issue in industrial policy has always been the conflict between promoting economic growth through structural adjustment and the political economy of protection. Of course, the two policy branches may overlap at some point. Furthermore, there is a permanent dichotomy regarding aims and objectives within the 'growth department'. Should government, for instance, leave the selection to the market mechanism and concentrate on improving the functioning of markets or should government itself selectively judge the relevance of particular projects?

How does one measure success in government intervention, be it qualitatively or quantitatively? In the last resort, success can only mean that industry has performed better through intervention and that this industrial performance has benefited the overall economy (a 'Schumpeterian' criterion). But what would performance have been without intervention? The Schumpeterian macro-performance criterion requires inter-temporal or international comparisons of different policy regimes. But even such comparisons can be misleading.

A prominent example is the relatively comprehensive prohibition of high-technology activities, as imposed by the occupation powers in post-war West Germany until 1955. It was a rather efficient industrial policy for downgrading industrial activities and promoting a brain drain. But this did not show up in macro-economic performance figures of the time, in which previously existing technological leads, for example in aircraft, missiles or computing, were dissipated.

In view of all these difficulties, only some tentative conclusions can be drawn on the effects of industrial policy:

(i) Structural policies in favour of selected declining sectors (like hard coal, shipbuilding, steel) have hardly contributed to successful restructuring. In most cases, designed to be temporary, they have led to permanent subsidization. 'Il n'y a que le provisoire qui dure', in this as in other respects.

(ii) Industrial policy has in many less favoured industries scarcely aimed at retarding industrial adjustment. Even a drastic decline in employment, for example in textiles, was considered with a certain benign neglect.

(iii) The funds of regional structural policy have been fairly evenly distributed among industries, though it is possible that the policy has mostly favoured declining firms. Not enough information is available to give a clear account.

(iv) The record of federal government and state governments in rescue operations for larger firms since the early 1970s has been one of frustration, while the banks seem to have performed somewhat better (AEG for instance). But this may simply be because the worst risks (particularly in crisis sectors) have been left to the state.

(v) Technology policy for growth sectors so far has not produced sectors growing on their own. Aircraft and nuclear energy are prominent examples. This is not to deny evidence of success at the micro-level, but the overall results do not seem to be overwhelming.

3.4 Trends which may prove critical

The West German economy is widely held to be strongly market-orientated. On closer inspection, things look somewhat different. The federal as well as the state governments intervene in the markets in a number of ways. Until recently, government intervention increased considerably over time. The current centre-right coalition has promised to reverse this in order to re-vitalize the economy. These attempts to strengthen the market side of the mixed economy have not made much progress so far. In the recent crises of the shipyard and steel industries, the federal government granted additional subsidies of several billion marks. This shows that in industrial policy, gradual changes, at best, are under way.

There are weak spots in the performance of West German industry that could limit capacity to adjust to future change. In the context of past industrial adjustment the following tendencies deserve attention:

(i)   The spread of protectionism: if this continues, it will not only affect the adjustment process but undermine industry's capacity for adjustment. First, adjustment is postponed in areas favoured by protection. Second, expectation of protection retards the search for anticipatory adjustment arrangements elsewhere. Third, protection discriminates against the unprotected so that relatively competitive industries are taxed to subsidize declining ones.

(ii) Declining supply elasticities: the responsiveness of industry to changing conditions seems to be more inert than, say, in the 1960s. This may be a consequence of the activities of public-interest groups but could also indicate that the internal 'dynamics' of industry have considerably declined. If so, this would make it all the more important to remove restrictions on, or introduce additional incentives for, innovation and investment.

(iii) Policy changes: as compared with the 1950s and 1960s, government intervention during the 1970s was more selective. Frequent changes in government priorities are in themselves a major problem for adjustment. Industry needs to plan for a longer time span than prevails in political decision-making. In recent years also, perceptions of economic policy have diverged considerably between the current coalition parties and the Social Democrats, not to mention the Greens.

(iv) Income distribution: in view of the 'big trade-off' between equity and economic growth (of which the trade-off between equity and efficiency is only part), in the 1970s redistribution issues disturbed political decision-making. This seems to be an important cause of declining supply elasticity. Since 1982, the federal government has so far made little, if any, progress in reducing social transfers, but has been vehemently criticized by the Social Democrats for dismantling the social welfare system. An important issue is whether redistribution controversies echo social attitudes, in which case these could change, or echo the structure of a society dominated by big interest groups (Thurow 1980), in which case they are not likely to.

(v) The educational system and labour supply: while more than 2 million people were still unemployed in 1986, employers complained of shortages of skilled production workers and qualified engineers, and not only in booming regions like most of Southern Germany, or sectors like information technologies. If industry is to expand further, training the jobless, including considerable numbers of university leavers like teachers, will prove crucial.

(vi) Industrial relations: the recovery after the second oil price crisis has been furthered by wage restraint. It remains to be seen whether the unions will tolerate a recovery of profit margins back to, say, pre-1973 levels. The metal-workers strike of 1984 indicates that more trouble might be ahead.

(vii) Exchange rate fluctuation: with the dollar exchange rate back to 2 marks in 1986, West German industry must overcome the hurdle of a highly valued domestic currency which could appreciate still further. The years to come will show how successful past restructuring has really been.

(viii) Deregulation: telecommunications are generally considered a key sector in modern industrial development. Among the leading industrial countries, West Germany seems to have a backlog in deregulation, in particular in comparison to Japan, the United States and Britain. The first steps have been taken: the federal government seems to be positively discussing denationalization, and increasing pressure for opening up markets is emanating from the European Commission. But opposition to deregulation is strong, in particular from the unions.

(ix) European Community: the recent amendment to the EC treaty has expanded the institutional competence of the European centre. The emerging European-style industrial policy could learn something from the experience (or failures) of German-style *Strukturpolitik*, British-style *industrial policy* or *planification à la française*. The larger internal market does not provide a guarantee for success where national experience has been frustrating. For West Germany, a 'low profile' approach aiming at minimum divergence from the policies of other member states (which would imply relatively strong and defensive interventionism) could involve high costs.

In sum, West German industry will have considerable difficulties to surmount in the future. Yet the assets are also substantial and the prospects do not look bad so long as industrial policy manages structural change by cutting back declining sectors and encouraging innovation and efficiency in the growth areas.

References

Börnsen, O., Glismann, H.H. and Horn, E.J. (1985), *Der Technologietransfer zwischen den USA und der Bundesrepublik*, Kieler Studien, 192, Tübingen, J.C.B. Mohr.

Breithaupt, K., Horn, E.-J., Klodt, H., Kriegsmann, K.-P., Neu, A.D. and Schmidt, K.D. (1979), *Analyse der strukturellen Entwicklung der deutschen Wirtschaft*, Kiel, Institut für Weltwirtschaft.

Der Bundesminister für Forschung und Technologie (1986), *Faktenbericht 1986 zum Bundesbericht Forschung*, Bonn.

Der Bundesminister für Wirtschaft (1984), *Hochtechnologien und internationale Wettbewerbsfähigkeit der deutschen Wirtschaft*, BMWI Dokumentation, No. 263, Bonn.

Commission of the European Communities (1983), *The Needs of New Technology-Based Enterprises*, Proceedings of the Symposium held by the Commission of the European Communities, Directorate General Information Market and Innovation, Luxembourg, 17–19 September 1982. Coordinators of the Symposium: G. Michel Gibb and Siegfried Neumann. Luxembourg: Infobrief (Banks and Industrial Innovation. Infobrief Series).

────── (1985), *Completing the Internal Market*, Com (85) 310, 14 June.

Dicke, H. and Glismann, H.H. (forthcoming), 'Troubled industries in Germany', in G.C. Hufbauer and H.F. Rosen, *Domestic Adjustment and International Trade*, Washington, DC, Institute for International Economics.

Dicke, H. and Trapp, P. (1985), 'Zur Ertragskraft von öffentlichen und privaten Investitionen', *Die Weltwirtschaft*, No. 1, pp. 70–86.

Donges, J.B. (1980), 'Industrial policies in West Germany's not so market-oriented economy', *The World Economy*, Vol. 3, pp. 185–204.

Donges, J.B. Fels, G., Neu, A.D., *et al.* (1973) *Protektion und Branchenstruktur der westdeutschen Wirtschaft*, Kieler Studien, 123, Tübingen, J.C.B. Mohr.

Donges, J.B. and Schatz, K.W. (1986), *Staatliche Interventionen in der Bundesrepublik Deutschland. Umfang, Struktur, Wirkungen*, Kiel Discussion Papers 119/20, Kiel, Institut für Weltwirtschaft.

Eckstein, W. (1980), 'The role of the banks in corporate concentration in West Germany', *Zeitschrift für die Gesamte Staatswissenschaft*, Vol. 136, pp. 465–82 (trans. from the German by Michael Hudson and Wolfgang F. Stolper).

Economists Advisory Group Ltd (1981), *The British and German Banking System: A Comparative Study*, London, Anglo-German Foundation for the Study of Industrial Society.

Fels, G., Breithaupt, K., Glismann, H.H., Horn, E.-J., Klodt, H., Kriegsmann, K.-P., Neu, A.D., Schmidt, K.-D., Schraad, N. and Wolter, F. (1981), *Die deutsche Wirtschaft im Strukturwandel*, Kieler Studien, 166, Tübingen, J.C.B. Mohr.

Gerken, E., Jüttemeier, K.-H., Schatz, K.W. and Schmidt, K.D. (1985), *Mehr Arbeitsplätze durch Subventionsabbau*, Kiel Discussion Papers 113/44, Kiel,

Institut für Weltwirtschaft.

Giersch, H. (1979), 'Aspects of growth, structural change, and employment—a Schumpeterian Perspective', *Weltwirtschaftliches Archiv*, Vol. 115, pp. 629–52.

Herdman, V. and Weiss, F.D. (1985), 'Wirkungen von Subventionen und Quoten: das Beispiel der EG Stahlindustrie' in *Weltwirtschaft* No. 1, Tübingen, J.C.B. Mohr.

Horn, E.J. (1982), *Management of Industrial Change in the federal Republic of Germany*, Sussex European Papers No. 13, Brighton, Sussex European Research Centre.

—— (1983), *Weltwirtschaftliche Herausforderung—Die deutschen Unternehmen im Anpassungsprozeß*, Beitrag zum Zweiten Strukturbericht an den Bundesminister für Wirtschaft, Kiel, Institut für Weltwirtschaft.

Jacobs, E., Orwell, S., Paterson, P. and Weltz, F. (1978), *The Approach to Industrial Change in Britain and Germany: A Comparative Study of Workplace Industrial Relations and Manpower Policies in British and West German Enterprises*, London, The Anglo-German Foundation for the Study of Industrial Society.

Jüttemeier, K.-H. (1984), *Deutsche Subventionspolitik in Zahlen 1973–1982*, Anlagenband zum Zweiten Strukturbericht des Instituts für Weltwirtschaft, Kiel, Institut für Weltwirtschaft.

Jüttemeier, K.H. and Lammers, K. (1979), *Subventionen in der Bundesrepublik Deutschland*, Kiel discussion Papers 63/4, Kiel, Institut für Weltwirtschaft.

Keck, O. (1976), 'West German science policy since the early 1960s: trends and objectives', *Research Policy*, Vol. 5, pp. 116–57.

Kommission für Wirschaftlichen und Sozialen Wandel (1977), *Wirtschaftlicher und sozialer Wandel in der Bundesrepublik Deutschland*, Göttingen, Otto Schwartz & Co.

Monopolkommission (1978), *Fortschreitender Konzentration bei Grossunternehmen. Hauptgutachten 1976/77*, Baden-Baden, Nomos Verlagsgesellschaft.

Pavitt, K. and Walker, W. (1976), 'Government policies towards industrial innovation: a review', *Research Policy*, Vol. 5, pp. 11–97.

Sachverständigenrat zur Begutachtung der gesamtwirtschaftlichen Entwicklung (1985), *Jahresqutachten 1985/86*, Bundestagsdrucksache 10/4295, Bonn, 22 November 1985.

Schmidt, K.-D. et al. (1984), *Im Anpassungsprozesszurückgeworfen—Die deutsche Wirtschaft vor neuen Herausforderungen*, Kieler Studien, 185, Tübingen, J.C.B. Mohr.

Studienkommission (1979), *Grundsatzfragen der Kreditwirtschaft*, Bericht der Studienkommission, Schriftenreihe des Bundesministeriums der Finanzen, No. 28, Bonn, Stollfuss.

Thurow, L. C. (1980), *The Zero-Sum Society: Distribution and the Possibilities for Economic Change*, New York, Basic Books.

4 France: the ambitious state

Patrick Messerlin*

One of the few points of agreement between the forty or so French governments since 1944 has been the need for an industrial policy. Such a policy, coloured by a 'Colbertist' philosophy of intervention, has often been regarded as typically French, by contrast with the market philosophy supposed to prevail in most European countries, and especially in West Germany.

This apparent consistency between so many successive governments may do no more than reflect a misunderstanding as to what an 'industrial policy' means. There are, in fact, at least two different ways in which one may be defined. (i) It may be understood as the sum of sectoral micro-economic measures applied to particular industries (Corden 1980)—encouragement of infant industries, new technology, creation of 'national champions', nationalization, regional distribution, and direction of resources to influence the labour and capital markets. (ii) It may be held to include, in addition, macro-economic policy. Here, as Corden emphasizes, fiscal and monetary policies exert a range of influences on industries not always explicitly understood and exploited; to take only one example, the French national plans have, for the most part, combined macro-economic objectives with a package of measures tailored to each sector of the economy.

This chapter employs definition (ii) as entailing the least distortion when the industrial policies of two separate countries or two different periods in the same country are compared. A basic assumption is that the state should act in ways entailing the minimum of discrimination, and any industrial policy should aim at avoiding distortion in existing markets where these are efficient.

The chapter is divided into five sections. Section 4.1 is concerned with the institutional and sociological background of French industrial policy since 1945. The next four sections deal with four relatively homogeneous periods which can be distinguished since 1945 in respect both of macro-economic and sectoral measures: 1944–58 (sect. 4.2), 1958–74 (sect. 4.3), 1974–81 (sect. 4.4) and 1981–6 (sect. 4.5).

---

* For a glossary of French organizations mentioned in this chapter, see the end of the chapter.

4.1 Industrial policy: the environmental background

This section aims to delineate the more important elements of the background to industrial policy: industrial relations, banking, and the role of the state and local bodies in particular. It tackles the nub of the theme: the difficulty of creating in France a stable 'national economic order', that is a kind of economic 'constitution' acceptable to established institutions and public opinion at large.

Industrial relations: the unions

Industrial relations in France seem often to be coloured by nineteenth century attitudes on both sides, but the potential for confrontation has been muted by the strong growth of the economy since 1948. Growth has been as much a constraint governments have to observe in order to keep the social balance on an even keel as a goal in itself. Obeying this constraint has at times proved expensive, as it was between 1970 and 1976, or 1981 and 1983, in terms of inflation and all its attendant costs.

Nevertheless, a certain stability in industrial relations has been achieved. This is a consequence of the political divisions among the French unions, which are much more marked than in the United States, Germany or Britain. These are particularly clear in the subordination of the CGT to the long-term objectives of the Communist Party, apparent also in the delicate relations of the CFDT, and to some extent the FO, with the Socialist Party. This did not, however, prevent an allocation of roles which ensures a certain stability. The CGT goes for confrontation, the FO for conciliation, while the CDFT oscillates between the two. This has been the source both of the weakness of the French trade union movement and of a certain stability in industrial relations, developing in parallel to the great era of political stability between 1958 and 1981.

Each union complements the other in a kind of 'imperfect cooperation'. The confrontational strategy of the CGT gives the FO and CFDT a negotiating margin. They get a quasi-free ride on the back of the CGT's strike force. At the same time, the cooperative attitudes of the FO and the CFDT let the CGT have a free ride on their backs by claiming for themselves credit for the gains negotiated on behalf of the 'working class'.

Some unions, of course, do better than others. The CGT has lost ground to the CFDT and the FO: the CGT, which obtained nearly 60 per cent of the votes in 1947, now gains close to 40 per cent. When then has 'imperfect cooperation' persisted? Leaving aside the fact that the growth of the economy has tended to mask disparities, there are four main reasons.

First, concessions negotiated were generally extended throughout the labour force through the 'conventions collectives'. No union, therefore, can offer its constituents gains plainly superior to those enjoyed by the others.

Moreover, the semi-institutionalized 'free rider' system deters excessive militancy in any particular union (which would penalize it financially while benefiting other unions) or excessive moderation (which would expose it to accusations of 'betrayal of the working class'). The resulting stability of industrial relations explains why the free-rider system has found favour with governments and with employers. Second, more than 85 per cent of union members are represented by three central confederations. The only others as powerful as the CGT, CFDT and FO are the specialist unions for agriculture, education and managers. Third, the unions are deeply involved at company level. By law, trade-union delegates may combine their functions with those of shop steward members of the 'company council' (*comité d'entreprise*) or workers' delegates to the council. They are allowed free time for union business. The company council plays an important part in determining working conditions but has only a consultative role in economic matters. Fourth, the internal organization of the unions also favours 'imperfect cooperation'. They, like the Employers Federation (CNPF) are loose confederations of sectoral federations. The complexity of the organization tends to perpetuate power at the top of the hierarchy and isolates union leaders from their members. Many a union boss has held office longer than the President of the Republic and has, moreover, been nominated rather than truly elected.

The cooperation between unions, being 'imperfect', is under constant threat, and the unions tend tacitly to seek government authority to perpetuate it much as producers' cartels do. The Socialist labour legislation of the early 1980s (the Auroux Laws) certainly tends to institutionalize such an 'imperfect cooperation' between the main union confederations. Intended to improve arrangements for representing the workforce, the Auroux Laws emphasize the 'exclusive' role of the unions; they sought to make more company information available to the workforce, but in practice spelt out the rights and duties of the company committee and the representatives of the cadres and workers more than they brought the new range of information to the notice of the workforce itself. The obligations prescribed in respect of wage bargaining are variations on the theme of the 'conventions collectives', particularly in the idea that only certain unions are big enough to qualify.

The banks

The main deposit banks were nationalized in 1946. After 1950, a range of regulations was introduced defining spheres of operations as between, for example, deposit and merchant banks (a distinction abolished in 1967), the Crédit Agricole, the Crédits Mutuels and a large number of specialized financial institutions. The rigidity of this system encouraged firms, when they were large enough, to go directly to the equity markets or, when they were 'crowded out' by government borrowing, to seek funds abroad. The banking system thus provided a strong stimulus to the larger firms, who alone could do this.

Accordingly, the banks seem to have played different roles depending on whether they were dealing with large or medium and small firms. The large firms had the edge on the merchant banks which in their case, played a follower's role, servicing mergers, capital issues and the like. This was accentuated when, following deregulation in 1967, the commercial banks began to offer competing services since they were able to draw on an extensive reservoir of deposits. Their close relations, as nationalized institutions, with the government were a substantial asset in a country where it was not always easy to forecast monetary policy.

In the case of small and medium firms (representing 60 per cent of industrial employment and including some of the most dynamic enterprises), the banks maintained their traditional and strategic role of advice and direction. Such firms did not command the resources or the expertise to enable them to operate independently of technical and financial advice. The banks also played a dominant part in assisting 'lame ducks', though account must be taken here of the growing intervention of the state in salvage operations. The state tended to impose political constraints on bank decisions in this sphere.

The state

France is often represented as the archetype of the centralizing state. Projects of any scope entailing regionalization have never succeeded, and programmes of devolution, including those of the socialists after 1981 have been most circumspect in tackling financial relations between central and local authorities.

This does not mean that nothing has changed. The public accounts show that local authorities undertake most public investment, their share rising from 71 per cent in 1973 to 76 per cent in 1981. On the other hand, local taxes account for less than 40 per cent of the income of local authorities. Consequently, they depend heavily on central grants. Moreover, the tax on professions, one of the main local sources of revenue, is politically controversial. Further, the interests of local authorities are represented in the Senate. The Senate has no right of veto and acts more as a 'shock-absorber' than a decision-making body.

The economic weakness of local authorities has important effects on industrial policy, for only one-tenth of subsidies on current expenditure and one-fifth of those on capital account are provided by them, and in any case, services (for instance, health and transport) rather than manufacture, probably take the lion's share.

Paradoxically, local authorities have been partly squeezed out of industrial policy by measures designed to loosen the stranglehold of the centre. For example, the Caisse des Dépôts et Consignations (Deposit and Consignment Office) was initially set up to replace direct Treasury management of municipal funds. As the municipalities' bank, the Caisse des Dépôts was excused paying interest on deposits. But the ministries began to take a hand in its management till the centre absorbed the funds the law required to be deposited in the Caisse des Dépôts. It was only in 1966, when a subsidiary body of the office was established for this purpose, that there was a reversion to the original intent behind the Caisse des Dépôts.

It is always difficult for an established authority to delegate to institutions powers which may be used against it, and as recent political developments have demonstrated, local authorities tend to act as a rallying point for the opposition. However, it seems that the recent devolution of power (*loi de décentralisation*) introduced by the socialist government since 1982 was effective and in favour of the Conseil Général (the local assembly at the *département* level) and specially its president. This new local power has so far been rather reluctant to tackle industrial problems.

The electoral cycle

The retention of power by the same coalition throughout the long term of office of the Fifth Republic (1958–81) obscured the fact that there is no consensus in France on economic and social policy. But this became clear on the accession of the socialists in 1981.

The lack of consensus is intensified by the swing of the political pendulum, not so much in the case of the President, whose election depends in the second round on the votes of the centre and whose even-year tenure of office ultimately favours the pursuit of a moderate and responsible policy, as in Assemblée Nationale, where a few votes determine the victory of one party or the other (except for the 1986 election, which was regulated by a different system of voting). The crushing majority of the socialists in the elections of 1981 reflected a swing of roughly 300,000 votes in an electorate of 12 million. In these conditions, the winning party finds it difficult to consolidate its position, yet fails to grasp the nature of the strong resistance which its economic and social policies encounter.

It is often claimed that the civil service is a stabilizing element in French policies because it gives independent advice to the government in power and because of the considerable body of high officials appointed to manage nationalized enterprises and banks. This should not be exaggerated. The spoils system operates in France and is no less influential because it works only at the top of the civil service.

4.2 Reconstruction and consolidation: 1944–58

The macro-economic debate that never was

On the morrow of World War II, most Frenchmen were aware of the links between the political, military and moral defeats of the 1930s and 1940s and the bad state of the economy at the time.

Thus, what France needed to recover from those disasters was not merely a straightforward reconstruction of the economy but an economic charter enshrining principles which would win general assent and enable France not only to avoid continuing to decline into an underdeveloped country but also to take its place among the leading economies of the world. There were three questions to consider: the distribution of ownership, the division of resources between the state and the free market, and the weight to be accorded to macro-economic and particularly monetary policy.

The nationalization of a number of basic industries (energy and communications mainly) along with the main deposit banks and insurance firms between 1945 and 1947 rapidly dealt with the first question. By 1947 it was accepted that the public sector had expanded far enough, but there was controversy about its function. Were the nationalized industries to be the outposts of a rigorously planned system or merely to be managed on principles of 'public service' which became less and less tangible with time?

But the debate on the other two questions never materialized. By contrast with Germany, which was in many respects in a similar predicament, there was virtually no resort to currency reform between 1944 and 1948. Instead, macro-economic policy at the time was not so much a guide in itself as a by-product of industrial policies single-mindedly dedicated to the expansion of output. Only a few politicians, such as Pinay and Mendès-France, saw the importance of monetary policy as a way of obtaining high growth at reduced social cost.

The social costs of inflation dawned only slowly on the dominant parties of the Fourth Republic (Christian Democrats and Socialists) as it began to undermine their political support. Between 1946 and 1948 inflation reached an annual average of 60 per cent. Hyper-inflation was a major factor behind the violent strikes launched by the Communists in the autumn of 1947 at the beginning of the Cold War. The government was saved from the consequences of all this by two factors. One was the Cold War split in the trade unions between the Communists and the rest. The other was the government's acceptance of annual autumn wage reviews as a *de facto* equivalent to a partial indexation of wages.

The failure to debate economic policy in these years is attributable not so much to the absence of economists with liberal views on the German model—the Liberal School was well represented, notably by Allais and Rueff—but to politicians deliberately turning a blind eye to the costs of growth, when pursued by the command economy methods favoured by the dominant networks in the state and the political system. To the extent that the government was aware of the importance of the debate on macro-economic policy, publicizing the cost that society was paying for growth during these years would have exposed the inadequacies of the administration and political regime.

Lacking an organic economic policy the French government resorted to *ad hoc* restrictions on credit, foreign exchange, wages and prices. Such quantitative measures were costly: between 1950 and 1958 the annual average growth rate was three percentage points lower than in Germany and one point less than in Italy. The average rate of inflation, at 5 per cent, was four points higher than in Germany.

Planning: an industrial policy?

Despite—or perhaps because of—this lack of consensus on a 'national economic order', Monnet did manage gradually to gain general acceptance of three points: that France was virtually an underdeveloped country; that what was required was modernization; and that an expansion of productivity should be vigorously pursued through planning.

Monnet insisted that the Plan should be based on consensus rather than diktat. The Commissariat du Plan was set up as a small team of experts servicing and coordinating a number of committees in which prominent individuals from labour, management and government worked together. His approach reflected the disillusionment of the French with the authoritarianism of Vichy and with the restrictive corporatism of the pre-war years and the politico-financial scandals to which it gave rise. He hoped that by insisting on the exchange of information and by confronting different projects and firms, the Plan would break up the defensive and backward mentalities inherited from the past.

By the time studies for the Second Plan began, it had become clear that this hope was not to be realized. This is well illustrated by the sectoral breakdown of the distribution of Marshall Aid to industry, which represented 16 per cent of all investment and one-third of all public investment between 1948 and 1951. This breakdown shows a remarkable similarity between France and Germany which cannot be explained by the fact that both countries were in a similar state of acute depression. Countries dispose of quite different natural endowments, and the poorer they are, the more investment patterns should take account of these. The conclusion is hard to avoid that the Monnet Plan was in fact copying the German model rather than proceeding on original lines.

This propensity to borrow not only from Germany but also Holland, Sweden, Austria and Japan was a feature of succeeding Plans. This gave rise to two important defects in economic management after 1945, and particularly in the 1950s.

First, the powerful nationalized industries took a disproportionate share of investment. Coal fought it out with electricity, while internationally the oil industry boomed; and the railways obstructed the development of the highway network. In general, there was such a concentration of effort on the primary industries that import substitution developed at the cost of exports, despite Monnet's desire to open up the economy to world competition. As a result, the rate of import penetration fell but export performance fell even more.

Second, by repeated intervention the authorities distorted markets, and because the role of markets was misunderstood, they were not allowed to work efficiently. The economy was deprived of reliable indicators, leaving the planners in no condition to withstand pressure groups. Amongst the market distortions of the 1950s, two deserve a special mention: finance and fiscal policy.

Finance

Between 1948 and 1958 there was no financial market worth the name in France. Astonishingly, the First Plan was launched with no clear idea of how the necessary capital was to be raised (Kruisel 1981). Access to funds was tied up in red tape and in effect rationed since finance was provided by the officially organized and controlled *circuits de financement*. The Plans and the interference of the state rapidly dried up the markets in this way.

The depletion of the money market was intensified by the reinforcement of state control over the banks following the nationalizations between 1945 and 1947. Credit was rationed through a spread of special agencies (Caisse des Dépôts, FDES, Crédit National, Crédit Agricole and so on), with access restricted to specified borrowers. The availability of finance for any particular industry thus became a key element in industrial policy. The system favoured the big cartels and discriminated against small and medium concerns.

Savings grew slowly in the 1950s—domestic savings from 8 per cent in 1950 to 10.5 per cent of total income of households in 1957 (Carré, Dubois and Malinvaud 1973). The real rate of return on fixed-interest bonds was from 0 to 1 per cent and variable return bonds from –2 to –3 per cent; the government, as the principal investor, had an interest in keeping down the cost of capital.

The poor performance of the capital market must detract from the favourable impression given by the rapid growth of investment between 1955 and 1959. The appearance of progress is highlighted by the comparison with the collapse of private investment in the early 1950s, due to the inability of private firms to compete for capital with the public sector and the contraction of investment opportunities in the shrinking French empire.

Taxes

Fiscal policy in the 1950s exerted a strong influence in favour of the large capital-intensive firms which were regarded as the only base for economic development. Such firms were favoured by long-term depreciation allowances on fixed assets and machinery. Between 1952 and 1955, a system of refunds in respect of social expenditure was introduced to stimulate exports. This, too, operated in favour of the larger firms, which formed a very large proportion of exporters. By increasing labour costs, high social charges also encouraged capital-intensive investment and production.

The opening up of the economy

While financial and fiscal distortions slowed down growth in the French economy in the 1950s, this did nevertheless develop at a high sustained level (an annual average of 4.8 per cent for the five years from 1954 to 1958 inclusive). This was associated with a gradual expansion of foreign trade.

Contrary to popular belief, France does have a free-trade tradition inherited from the nineteenth century. This has been obscured by the period of severe protectionism in the 1920s and especially the 1930s. Even then, France's protectionism can be overstated. Between 1925 and 1936 the sum of French exports and imports taken as a percentage of GNP was roughly similar to that for Germany and equal to 75 per cent of the corresponding figure for Britain. France's protectionist reputation is due rather more durably to two post-war aspects of its trade policies, both of which were dominant in the 1950s and, interestingly enough, are still evident in the 1980s. The first is the tendency to seek to limit free trade to a preferential area: the French Empire from the 1930s to 1950s, and the EEC since the late 1950s. The second is a tendency to rely on non-tariff barriers for protection.

After World War II, in the pursuit of industrial revival France, like many developing countries, first pursued implicit policies of import substitution. These gradually gave way to export promotion as markets opened up abroad. The reason was that industrial modernization, involving growth and rising productivity, entailed the import of so many capital goods from the United States and elsewhere that the country's chronic trading deficits could only be covered by more exports, and these demanded a competitive approach.

Accordingly, during the 1950s, the idea gradually emerged of free trade limited to 'comparable', that is European, industrial economies. World-wide free trade still seemed too risky; competition limited to European producers seemed acceptable. The last Fourth Republic governments established the EEC formally between 1957 and January 1958. But the authorities, sensitive to the political costs of devaluation, and in the face of domestic inflation fuelled by the Algerian War, maintained a complicated system of import levies and export subsidies effectively isolating France till October 1957.

It was then replaced by a standard 20 per cent levy on all overseas dealings. This helped to restore balance-of-payments equilibrium. By December 1958 the last government of the Fourth Republic, under de Gaulle, was able to introduce an open devaluation of 17.6 per cent. This marked the effective commitment of France to the European customs union gradually set up in the next decade in the EEC.

Collusion on the domestic markets

The way in which markets work inside France, especially as regards the effective level of competition, is one of the most difficult of all the issues raised by industrial policy, and very divergent views have been expressed (McArthur and Scott 1970; Carré, Dubois and Malinvaud 1973). Certainly, the relatively autarchic nature of the domestic markets during the 1950s tended to weaken competition and favour monopolistic competition. At the same time, the catching-up process gave rise to competition between old-established firms and innovating newcomers. In general, a sort of 'imperfect collusion' seems to have obtained during the period. Collusion was certainly widespread, but collusive arrangements can yield very quickly to competitive pressures in some cases.

The authorities had to consider three points: to maintain public regulatory measures, to freeze controls and thereby to close entry to newcomers. First efforts between 1949 and 1951 to get rid of wartime control measures reduced their application by the late 1950s to agriculture, primary products (coal, oil, aluminium, nickel, cotton and paper), housing and transport.

Price controls during the 1950s seem to have had limited impact. By resorting to discounting arrangements and by introducing new descriptions of products, traders were able to circumvent listed prices. Price controls tended to be variable and intermittent, with periods of relative freedom succeeding periods of freeze. All this suggests that price controls had in fact little effect on prices in the long term, except for industries like steel, which are specially sensitive to boom and slump. For these, price controls applied strictly at the top of the boom—when profits are made for the whole trade cycle—seriously undermined their profitability over the long term.

After the corporatist system of Organizing Committees was established by the Vichy government, elevating cartelization to the rank of a public benefit, a regulation of June 1945 prohibited agreements in restraint of trade (*ententes*) but only in general terms. The Pinay government introduced legislation establishing a Technical Commission on Cartels set up in August 1953. This too played only a minor role.

It was, rather, the actual play of market forces, in conditions of growth, that brought in the breath of competition. There were several sources. Pressure of competition from countries like Germany and Holland broke up some of the weaker cartels. Other industry associations lost their hold on their sector as growth differentiated the interests of the member firms. some came to represent the marginal firms in trouble. Others, on the contrary, became spokesmen for the more dynamic firms determined to increase their market shares. Such developments put pressure on the cartels and go a long way to explain the 'imperfect' nature of the collusion which obtained.

The growth of the 1950s

During the decade, French growth was indeed higher than in Britain and the United States, but more importantly, it was lower than in Germany and even Italy, and at the cost of higher inflation. The numerous distortions built into highly protected markets seemed to sap the dynamism of the catching-up process.

If one compares 1948 and 1958, growth embraced all the broad sectors of the economy, with energy and non-food manufacturing (in that order) well to the fore, doubling in volume against a GDP growth of two-thirds. Nevertheless, because planning tends to overemphasize investment in energy and intermediate products, the next period, from 1960 to 1965, brought a spate of difficulties, in coal, steel and shipbuilding, all of them industries heavily stressed in the first and second plans. Growth on the import substitution, autarchic, model was running out of steam. If the debt ratios of firms remained stable at a low level, gross savings and profit margins, in terms of value added, tended to fall. The capital–output ratio fell between 1950 and 1960, although less rapidly towards the end of the period owing to the development of private investment in response to the opening up of European markets. Overall productivity improved steadily throughout the period, while the galloping inflation of the late 1940s eased markedly between 1952 and 1957.

There was no employment problem in the period under review. By contrast with other growing countries there was complete stagnation of the labour force at around 19.5 million, but there were considerable transfers of labour between sectors. Agricultural employment fell from 36 per cent of the total workforce in 1948 to 27 per cent in 1954 and 20 per cent in 1962. Up to 1954, employment in industry was the sole beneficiary of these transfers, since its part of the total workforce rose from 29 per cent to 36 per cent. Thereafter, transport, commerce and other services absorbed 60 per cent of new hands coming on the market.

4.3 The acceleration of growth: 1958–73

From 1960 to 1973, growth improved on average by one annual percentage point over the 1950s: it is only at this time that the catching-up process became a full success. The average annual rate of 5.5 per cent exceeded that of Germany by 0.5 per cent. Annual inflation ran at 4.5 per cent, which brought the inflation gap with Germany down to 1.6 percentage points in between 1970 and 1973 compared with three percentage points in the 1950s. This improvement was due to the four following points: increasing participation in the competitive markets of the EEC; the government's adjustment to a new role in a more open economy, which reduced its powers in some respects; new opportunities opened up by the population boom and immigration; a greater political stability, which allowed the governments of the Fifth Republic to follow more coherent macro-economic policies than those of the Fourth.

New macro-economic policies

It was the freer trade obligations undertaken in the Treaty of Rome and the Kennedy Round which shifted the emphasis from autarchic growth in the 1950s to exchange rate and price stability as the prime objective of the 1960s. As a result of the efforts of the government to reduce the accumulated distortions of the 1950s, growth was more rapid than ever before. It was not, however, till the Stabilization Plan of 1963, when the inflation of the 1960s reached its peak (over 5 per cent per annum), that priority was given to monetary policy: it was at this time that the constraints from the EEC began to make their effects felt on French macro-economic policies.

The Stabilisation Plan of 1963 was the first substantial piece of macro-economic control undertaken in France. It accepted the idea that the three goals common to all economic policies—price stability, the external balance and full employment—were not all equally obtainable at the same time. In practice, the government put stable prices and external equilibrium first and growth and full employment second.

The circumstances were relatively favourable. The monetary reform of 1958 and the new political stability gave new confidence to business despite the troubles associated with the end of the Algerian War from 1961 to 1962. In addition, the franc was undervalued after the large 17.5 per cent devaluation of 1958, and this led to a surplus on current account which gave a further boost to confidence. Above all, a fairly strict budgetary policy and higher taxes converted the deficit of 3 per cent of GDP in 1956 to a surplus of 1 per cent in 1961, despite rising expenditure.

From the mid-1960s the deficit on external account began to reappear, suggesting that the slack afforded by devaluation had been taken up. Until 1968 the authorities tried to be strict and deflationary in their macro-economic policies in order to maintain the exchange rate. However, these efforts were only partially successful: between 1969 and 1971 the franc fell to 10 per cent against the dollar and 30 per cent against the mark. This seemed to stabilize the situation in so far as from 1971 to 1980 there was a gradual improvement of the franc against the dollar and deterioration against the Deutsche mark.

As a result of this reordering of priorities, the 1960s produced a decisive change in the role of French planning. At first, the development plans were raised to the level of a 'fervent patriotic duty' by de Gaulle, who, it should be remembered, authorized the first Monnet Plan. But soon central investment planning in direct line of descent from Monnet gave way to macro-economic controls accompanied by sectoral measures in specific areas—in brief, explicit industrial policies for the first time since the reconstruction period immediately after the war.

Two phases of this macro-economic control can be distinguished. From 1963 to 1968, budgetary stability and monetary restraint prevailed, with taxation at a steady level (tax reductions making up for the uncontainable rise in social security contributions). From 1969 to 1973, monetary policy was relaxed, money supply increased and with it the rate of inflation and interest rates. In this period the weight of investment in the public sector and nationalized enterprises fell steadily in terms of GDP. All this suggests, on the face of it, a partial disengagement of the state, as a natural consequence of increased reliance on macro-economic controls. In fact, however, the reality was more complicated and the break with the past less clean than it looked. The limits on the disengagement of the state can be gathered from the measures used to stabilize prices.

First, the spasmodic price freezes of the 1950s give way in the 1960s to a much more systematic supervision of industrial prices and distribution margins, notably by way of 'price moderating contracts' with the industry associations. From 1966 such contracts accounted for four-fifths of industrial production (Stoffaes 1978).

Second, monetary policy did not eliminate financial distortions. The channels of finance continued to be rigidly segmented and interest rates were controlled through the near-complete nationalization of the banks. Preference given to agriculture and housing resulted in distortions which are exemplified by the existence side-by-side of negative and positive real interest rates—for example, savings banks, -3.2 per cent; building societies, -0.4 per cent; Treasury Bonds, 1 per cent; public sector loans, 2.25 per cent. The effects of this policy were accentuated by the weakening of the capital position of private enterprises and the increase in their indebtedness. This increased the risks for shareholders, which was all the more disturbing as short-term interest rates were higher than long-term ones.

Third, tax incentives were used by successive governments to direct investment to priority sectors. The combination of tax reliefs and low interest rates encouraged firms to move into debt and run down their own capital, making them vulnerable to the higher interest rates prevailing from 1974 to 1982 and the oil price crisis. Budgetary devolution around 1963 caused some transfer of central expenditure to local authorities. This enhanced local financial difficulties, labour costs were increased by an unrestrained growth in national insurance contributions, and the flexibility of labour markets was impaired by a system of agreements between the authorities and the unions introduced to cope with the social unrest following the events of May 1968.

In short, though intervention in the style of the 1950s lost much of its importance, particularly in view of the growing complexity of the economy, the authorities hit on other methods to maintain the role of the state and limit the impact of macro-economic policies. The true limits to state intervention resulted mainly from a radically new environment based first on the increase in the supply of labour and second on the opening of the French economy to the world.

A radically new environment

Population. After the war, there was a surge in the birth rate and by 1960 population was growing faster in France than in most other industrialized countries. Until then the working population had remained static at around 20 million. This helps to explain the low level of unemployment (1 per cent right up to mid-1960s) and the maintenance of a relatively long working week rising to a peak of forty-six hours in 1962.

Only after 1962 did the labour force begin to grow. This, of course, increased the importance of production growth to provide jobs. All estimates suggest that the level of technical qualification of this growing population was rather low.

As in other countries, immigration was an obvious means of relieving labour shortages especially in unattractive jobs. Immigrants came mostly from Spain, Portugal and France's former African empire. Immigration policy was not restrictive right up to 1974, and the unions were content to associate immigrant workers with their own wage bargaining. In 1973 the main concentrations of immigrant workers were in the transport industries (one-quarter of the labour force) and metal-working (one-sixth). Immigration did not preclude a rise in wage costs. After 1970 these costs increased faster than the growth of the economy, till in 1974 there was a wage explosion.

On balance, the growth of the French economy between 1960 and 1973 was principally based on an increase in the supply of labour. Christensen, Cummings and Jorgenson (1976) ascribe France's excess of growth over her neighbours entirely to this factor.

Freer trade. Throughout the 1960s, French exports held a stable market share of 8 per cent of world trade, only reaching 9 per cent from 1972 onwards. However, the direction of trade changed completely under the stimulus of the Kennedy Round and the development of the EEC. By 1968 European markets had practically replaced the markets of the old French Empire, and thereafter both imports and exports took off. Whereas in 1958 import penetration and export oscillated around 10 per cent of consumption and production, by 1968 a level of 17 per cent was reached, and by 1978 it had risen to 25 to 30 per cent.

The exposure of France to the European market in the late 1960s took place in a particularly stable and helpful economic and political environment, and it was accompanied by some improvement in the terms of trade. At the same time, the opening up of the French economy has taken place mainly since the late 1960s. This puts in proper context the argument that free trade vitiated French planning. Planning had already met its most important challenge with the Stabilisation Plan of 1963 well before the opening up of the economy.

The 'industrialist' policy

The challenge of the European and, thereafter, world markets forced the authorities to face old problems of how to adjust inefficient industries and build up future growth sectors. To tackle these issues, the planning approach looked too inflexible. At the same time, though macro-economic measures promoted price stability and growth in general, they could not meet the special needs of industrial sectors in particular. From this arose a system of specific industrial policies to the point where, at the beginning of the 1970s, industrial policy constituted an important arm of state intervention.

This phase of industrial policy was dominated by three characteristics: (i) an almost exclusive preoccupation with manufacturing, regarded as the sole source of wealth creation and economic dynamism; (ii) a search for economies of scale via the creation of 'national champions' large enough to compete internationally, with little attention paid to the costs of mergers and to competition policy; (iii) emphasis, sometimes more verbal than practical, on the technologically advanced industries.

This policy developed against the background of an industrial sector which was undergoing steady and rapid change. Up to 1968 its conditions were stable with a ratio of gross profit to value added of 45 per cent and an indebtedness below 3 per cent of value added. This reflected the relative stability of wage costs and the weak incidence of interest rates in real terms. But after 1968, wage costs rose substantially and profit margins declined. By 1974 indebtedness had doubled compared with 1966 and profits were massively squeezed. One of the motives for the rise in industrial policies was to make up for the general deterioration in these years of the economic and financial conditions in which industry operated.

National champions. Faced with the 'German miracle' and 'American challenge', the authorities sought 'national champions' with sufficient stature to meet foreign competition. Since there was none, the state set about creating them. Directly and indirectly it engineered mergers and takeovers by a policy of tax incentives including remission of capital gains tax, medium- and long-term credits and direct government intervention. As a result there were twice as many mergers in the second half of the 1960s as in the whole of the 1950s. The contemporary shape of major companies like CGE (heavy electrical), PUK (aluminium and chemicals), Saint-Gobain (glass and public works),

Rhône-Poulenc (chemicals), DNEL (steel), SNIAS, Dassault and Bréguet (aerospace), to quote only some of the more important, was established in this period.

The creation of national champions has had a number of implications for the market, some of which are obvious, others less so. To begin with, it has created a large number of national monopolies. These are not likely to be effective in a period of open markets where international standards set competitive norms. But when, with recession, protectionist measures spread, the potential effect becomes much more restrictive. Second, in theory at least, firms that are given larger economies of scale on the domestic market may not be stimulated to export more, as the government hoped. Third, the national champions are to be found almost exclusively in the capital goods and intermediate goods sectors of manufacturing.

In addition, the national champions policy has been interesting for what it has revealed of the motivations of the state. Horizontal mergers of firms have been encouraged; but vertical integration on the German model, which might make firms better able to adjust internally but also less open to pressure from the authorities, has been actively discouraged (e.g. CGE-Thomson in electronics in 1969 and Usinor-DNEL in steel in 1974). Similarly, the opponents of some major spontaneous private mergers have been encouraged and supported by the state (e.g. to prevent the attempted take-over of Saint-Gobain by BSN).

It was only at the end of the Pompidou Presidency that the policy of 'national champions' began to be questioned. Jenny and Weber (1974) and others later (de Vannoise 1977) highlighted the fact that, other things being equal, the mere size of an enterprise seemed to react adversely on its profitability. Moreover, the profitability of national champions seemed to be lower than in other firms in the same line of business and their indebtedness higher by between 30 and 35 per cent. As the national champion policy gained ground, its costs in terms of declining efficiency tended to offset the gains of economies of scale, and there were some glaring setbacks, for instance in computing and to a lesser extent aerospace. Paradoxically, the policy even favoured foreign penetration, for the amalgamation of small firms created units with a large enough share of the market to attract foreign buyers.

National champions also had a paradoxical effect on regional policy. The choice of the Lorraine region for the location of Sacilor, de Wendel-Sidelor and Sollac ignored the principle of siting steel plants with access to the sea. Fos-sur-Mer, which observed that principle, then put one steel region in competition with another, so that far from subordinating industry to regional policy, regional policy was determined by the needs of industry. Foreign firms chose their location unconstrained by French precedents but benefited substantially from regional development assistance.

In short, competition was not a government priority in the 1960–73 period. However, there was one key sector where the authorities did promote it. This was in the retail trade. In the 1950s this was very backward. From 1960 on, there was an explosion of supermarkets and hypermarkets. This was disliked by manufacturers, who tried to promote measures in restraint of trade on the distributors. The authorities frowned on these efforts and opposed them.

Advanced Technology.   The 'national champions' policy aimed at asserting a 'French presence' in advanced technology as well as at reaping economies of scale. At the beginning of the 1960s, expenditure on R & D was stepped up, initially with the emphasis on defence (absorbing 35 per cent of R & D outlay by 1970). But there was a considerable spin-off which benefited civilian development, notably in nuclear power reactors and aerospace (Airbus).

It is difficult to say if French R & D strategy in these matters was one of innovation or imitation. The 1960s may have leaned to innovation, but after some resounding failures (like the abandonment of the French natural uranium reactor system in 1969) the 1970s seemed more inclined to complement R & D elsewhere.

Expenditure was concentrated on nuclear energy, aerospace and electronics. In aerospace, where conditions particularly encourage state intervention, France came to be recognized as an important partner in state-sponsored joint European ventures. Military aviation, centred on Dassault, was the core of this development. On the other hand, to be really competitive it was necessary to achieve at least a European market base and, since this was only spasmodically attained, it is no surprise that production was sold to the state and that Dassault absorbed subsidies of the order of 106,000 francs per employee in 1974! Though the government took an interest in nuclear energy development at the highest levels, including the President and the Prime Minister, the basic effort was provided by the EDF to the point where it was argued that the state was losing its power to make independent judgements. In electronics, the whole field of computer development and operation, the lack of any solid expertise in the industry made it difficult for the authorities to deal with the essential problems. In consequence, decision-making was dispersed among a large number of agencies which tended to dilute the effectiveness of the considerable level of R & D outlay deployed in this field (30 per cent of sales from 1960 to 1970).

The public R & D effort in France was spread over as many as thirty agencies reporting to fourteen government departments, all jealous of each other. The disadvantages of this dispersion of effort were to some extent mitigated by the existence of some large and well-developed research bodies, such as the DGRST and the CNRS, but it remains true that the complexity of the general structure coupled with bureacratic interference had a bad effect on the economic climate for R & D.

Nationalized industries and public procurement. From 1960 to 1974 the share of the nationalized sector in industry remained static at the immediate post-war level, employing 10 per cent of the non-agricultural workforce and producing 12 per cent of gross value added in the non-financial sector. Nationalized firms operated in eight main sectors: energy, car manufacture, aerospace, transport, telecommunications, banking, insurance and data processing.

When they were set up, in 1945–6, the nationalized firms were supposed to form an industrial and social strike force, but it is difficult to estimate how far they achieved this between 1960 and 1974. Many of them enjoyed a clear market monopoly, in fact if not in law, and many of the others dominated the market either in terms of labour or sales—as in the case of Renault, for instance. Generally, nationalized firms seemed to be technologically advanced during this period and particularly capital-intensive. Finally, they were subject to regulation by the authorities and manipulation by pressure groups. Le Pors and Prunet (1975) have shown that between 1962 and 1972, between 81 and 89 per cent of industrial subsidies to industry and transport—leaving aside rebates on social costs—went to the public sector and only 10 to 20 per cent to the private sector. The eight main nationalized enterprises were subsidized to the tune of 15 per cent of their value added between 1967 and 1973. All these features leave a fairly solid impression that nationalized firms were neither efficient nor aligned in the 1960s on market norms.

There was no sign as yet of what in the late 1970s was to be called 'silent' (or creeping) nationalization. If there was anything that deserved this name, it was to be sought in public purchasing rather than production. Government-funded purchases amounted to between 12 and 16 per cent of the market for energy, engineering, construction and civil engineering, 30 per cent for electrical engineering and electronics, and 35 per cent for shipbuilding and aerospace. The roster of suppliers coincided in most cases with the national champions promoted by the state.

4.4 The Barre period: 1976–81

During this period, starting with the energy crisis of 1973–4, the authorities had to make a judgement whether or not France was facing an economic crisis and, if it was, what part the state should play in resolving it. The Chirac government (1974–6) interpreted the problem as a short-term recession calling only for short-term macro-economic measures. In September 1976, on becoming Prime Minister, Raymond Barre presented the first official analysis to recognize the full breadth of the problem. Instead of merely pointing to the danger of inflation arising from the oil price shock, he concentrated on the problem of adjustment to the new environment, which favoured petroleum exporting countries and flexible industrial economies able to adapt their output and exports to new world patterns of demand. France had to move in that direction.

To encourage dynamism and flexibility the government resorted to a quite new policy which had the following broad objectives: to retain as much as possible of the 'social-democratic' welfare policies the government had inherited and to try to liberalize goods markets in the hope of improving the financial situations of French firms. This difficult strategy—trying to reconcile a slow liberalization of the labour and capital markets with a much faster liberalization of goods markets—was followed with some success from 1977 to 1980. But it was dealt a blow in 1980 by the second oil shock, then cut short by the Socialists in 1981, only to be taken up by them in 1984.

Social and wage policy

The government tended first to avoid social conflicts by retaining the main social benefits of the prosperous earlier years, despite economic constraints which narrowed further with the second energy crisis of 1979–80. It tried, on the one hand, to maintain the collective bargaining and minimum wage policy (SMIC) which mattered to the labour unions and, on the other, to bring wages down to the long-term levels dictated by the persistent slowing down of growth and increase in unemployment after the second energy crisis. The system of negotiated wage agreements between the labour unions and employers introduced in the early 1970s was maintained until 1981 and was particularly effective in the civil service and nationalized enterprises.

The results of the wage policy can be illustrated by the comparative movement in real terms of the SMIC and the average hourly wage rate. Up to 1968 the SMIC declined steadily in relation to the latter, but after 1969 the trend was reversed until, between 1973 and 1976, the SMIC exceeded the average hourly rate by 3.1 per cent. After 1976 the rate of increase of both indicators steadily declined (from 4.7 per cent in 1976 to 1.8 per cent in 1980), suggesting that costs had begun to be brought under control.

However, the combined effect of rising labour costs and external oil shocks increased unemployment. Unemployment began to appear in France in 1975, rising to 2.8 per cent of the working population in 1974, 4.7 per cent in 1977, and 6.3 per cent in 1980, when there were more than 1.5 million out of work.

Existing unemployment insurance arrangements did not help to solve the problem. Most of the unemployment insurance arrangements were instituted at the end of the 1960s—a period of prosperity—and were quite generous. As a consequence, the demands on the system grew explosively after 1974. In 1979 the government was obliged to set in hand a first reform of the system designed to reduce discrepancies, bring down the costs and shorten the periods of benefit.

All this implied increased budget transfers and social security payments.

They accounted for 35 per cent of the total budget in 1960 and 47 per cent in 1975, rising by a further 4 per cent between 1976 and 1980, while the yield from company taxation fell away consistently from a starting point before 1974. This was counterbalanced by an increase in social contributions which accounted for 40 per cent of consolidated public income in 1980. The unemployed benefited most: health contributions declined while pensions remained static.

The extent to which the Barre government achieved the social peace at which it was aiming can be illustrated by two facts. First, the Socialist CFDT, one of the three leading trades unions, whilst still in opposition, decided to adopt a more cooperative attitude to the government. Second, in terms of days lost by strikes in France as against Germany on the one hand and Britain on the other, the record was twice as good in 1977–80 as in 1974–6.

Industrial policy: a major change in perspective

Between 1945 and 1976, price control enjoyed unquestionable legitimacy in the eyes of the authorities. The Barre government operated a major change in this respect, even if two major shocks (the second oil shock of 1980 and the presidential election of 1981) put a provisional end to this approach. Price decontrol had two objectives. The first was to improve the financial climate for private enterprise, which had suffered between 1974 and 1976 from a further decline in profit margins coupled with a rising burden of debt and high rates. The second was to release the forces of competition and reduce distortions, whether due to state interference or private collusion. The two were linked: better finances would make little sense without appropriate signals to guide subsequent investment decisions. However, these two objectives were not equally successfully achieved.

There is evidence of substantial readjustments of company strategies in the Barre period. An enquiry conducted by the Crédit National in 1981 showed that 56 per cent of firms had developed new products in their traditional field of manufacture and 21 per cent had developed products in new fields. Finally, 1979, the year following the decontrol of prices of industrial goods, saw a pronounced return to the level of self-financing of the end of the 1960s. A Banque de France study of 1980 showed that firms recovered 2 to 3 per cent of value added compared with the preceding year, due primarily to the improvement in finances and also to the slowdown in wage costs discussed earlier. From the third quarter of 1979 conditions began to deteriorate again. This was due to the second oil price shock and uncertainty about the outcome of the presidential elections, with its threat of a reversal of economic policy. Firms were finding it difficult to envisage new profit opportunities and, as always where social-democratic policies prevail, high labour costs acted as a disincentive in time of slump.

Concerning the freeing of markets, the control system to be dismantled was extraordinarily complex. For instance, in the first three months of 1976 the Official Price Bulletin listed at least 100 price-maintenance agreements in respect of industrial products and fifty-five public decisions on price regulation. Accordingly, decontrol came into force slowly between June 1978 and March 1981. For manufacturing the key dates were August 1978 (decontrol of prices of all production goods) and January 1980 (decontrol of mark-ups in wholesale and retail trades).

Contrary to expectations, price decontrol did not produce major inflationary pressures. The rate of inflation stayed at around 10 to 13 per cent from 1976 to 1980, accompanied by an annual growth of the money supply of around 10 to 12 per cent. Monetary policy amounted essentially to a complex credit framework counterbalanced by a tight budgetary policy. The deficit explains the closing of the gap between inflation rates at home and abroad. At the same time, the nationalized industries experienced a rise in prices of 2 to 3 per cent above the private sector. This seems to have been due to their rigid labour costs, to a lower productivity that required urgent investments to cut costs, and to a poor financial situation.

The act of 19 July 1977 established the first real anti-trust law in France, under the supervision of a Commission on Competition, which was given three tasks: (i) to take legal action in cases of abuse of monopoly power; (ii) to advise on merger operations potentially able to inhibit competition; (iii) to advise the government on all matters affecting competition. The Commission enjoyed considerable independence in the recruitment of staff and investigators. But it remained largely dependent on the government for the cases referred to it. This turned out to be a crucial problem. In the first three years, when the Barre government was not under too great pressures, the Commission held enquiries in specially sensitive areas such as domestic appliances, car repairs, drugs and fertilizers, and imposed some heavy fines. The major restraints of trade brought to light were the rigging of prices and tenders, market-sharing arrangements, exclusive agencies, cartel discounts and block purchasing deals. But in 1980–1, when the government was facing the oil shock and the pressures of the presidential elections, the Commission's activities decreased substantially.

In a medium-sized economy, like the French, foreign trade has a major impact on the competitiveness of industry. As the French economy opened up to the point where France became the fourth largest exporter in the world, it encountered two problems.

The first concerned exchange rate policy. By the end of 1977, inflation in France had eroded the differential between the mark and the franc. The Barre government then broke with the immediate past by treating the exchange rate as a constraint to which the domestic economy must adapt. The strength of the franc against the dollar up to mid-1980 and against the mark up to March 1981, reflected the recognition by international financial markets of the relative prudence of French management compared with other industrial countries. Again, 1980 appeared to be a turning point: there was at that time a deficit on current account. The possibility that the franc might be overvalued came into question.

The second problem concerned import penetration, which became a hot political issue. Apart from a few industries such as glass, industrial chemicals, precision instruments, some textiles and leather, it was contraction of demand and growth in productivity, rather than import penetration, which forced industry to face up to adjustment (Messerlin 1982). However, like most industrialized countries during these years, France accused some Third World countries of unfair competition. She took a hard protectionist line during the Multifibre II negotiations and in the EEC's Davignon cartel for steel. But the fact that developing countries proved a major market for France (whose deficits were primarily with industrial markets) placed clear limits on this kind of protectionism.

Subsidies and aid to industry. The dismantling of price controls was not undertaken without any industrial policy. Again, 1980 was a watershed. Before 1980 the Barre government used existing agencies or arrangements for industrial purposes, while considerably slowing down their activities and the global amount of subsidies. After 1980 new institutions appeared and state aid to some sectors (steel) increased.

The subsidy rate (i.e. subsidies divided by value added) in manufacturing decreased from 2.5 per cent in 1976 to 2.3 per cent in 1977 and 1.8 per cent in 1978. This rose again in 1979, essentially because of aid to steel. During this first period, traditional agencies remained in charge of industrial readjustment assistance, with their traditional field of intervention: FDES for heavy industries; IDI, which was only modestly funded, for firms showing promise of rapid development; the Ministry of Industry; CODEFI for firms with less than twenty-five employees in temporary difficulties; and finally CIASI for larger firms. CIASI and CODEFI dealt with firms individually. FDES was concerned with sectors across the board (machine tools, printing, furniture, footwear, etc.).

In 1979–80 progressive changes arose in the institutions of public support and mirrored a change in the direction of industrial policy which tended to become more 'interventionist' and active. First, specialized bodies were set up to deal with bankrupt sectors (e.g. CAPA for steel). FSAI was formed in 1979 to tackle difficult pockets of depression and unemployment in the North, Lorraine, the Loire and Marseilles areas. Whatever the original purpose of all these organizations, the safeguarding of jobs and local employment became their overriding purpose. Letting 'lame ducks' die became exceptional. The government, in search of a more aggressive industrial policy, set up in 1979 (i) CODIS, concerned with areas showing promise of future technological development; (ii) CIDISE, using 'participatory loans' to assist small, dynamic but undercapitalized firms in food processing and textiles; (iii) ANVAR, for new enterprises (25 per cent of its assistance went to firms established less than two years previously) and enterprises with a nation-wide spread; ANVAR was the key agency for revitalizing R & D, which caught up with Germany and Japan (2 per cent GDP in 1977).

The nationalized industries. The fact that the index of investment of nationalized enterprises was 200 in 1979 (1971 = 100) compared with an overall index of 130 and an index of 118 for private industry, suggests that the public was more dynamic than the private sector. In fact, this counter-cyclical public investment was confined to nuclear energy and telecommunications. Other public investments grew at about the same level as private industry. The distinction in fact was not between nationalized and private but between energy and communications on the one hand and the rest on the other. The revival of the public investment programme between 1974 and 1981 was essentially based on high returns to capital from energy saving.

After a pause between 1966 and 1970 the nuclear programme was resumed with a programmed generation of 8,000 megawatts during the Sixth Plan. In 1973 the programme was trebled. A uranium enrichment plant was set in hand, and a firm specializing in pressure vessels (Framatome) established. Prospecting for uranium world-wide (particularly in Niger, Gabon and Canada) was stepped up. From 1980, connections with the national grid were proceeding at the rate of one every two months with a saving of 15 million tons of fuel oil a year in 1981 and 1982.

It is still too early to judge whether the nuclear programme was an economic as well as technical success. It is sometimes estimated that with oil at 15 dollars per barrel — let alone 10 dollars — nuclear energy is unprofitable. Again, since the price paid by the consumer depends on the cost of the fuel or gas needed to supplement energy supply, the advantage of nuclear energy must be analysed in terms of the surplus profit of a monopoly production group, namely EDF with Framatone-Alsthom-Atlantique and the supporting civil engineering firms. It is doubtful whether such a firmly based monopoly would pass on this surplus to the consumer. Three official reports between 1979 and 1983 reveal a drift in cost of the order of 10 to 15 per cent largely owing to the disappearance of competition at the power station level. Finally, an increase in the domestic supply of energy is not all gain. Between 1973 and 1979 the energy supply needed to produce one dollar of GNP fell annually by 1.3 per cent in France, but by 1.7 per cent in the United States and 2.6 per cent in Japan.

Telecommunications lagged behind right up to 1975 when there were still only 13.4 telephones per 100 households and an average of eleven months delay in providing connections. The telephone was expensive. Installation charges amounted to half a month's pay at minimum wage rates (SMIC). From 1970 onwards massive investments were undertaken in the system. From 1975 the Seventh Plan accorded priority to the telephone, and connections rose from 7 million to 16 million by 1980. Installation costs were reduced and deposits eliminated.

Between 1975 and 1981 half the priority funds of the current Plans were devoted to telecommunications. From 1969 to 1974 the authorities gave a monopoly to the CGE—in order to raise it to the level of Siemens—but in 1975 Thomson was brought in. This duopoly was modified from time to time, however, by the introduction for technological reasons of foreign equipment, especially in telephone exchanges (a policy not confined to telecommunications).

The two investment programmes described above (by far the most significant) posed two problems which are still relevant today. First, the nationalized industries had to raise their finance by borrowing on the money markets (for 25 per cent of their needs in 1970, rising to 50 per cent in 1980), including a considerable recourse to foreign markets. The leading nationalized industries were responsible for 26 to 28 per cent of all loan issues between 1976 and 1979 following the oil price crisis. the indebtedness of the EDF alone—including foreign debts—amounted to 140 billion francs. This obviously made the nationalized firms' finance heavily dependent on foreign exchange movements, and any costs had to be met by the state.

Second, the size of this investment effort produced a kind of 'silent nationalization' as big private firms became tied to public corporations. This 'silent nationalization' was due to three influences: (i) the pressure from the authorities directed to avoiding layoffs or maintaining key industries (for instance, the takeover of paint firms by CDF-Chimie, and Rivière Casalis— agricultural machinery— by Renault); (ii) the relative ease of takeover as compared with the legal complexities entailed in privatization; (iii) the dynamism of nationalized companies.

This dynamism has several causes. Some companies are dynamic simply because they were, over the years, in the leading sectors of the economy (e.g. energy), some because they enjoyed a near monopoly in the purchase of essential equipment (e.g. EDF, SNCF or the telecommunications firms) and could in consequence easily develop 'silent nationalization' upstream. Finally, there are companies, like Renault, which are in an extraordinarily privileged position since they seem to enjoy complete freedom from regulation in respect of fixed assets, pricing and wages policy. It has been calculated that if Renault had pursued the same dividend policy as Peugeot since 1980, it would have had to quadruple its payments to the state. Further, Renault enjoys government credits at a preferential rate of 9 per cent and is minimally taxed because its profits are (apparently) deliberately concealed. Against this, it has probably been forced to refrain from redundancies far longer than it would have liked.

The banking sector also experienced 'silent nationalization' in this period. Three factors played a part: (i) the system of participatory loans operated by FDES (Clause IV of the law of 13 July 1978), although intended as a form of pump-priming to draw in extra private finance, gave the state a *de facto* interest as a shareholder in firms; (ii) IDI, specially concerned with the top level of medium-sized firms and provided with only modest funds, spread over nearly every field of economic activity; (iii) the establishment of specialized state-owned banks such as the Crédit d'Equipement and regional development agencies for the benefit of medium-sized and small firms. These agencies operate with precisely the customers who would be best served by private banking.

4.5 The Socialist period: 1981–6

In May–June 1981 the Socialist–Communist–Radical coalition, led by François Mitterrand, came to power following presidential and parliamentary elections. In July 1984 the Communist Party withdrew from the government and the Socialists governed alone until March 1986, when new parliamentary elections gave the majority to the right-wing coalition. During these five years, industrial policy mirrored the U-turn in macroeconomic policy: there are few things in common between the expansionary and 'voluntarist' industrial policy of 1981–3 and the policy of readjustment to competition ('flexibility and modernization') of 1983–6.

Macro-economic policies vs industrial policies

In June 1981 the first Socialist government under the Prime Minister, Pierre Mauroy, pursued demand reflation in pure Keynesian style. As the world economy was in deep recession and domestic supply, hampered by the wage and other cost increases imposed by the government, did not respond, the trade deficit soared. Three devaluations of the franc followed between October 1981 and March 1983. From the first devaluation to the second, which came nine months later, in June 1982, the government renounced reflation and imposed a four-months price and wage freeze with tight price controls. Nevertheless, as no major changes were made in fiscal-monetary policies, a third devaluation followed in March 1983. By that time the value of the franc had dropped 19 per cent against the Deutsche mark compared with 1981. Further, France's long-term international debt doubled from 27 billion dollars (at the end of 1980) to 54 billion dollars (at the end of 1983).

The Mauroy government was obliged in March 1983 to make a complete U-turn and adopt an 'austerity' programme in order to curb inflation and restore the foreign and social security balances. This involved a classic mixture of budget cuts, increased taxes on households and a tighter monetary policy in 1985. Total taxes (*prélèvements obligatoires*) rose as a proportion of GNP from 42.5 per cent in 1980 to 45.4 per cent in 1984 and remained at this level thereafter.

Both inflation and the trade deficit were halved from 1981 to 1985 (inflation from 12 per cent to 6 per cent—and 3 per cent expected in 1986—and the trade deficit from 2.9 per cent of GDP to 1.2 per cent), but at the cost of the lowest growth rates since the war (oscillating around 1 per cent a year) and stagnant industrial output. The results are bad compared both to France's main industrialized competitors and to the earlier performance under Barre.

Reflation in 1981–2 had a severe impact on labour costs. The Mauroy government favoured real wage increases by both increasing the minimum wage and the weight of the 'indirect' wage (social security, paid holidays), which rose from 40 per cent to 43 per cent of all labour costs. In 1982 President Mitterrand also imposed a reduced (thirty-nine hours) working week with constant wages. This was supposed to stimulate employment through job-sharing, but it has been estimated that only 60,000 jobs were saved, at the cost of labour-intensive industries such as coal or textiles which the government wanted to promote.

During this U-turn of 1983, the Socialists introduced partial indirect 'de-indexation' by adjusting wages on the official inflation target for the coming year. Given a declining target for inflation, this introduced systematic wage lags with respect to prices. These lags and the increased taxes of the austerity programme led to a fall in net real wages of 1.6 per cent in 1984. Benefits to the long-term unemployed were cut in 1983, and the youth employment schemes of 1984 (*travaux d'utilité collective*) provided wages below the SMIC (the national minimum wage).

The U-turn also affected industry via indirect taxes and subsidies. Apart from the distortions introduced between industrial sectors by (tax-subsidy) differentials, the end of the period differs from the beginning under two main heads. First, tax rates reached a level where the authorities could no longer raise new resources at a politically acceptable cost. Second, the reflation of 1981–2 had expanded the incompressible part of the budget, since the debt service had risen and 200,000 new civil servants, who were legally secure against redundancy, had been hired to bolster employment. As a result, any reduction of the budget deficit implied cuts in public investment and transfers to firms. The financial scope for industrial policy became severely limited.

A new round of nationalizations

The nationalization of five major private firms (CGE, Pechiney, Rhône-Poulenc, Saint-Gobain and Thomson, hereafter the Five) and all the major banks was 'a prime objective' of Mitterrand's electoral programme of 1981. Then Sacilor, Usinor and CGCT were added, and the state became a majority shareholder in Dassault and Matra.

The reasons for this bout of nationalization still remain obscure. Most of the banks were profitable. None of the Five was in a desperate situation, although Pechiney, Rhône-Poulenc and Thomson faced severe adjustment problems. Sacilor and Usinor (steel) were already quasi-nationalized, while Dassault and Matra, heavily dependent on government defence programmes, were flourishing. Non-economic arguments seem to have been dominant. Many Socialists fell back on the view expressed in 1944 by Mendès-France, Moch and Philip of a three-sector economy with nationalized industries as the 'locomotive' and the private sector under strict control through the state-owned banks. Nationalization finally formalized the traditional French policy of 'national champions' (Zinsou 1985).

The public sector jumped in 1981 from 8 per cent to 23 per cent of manufacturing value added (more than 30 per cent in energy, steel, non-ferrous metals, glass, base chemicals, electronics, cars, aerospace and ships). The remaining private ´banks now accounted for only 1 per cent of all deposits and loans. This extensive nationalization process had three crucial outcomes.

First, state-owned firms now provide more than 25 per cent of local employment in seven out of twenty-three French regions (including the Paris area) and for less than 15 per cent in only six. Political devolution (*décentralisation*) has been heavily counterbalanced by economic national-ization.

Second, the statutory process of nationalization took a long time: after nine months of political and legal battles it really only ended in mid-1984 when the boards were completely set up and the new contours of the firms more or less stabilized. It triggered off intense rivalries between the firms themselves (each trying to annex good parts of the others and sell off its bad ones) and between the firms and the government about the degree of free-dom of management. As a consequence, nationalized firms were fully manageable only in 1983-4.

Third, in the process, most of the efforts to diversify made by the Five during the 1970s were reversed. For instance, Saint-Gobain had to sell its electronics division (Bull-Olivetti), created in 1980, to the new Bull firm and to ATT, and its component and military activities to Thomson. Thomson had to sell its telecommunications activities to CGE, which then enjoyed a monopoly of French production.

Economic theory would lead one to expect such developments. Diversifi-cation is one of the few means at the disposal of a private firm for contending with increased uncertainty. Public firms, however, can rely on government protection against risk and can be more specialized: nationalization allowed the newly nationalized firms to be less cautious. It can even be argued that they tried to 'capture' the public authorities when the contours and strate-gies of the newly nationalized firms had to be decided. Four of the big Five seem to have been obvious winners (CGE, Rhône-Poulenc, Pechiney and, to a lesser extent, Thomson).

This hypothesis is reinforced by the planning contracts drawn up between the government and nationalized firms. The planning contracts, signed in summer 1982 and renewed each year, were designed to justify the state doling out funds to firms that were supposed to be profit-maximizing. Initially, all the public firms (new and old) opposed the contracts which they saw as limits on their freedom. But they quickly learnt to manipulate them to their own profit. The firm announced broad goals (investments, R & D, jobs) it 'intended' to achieve and quantified them only for the coming year. In response, the government announced the funds (capital funds and 'participative loans') it would grant the firm that year. Such contracts hardly sufficed to let the government monitor the firms, as the CGE-Saint-Gobain deal soon showed. They also contained strategic commitments by government, for instance to fund redundancies, that the firms could exploit.

The time lost in establishing the new nationalized firms makes it hard to draw up an empirical analysis of their performance. The process has also concealed some of the losses of the public sector, when the wealthier firms were obliged to buy the unprofitable activities of others. Consequently, the best approach for establishing the cost-benefit of these nationalizations is to use data aggregated over several firms and to compare average results for 1977–80 and 1982–4. Such data suggest that a highly sceptical judgement of their performance is in order, as shown by Table 4.1, which throws light on the five main supposed advantages of nationalization.

First, nationalized firms were supposed to be 'job-machines'. In fact, the new ones reduced their labour forces by more than the rest of manufacturing: the Five represented 9.5 per cent of the manufacturing labour force in 1981 but 8.9 per cent in 1984.

Second, nationalized firms were supposed to help 'reconquer the internal market'. In fact, sales in France were quite stable after 1980. The ratio of domestic sales to domestic consumption decreased for the Five (7.1 per cent in 1981 versus 6.5 per cent in 1984).

Third, nationalized firms were to be the spearhead of French 'modernisation'. Investments did increase both in physical capital and in R & D, but at the cost of sharply increasing long- and medium-term debt and subsidies.

Fourth, they were to be profitable. Average net returns have fallen between 1977–80 and 1982–4. The later period was much more internationally depressed than the former, but the results hold even for 1984, a relatively good year. When subsidies (on which only rough estimates can be made) are excluded from net profits, the balance sheets of the nationalized firms justify some anxiety. Net results for 1984 for some like Bull, which never previously turned in good results, give a better impression. It is hard to tell how real this is, because a substantial portion of Bull sales derives from the obligation to 'buy French' in schools and universities.

Finally, nationalization was to stop the 'process of selling off parts of France's industrial wealth to foreigners'. However, substantial parts of the newly nationalized firms, accounting for some 5 per cent of total turnover, have been sold to foreigners since 1982.

Table 4.1. Selected indicators for nationalized firms in manufacturing, 1977–85 (billions of 1980 francs, except where otherwise stated)

Indicators	Group of Five†				Group of Nine†			Group of Twelve†		
	1977–80	1980	1982–4*	1984	1980	1982–4*	1984	1980	1982–4*	1984
Work force (000s)										
In France	628.3	635.5	548.6	527.3	681.5	610.1	591.8	999.6	951.7	934.9
Turnover										
French market	182.7	439.5‡	392.7	379.9	485.7‡	445.5	435.5	758.6‡	703.9	646.8
Abroad		190.3	182.4	189.0	215.1	214.3	226.8	333.4	342.3	358.2
Value added		87.0‡	79.7	79.2	102.8‡	98.9	101.4	167.8‡	168.2	168.2
Labour costs		103.3‡	102.7	109.8	112.3‡	115.4	125.4	165.6‡	174.1	190.0
Investment										
Total	11.7	13.7	13.0	13.7	14.1‡	15.1	16.3	24.1‡	25.7	27.1
Industrial	8.7	9.4	9.7	10.9	10.4	10.9	12.4	17.5	20.0	22.2
R & D										
expenditure	7.8	8.3	8.6	9.7	9.3	9.7	11.0	11.4‡	12.1	13.5
Long-term cost		30.9‡	34.0	35.9	37.0‡	42.9	45.8	79.6‡	94.6	106.2
Net profits§										
Incl. subsidies	2.3	0.6	−1.4	2.4	0.1	−3.9	0.8	−1.6	−15.9	−18.4
Excl. subsidies	2.3	0.6	−2.5	1.7	0.1	−5.3	−0.7	−1.6	−24.9	−27.6
State equity funding	0.0	0.0	2.2	0.9	0.0	3.3	2.4	0.0	6.5	8.0

* Figures for the four-year periods are simple annual averages.
† The Five are CGE, Pechiney, Rhône-Poulenc, Saint Gobain and Thomson; the Nine are the Five plus Bull, CGCT, CDF-Chimie and EMC; the Twelve are the Nine plus Sacilor, Usinor and Renault.
‡ 1981.
§ 'Résultats nets consolidés'.

Sources: Rapport du Sénat sur les Entreprises Publiques, 1983. and ibid. 1985; Ministère du Redéploiement Industriel, Observatoire des Entreprises Nationales, Le Secteur Public en 198 . . ., various years, Paris, La Documentation Française.

Industrial policies: the big 'swing'

In 1981 the Mauroy government decided that even mature industrial sectors should expand their output and increase employment. Official targets required coal output to rise from 20 million to 30 million tons between 1980 and 1990 (instead of previously planned cuts of 8 to 10 million tons), steel from 21 million to 24 million between 1981 and 1985 (instead of cuts of 3 million tons), and so on. The textile, machine-tool and paper industries were to 'reconquer the internal market' and increase output by 10 to 15 per cent (in volume). The government subsidized the hire of 8,000 new miners in coal (90 per cent from Morocco), 10,000 workers in steel and a few more thousand in textiles.

Yet output in the sectors concerned continued to fall (for instance, coal by 13 per cent, steel by 15 per cent) and only rose by 1.5 per cent in textiles. Employment fell 3.5 per cent in coal, 6 per cent in steel and textiles, 5 per cent in machine tools and 4 per cent in paper. Yet subsidies doubled in most of the selected sectors (Dutailly 1984). These direct costs do not take account of the indirect costs of the increased protectionism necessary to implement the policy. These involve non-tariff protection (compulsory use of French for all documents, a more systematic use of Article 115 of the Rome Treaty, severe exchange controls) and 'Buy French' public procurement. The rising US dollar and the rules of the EEC prevented a more dramatic move to protection.

With the U-turn of 1983, restructuring (*modernisation*) became the official watchword. But the financial situation of French firms was desperate after the inflation of 1981–2. Jenny and Weber (1984), using a sample of 817 big firms, have estimated that the rate of profit dropped from an already unfavourable –0.7 per cent in 1980 to –11.6 per cent in 1982, while the debt–asset ratio rose from 68 per cent to 72 per cent. The government was now trapped between its desire to give more money to 'sunrise' sectors, the political necessity of avoiding generalized collapses in several crucial sectors (cars, tyres, nuclear power plants, engineering) and the budget constraints of deflation.

First the government came back to Barre's policy of closing down excess capacities in declining sectors, with more determination in some cases. Massive redundancies followed: 30,000 jobs in coal, 25,000 in steel, 5,000 in shipbuilding. No targets were specified for other sectors, but it was clear that similar action was expected of the relevant firms. The government even sold off some of the firms it massively subsidized in 1981–3. The process was very costly, since the government-funded redundancy schemes added to the budget deficit.

Second, the government felt politically obliged to subsidize troubled firms in crucial sectors. One was the car industry, which was near to collapse in 1983 because of market errors, the state's 1981–2 veto on redundancies, rising labour costs and prices that were held back by the slump in demand

and increased competition. The nuclear power and engineering industries were in bad shape because of world recession.

As budgetary constraints reduced the scope for subsidies, these were granted in indirect and hidden ways. Banks were made to buy voting shares in firms in trouble, like Creusot-Loire (special steels and nuclear power plant), Poclain (civil engineering) or La Chapelle-Darblay (paper), at the same time as these firms were being bought out by foreign enterprises. Some redundancies were financed by institutions which are not normally involved in such operations, such as the insurance companies. The government also imposed agreements on firms with the potential to subsidize one other; for instance, EDF and CDF signed a contract on coal deliveries (1984–8) which was initially a subsidy of EDF to CDF estimated at 0.9 billion francs. Public procurement was exploited to the hilt. For instance, the PTT (the French telecom authority) was forced to pay artificially high prices to CGE for phone equipment and to allocate most of its earnings to finance the *filière électronique* (Bull, CGGT and Thomson) so that service prices were massively increased.

Naturally, there remained relatively little finance for funding the 'third industrial revolution'. The government proposed to invest 60 billion 1982 francs in electronics between 1982 and 1987. However, it was never able to do so and its effort tailed off steadily from 1984 onwards. French funding fell to half the Japanese in 1984: if 'catching up' was the real problem, French efforts were hopeless. More important, the nationalization of Bull, CGCT and Saint-Gobain cut the French national champions' international links. Honeywell's stake in Bull was cut to 20 per cent from of 47 per cent. The Olivetti stake bought by Saint-Gobain in 1980 was sold to ATT in 1982.

To summarize, the 1983–5 industrial policy seems to have been largely dominated by the need for short-term adjustments to the effects of macro-economic policies rather than by strategies for modernization (Adams and Stoffaes 1986; Bfalassa 1985; Cohen and Bauer 1985). Moreover, the forms taken by adjustment added to the distortions in the French economy. Two examples illustrate this. First, the 1982–3 *plan textile* granted subsidies to firms both for labour and investment, so that the industry was unsure whether to pursue capital-intensive policies or not. Second, the costs of subsidizing jobs varied in the order of 1 to 20 as between different firms in 1983. Economic theory suggests that the main result of such massive distortions is increasing efficiency losses. Recent results presented by Malinvaud (1986) are consistent with this. The net profitability, defined as the difference between the real rate of profits and the real interest rate, of private French firms decreased from +4.4 per cent in 1979 to –3.6 per cent in 1982, improved slightly to –1.6 per cent in 1983, but worsened again to –2.4 per cent in 1984.

4.6 French industrial policy: an exercise in futility?

This chapter has taken the view that during the three last decades French industrial policy was ineffective: it did not achieve its announced goals and was sometimes a costly exercise in futility. This perspective goes against the common view—which sees French industrial policy as one of the most successful in the world—and leads to two questions. First, how is it possible that all the institutions created during these thirty years to conduct industrial policy could have been so ineffective? Second, what were, instead, the driving forces of French growth during these decades?

Appearance and reality

The French state has been an ambitious state over the past thirty years. It almost disappeared during World War II, and this induced it to prove itself by creating a host of institutions to fight new battles—to create new economic and industrial policies. Studies examining the 'success' of French industrial policy generally focus on this institutional proliferation and on the objectives given to these institutions. However, these are appearances. The real world was different because all these agencies faced two major problems.

First, an institution can be effective only in so far as it is supported by a 'consensus' on the rules of the game. During these three last decades no such consensus was achieved on industrial policy, and the French state oscillated between two different approaches, each equally well represented among the major political streams. These two approaches have agreed on one thing: the firm—and not the market—as the key issue in the economic and industrial debate. The first of these approaches—supported by people as different as Jean Monnet, President Pompidou or Pierre Mendes-France—takes a positive view of the firm and, accordingly, sees the public role as one of supporting and protecting French firms, if necessary in the face of market forces. In other words, this first approach favours firms over markets. The second approach takes a negative view of the firms, seeing them as the focus of social exploitation. This approach is well represented across the whole political spectrum, from the Marxists of the Communist or Socialist parties to those who share a nostalgia for 'pre-industrial' economic organization in the parties of the extreme right.

One of the best illustrations of this emphasis on the firm in both approaches—and of the weak influence of those who believe in markets—is the way in which French political parties are completely incapable of analysing and benefiting from the foreign experience of deregulation and privatization of ownership. This experience suggests that deregulation, that is increased competition and an emphasis on well-functioning markets, is more important for domestic economic welfare than privatization, that is the emphasis on whether the firm is publicly or privately owned.

Second, in order to be effective, an industrial policy would need to be focused on a strictly limited number of public actions. This follows from the limitations on public funds available for intervention and the large size of the markets in which the state would like to intervene. The best illustration of this is the socialist policy of 1982–3: public funds were already shrinking while the scope for intervention was still increasing, so that the gap between appearance and reality reached a peak. In fact, the multiplication in the number of agencies of industrial policy during the ten last years can be interpreted as an index of inefficiency in industrial policy. This need to focus on a limited number of actions follows from another consideration: to make sense—good or bad—an industrial policy should favour some industries. By the same token, it also means that it has to disfavour all the others. But the fact that the French state was ready to support any firm, as long as it was not too small, against the working of the market made the French authorities vulnerable to any pressure group: the ambitious state was indeed easily captured.

The invisible hand behind the ambitious state

French growth during the three last decades was the outcome of two opposing forces: trade liberalization and industrial policy. The first force tended to increase existing opportunities for rapid growth. The second tended to decrease them because of the distortions introduced in many markets by public actions. However, what matters here is the relative, rather than absolute, strength of these two forces.

During the 1950s, industrial policy was relatively stronger than trade liberalization. This was a striking difference with Germany and Italy. Indeed, France did not catch up with these two countries: French growth was lower than in Germany or in Italy. On the other hand, it can be argued that French growth was higher than in Britain or the United States; but, as Olson (1982) convincingly argued, it is inaccurate to compare countries with political continuity—such as the victors of World War II—with countries whose political life was disrupted, such as the vanquished of the same war, among them France. Although there was no catching up process in France during the 1950s, French growth was fortunately quite respectable in absolute terms. This was the result of two forces: the massive flow of cheap labour from agriculture to industry and the fact that the industrial policy of this early period was so crude that most of the markets of an economy still close to wartime autarchy and based on small firms were beyond its reach.

During the 1960s and the 1970s, trade liberalization became stronger than industrial policy. International competition became the dominant feature not only between firms on the goods markets but also—and crucially for

French policy—between states at the level of macro-economic policies. More and more frequently, the macro-economic choices the French state was obliged to make for France to compete industrially with Germany tended to negate the potential impact of the industrial policy interventions made at the same time. Alignment on the most efficient economy—the economy the most dominated by market forces and a stable state—became the rule: the invisible hand of European and world markets became the driving force behind the ambitious state.

European construction has played a crucial role in this past balance between trade liberalization and industrial policy. The influence of the European Community will be even more crucial for the evolution of the French economy during the next decade. If the European Community is still able to tilt the scales towards trade liberalization—either by a genuine move towards freer trade or by unilateral decisions by some member states (e.g. British deregulation of financial markets)—the same balance as that prevailing during the 1960s can be expected. If not, it is likely that France will be one of the member countries that will suffer most from a relative closing of the European Community.

References

Adams, W.J. and Stoffaes, C. (1986), *French Industrial Policy*, Washington, DC, Brookings Institution.

Bfalassa, B. (1985), 'La politique industrielle socialiste', *Revue 'Commentaire'*, No. 30, Summer.

Carré, J.-J., Dubois, P. and Malinvaud, E. (1973), *French Economic Growth*, Stanford, Calif., Stanford University Press.

Christensen, L.R., Cummings, D. and Jorgenson, D.W. (1976), *Economic Growth, 1947–1973: An International Comparison*, Cambridge, Mass., Harvard Institute of Economic Research.

Cohen, E. and Bauer, M. (1985), *Les Grandes Manoeuvres Industrielles*, Paris, Pierre Belfond.

Corden, M.W. (1980), 'Relationships between macroeconomics and industrial policies', *The World Economy*, Vol. 3, No. 2, September.

Dutailly, J.-C. (1984), 'Aides aux entreprises: 134 milliards de francs en 1982', *Economie et Statistique*, September.

Kruisel, R.F. (1981), *Capitalism and the Modern State in France: Renovation and Economic Management in the 20th Century*, Cambridge, Cambridge University Press.

Jenny, F. and Weber, A.-P. (1974), 'L'évolution de la concentration industrielle en France de 1961 a 1969', *Economie et Statistique*, No. 60, October.

Le Pors, A. and Prunet, J. (1975), 'Les transferts entre l'état et l'industrie', *Economie et Statistique*, No. 66, April.

McArthur, J.H. and Scott, B.R. (1970), *Industrial Planning in France*, Boston, Mass., Harvard University Graduate School of Business Administration.

Malinvaud, E. (1986), 'Mise à jour', quoted in B. Balassa, 'Bilan de la politique socialiste', *Revue 'Commentaire'*, Vol. 9, No. 33, Spring.

Messerlin, P.A. (1982), 'Reconquête du marche intérieur ou protectionnisme?' in H. Bourguinat, *Internationalisation et Autonomie des Decisions*, Paris, Economica.

Olson, M. (1982), *The Rise and the Decline of Nations: Economic Growth, Stagflation and Social Rigidities*, New Haven, Conn., Yale University Press.

Stoffaes, C. (1978), *La Grande Menace Industrielle*, Paris, Le Livre de Poche, Collection Pluriel.

de Vannoise, R. (1977), 'Etude économique et financière de 18 groupes industriels français', *Economie et Statistique*, No. 87, March.

Zinsou, L. (1985), *Le Fer de Lance: Essai sur les Nationalisations Industrielles*, Paris, Olivier Orban.

Glossary of institutions

ANVAR	Agence Nationale pour la Valorisation de la Recherche
CAPA	Caisse d'Amortissement pour l'Acier
CDF	Charbonnages de France
CGT	Confédération Général du Travail
CFDT	Confédération Française du Travail
CIASI	Comité Interministériel pour l'Aménagement des Structures Industrielles
CIDISE	Comité Interministériel pour le Développement des Investissements et le Soutien de l'Emploi
CNPF	Comité National du Patronat Français
CNRS	Centre National de la Recherche Scientifique
CODEFI	Comités Départmentaux d'Examen des Problèmes de Financement des Entreprises
CODIS	Comité Interministériel d'Orientation pour le Développement des Industries Stratégiques
DGRST	Délégation Générale de la Recherche Scientifique
EDF	Electricité de France
FO	Force Ouvrière
FDES	Fonds de Développement Economique et Social
FSAI	Fonds Spécial d'Adaptation Industrielle
IDI	Institut de Développement Industriel
PTT	Postes, Telephones et Telecommunications

5 Italy: the weak state

Pippo Ranci[*]

Since practically all economic policies, including some not strictly economic, affect the performance of industry, the definition of industrial policy is highly subjective. I have followed a middle course, concentrating on industrial policies rather strictly defined as government actions directed at producing effects on industrial structure and performance, and referring only briefly to other policies which appear to have been particularly important in shaping industrial change in Italy. Macro-economic issues have been important for industry, but the broad lines of these are well known, while a detailed reporting of the short-term vagaries of Italian macro-economic policy would be lengthy and less relevant to our topic.

Italian industrial policy is described in section 5.2, with a rather schematical subdivision of the period into four subperiods. Some important aspects of the environment are sketched in section 5.1 before the story is taken up in section 5.2. Issues, policies and instruments are analysed in some detail in section 5.3, where a synthetic approach dealing with the main areas of public intervention in industry is superimposed on the chronological approach to section 5.2.

5.1 The environment for industrial policy

Structural dependence on imports

The external constraint has always been the main concern behind governmental action on the supply side. Once the decision in favour of trade liberalization was made in the post-war years, Italy had to face the problems of a small open economy with a structural trade deficit. The lack of domestic raw materials has long been recognized as a main weakness. Rapid post-war growth brought the energy problem to the fore.

The rapid rise in energy consumption coincided with a massive shift to oil.

* I greatly benefited from the comments of Giovanni Dosi and Michele Salvati on an earlier draft of this chapter.

In 1973 among industrial countries, Italy was second only to Japan in the share of energy needs met by imported oil. In 1971 primary electric (mostly hydro) power accounted for 10 per cent of total energy consumption, natural gas for 9 per cent and the remaining 81 per cent was made up by oil (73 per cent) and coal (8 per cent) imports. An ambitious programme of nuclear generation, with some attempt to develop national research, was started in the late 1950s, and halted in 1963 by a political quarrel believed to have been instigated by the oil lobby. With the 1973–4 oil shock the share of Italy's merchandise exports required to pay for imported oil jumped from 17 to 33 per cent (cf. Japan, 45 per cent; France and Britain, 25 per cent; Germany, 15 per cent).

The consequent adjustment in the energy balance was carried out almost completely on the demand side. Net energy imports in 1983 were about the same as in 1973, while GDP had grown by 20 per cent. This remarkable performance is almost completely due to saving in industry and services other than transport. Change in the industry mix was of great importance. On the supply side, the nuclear programme has been slowly resumed; a number of coal-fired power stations are under construction or planned; imports of natural gas have been stepped up.

Besides energy, Italy's traditional pattern of importing raw materials and exporting manufactures still prevails, with some qualifications. Import penetration has been increasing, with some acceleration in the last five years. The trend affects all classes of manufactured goods, and is particularly strong in intermediate products, underlining a shift away from the early stages of production processes.

Although increased imports have been matched by increased exports, manufacturing exports appear to be strongest in two of Pavitt's (1984) four classes: *traditional* products such as textiles, clothing, shoes, steel, furniture, and *specialized suppliers* including most engineering products, rather than *science-based* and *scale-intensive* products (Onida 1986). This pattern of import penetration and export specialization defines the evolving nature of the foreign trade constraint.

Regional dualism

The historical difference in the level and structure of incomes and employment between the North and the South of Italy was immediately seen as a major policy problem in the years of reconstruction. A better balance in the geographical distribution of industry has been a major goal of industrial policy.

The small firm and the informal sector

Italian industry clearly has a higher share of small business than other industrial countries. The average size of plants rose until the early 1970s, but in the following decade the trend was reversed. Large organizations have been considered a weak point in the economy, particularly in the public sector. Small firms in a given sector often congregate in one location and create significant external economies in manpower, technical skills, services and entrepreneurship.

Among small firms, commercial ability goes hand in hand with simple management and accounting techniques, and a widespread habit of tax avoidance through legal loopholes or straight evasion. This limits the scope of industrial policy: tax incentives are unpopular and have a limited impact. The provision of educational and advisory services to the small entrepreneur is much talked of and would have more scope if handled by a more competent and efficient public administration.

Cottage industry is important, particularly in clothing and knitwear, leather and shoes. The infringement of labour and tax laws is widespread here, as in construction and numerous other services such as automotive repairs. Tolerance of evasion may be regarded as a sort of involuntary industrial policy, but the cost advantages are partly offset by the weaker incentives for quality improvement and technical advance, and the damage to more industrially minded and law-abiding entrepreneurs.

Political institutions and public administration

The degree of stability in policy-making is difficult to assess. Governments change very rapidly, the relative strength of political parties is exceptionally stable, and the pattern of coalitions and the turnover of prime ministers are in between.

As a result, while the basic tenets and objectives of economic policy change very slowly, the short duration of governments weakens all actions, since most initiatives have to be abandoned at some intermediate stage and started again from scratch when a new government or minister takes over. By spinning out the enactment process beyond the tenure of a government or a minister the whole thing can be renegotiated with their successors; individual ministers tend to neglect long-term measures over which they know they have little influence, and concentrate on immediate issues. Hence there is a kind of continuity in the general orientation of economic (including industrial) policy, which goes with a tendency to paralysis at the operational stage.

The quality of public intervention is also lowered by a generally low level of skills, organization and equipment in public offices. Not much has changed since Joseph LaPalombara (1966) wrote:

An equally nagging problem involves the technical data-gathering capacities of the bureaucracy. My research has shown not merely that bureaucratic agencies are extremely ill-equipped in this regard but that they tend to become dangerously dependent on the kind of data that certain interest groups provide. Thus, to cite an important example, the degree to which the Ministry of Industry and Commerce must rely for information on the data-gathering facilities of the General Confederation of Italian Industry is both striking and perplexing.

Financial aspects

Italian industry has long been highly dependent on bank credit, due to the slow development of financial markets and of the stock exchange, a serious handicap, given the oligopolistic character of the banking system and the lack of a diversified supply of banking services. Leasing and factoring were introduced rather late in the 1970s, and the development of merchant banking has been an important issue only in recent years.

Large firms greatly increased their indebtedness in the 1960s, when investment opportunities were abundant and subsidized credit was available for investment in the South. This happened again in the 1970s, as a result of poor economic performance. Indebtedness at fixed interest rates was a blessing in the years of rising inflation (1970–7). New debts were a bargain as long as real interest rates were negative (1977–9). During the 1980s there was a rapid shift away from loans into self-financing and equity financing.

5.2 A historical sketch of Italian industrial policy

The main issues of the 1950s

At the end of the war the main economic task was reconstruction, complicated initially by an acute imbalance between demand and supply, then a surge of inflation in 1948–7 and an acute shortage of foreign exchange. By 1948 the stabilization manoeuvre had been carried out successfully and American help had eased the external constraint. Pre-war levels of production were reached around 1950. The ECA Country Study on Italy of February 1949 indicated that production had attained 90 per cent of the pre-war level in October 1947 before falling in response to the credit restrictions (see Graziani 1979, p. 143).

Inseparable from reconstruction were three main objectives:

(i)   to remove the external constraint permanently, that is beyond the Marshall Plan effect;

(ii) to reduce structurally high unemployment;

(iii) to narrow the gap in employment, living standards and productivity between the North and the South.

The current-account deficit, though highlighted by lack of foreign exchange reserves, was not excessive in the early 1950s and moved into surplus for most of the period 1958–73.

Around 1950 there were between 1.6 million and 2 million unemployed, that is between 7.5 and 9 per cent of the labour force, the lower figure indicating registered unemployment, the other an official estimate. (See Graziani 1979, p. 21, who thinks this was an underestimate. For a discussion of the employment figures, see also Lutz 1962.) Some hidden unemployment may be assumed, particularly among the 8.6 million employed in agriculture (44 per cent of total employment). In 1959 (the year when a consistent data service starts) the activity rate was 45 per cent, with unemployment at 7 per cent. The rapid growth of the economy in the 1950s was needed merely to produce jobs for those leaving agriculture: farm employment had fallen to 34 per cent of total employment by 1959. Unemployment fell by only a small amount, and this was probably due to emigration. In the interval between the censuses of 1951 and 1961 total emigration amounted to 1.3 million people.

A notable improvement was achieved in the 'miracle' years up to 1963. The overall unemployment rate was brought down to 4 per cent. The growth of industrial employment was then halted by the acute imbalances it had generated. There was full employment of males in industrialized areas. Internal migration, which had been at an unprecedented rate, was hindered by the shortage of houses and services. The policy of full employment could only go further through greater resort to structural policies.

The policy orientation of the 1950s: free foreign trade and a 'mixed' domestic economy

A 'free market' policy prevailed between the end of the war and the end of the 'economic miracle' (1963). But while free trade was in favour, internally there were two exceptions, in the state-owned industrial enterprises and in the new effort to develop the Mezzogiorno. The double straight-jacket of the fascist corporate state and of wartime controls was rapidly shed. Protection was discarded, and Italian governments wholeheartedly supported European economic unification. There was no wave of post-war nationalizations as in France and Britain. The existing large share of state holdings in industry and services was inherited from the previous regime and its great rescues of the 1930s. This was supplemented by a few rescues of military-oriented engineering firms in need of reconversion (such as Breda) and by some development in the energy sector (AGIP). The state holding sector, on the other hand, was organized under a 'mixed economy' philosophy, with a programme of joint public–private ownership destined to enjoy a certain renown just when it was starting to collapse (Holland 1972).

The economic policies of the 1950s can be better understood if we look at the main streams of ideas and interests behind them. The free-market orientation was politically convenient since it marked a neat break with fascism. On the other hand, the ruling economic class was half-hearted in its support for the open economy. Recognizing that reconversion to peacetime production required some public intervention, and accustomed to feather-bedding, many industrialists saw some advantages in the corporate system. An important section of industry, though, was in favour of free trade, and it won.

The managers of the state enterprises consituted a distinct section of the ruling economic class. Among them a dynamic view prevailed, envisaging the opportunities for public investment in basic sectors such as steel and energy, where the amount of finance required, the degree of risk, and the possible clash with foreign interests deterred private capital. The argument for public intervention in such 'strategic' sectors was well supported by the theoretical work on latecomers in industrialization, although it met some opposition from free-marketeers such as Luigi Einaudi.

The workers' movement was divided after the split of 1947 in the trade unions and had very little say in policy. The Communist Party had no influence on economic policy decisions. It supported a limited programme of nationalizations, aiming at bringing the greatest concentration of private power under public control.

The world of the intellectuals and political reformers was dominated by *liberali* (very much free-market orientated and less keen on reform than the English word 'liberal' suggests). Southern social scientists were deeply committed to the rebirth of the Mezzogiorno and provided respectable intellectual support for land reform and industrial inventives programmes there. But, though the weak economy of the south was vulnerable to a policy of free trade, Southern tradition was in favour of such a policy. The switch from free trade to protection in the last two decades of the nineteenth century had been imposed by Northern industry against the interests of Southern agriculture.

Finally, politicians of the ruling Christian Democratic Party (DC) had no great economic tradition and initially yielded to the orthodox free-traders in the field of macro-economic and foreign-trade policy. De Gasperi was mainly interested in the political integration of Italy into Western Europe and accepted all its economic implications. The free-trade choice did not entail the rejection of any credible alternative as it was closely tied up with the general choice in favour of Western integration.

For several reasons the DC began to drift away from free trade after the stabilization years 1947–9. It had close ties with a large labour union (CISL). The Catholic movement was traditionally hostile both to capitalism and collectivism. Needing to deny room to the Marxist left, the DC was compelled to embrace a mixed economy, combining a strong measure of state intervention to help the Mezzogiorno with a certain amount of social policy and a basic free-trade system. To retain power, the DC had to work out a way of cooperating with the state apparatus, which had not changed much since fascist times and was less at home with general economic management and macro-economic policy than with direct deals between government and single firms. Last but not least, the DC relied on financial support from private and public industry which wanted something in exchange.

Inside a basic free-trade system, three main elements of intervention developed in addition to the land reform of 1950:

(i)   a set of instruments designed to foster development in the Mezzogiorno, centered on the institution of the Cassa per il Mezzogiorno in 1950;
(ii) a number of sectoral programmes carried out by state enterprises in such 'strategic' sectors as mining, steel, oil and gas, and fertilizers (although some of these initiatives were undertaken independently by state enterprises, and only later recognized as programmes by the state);
(iii) a framework for indicative planning—the so-called Piano Vanoni (see Ministero del Bilancio 1967).

1963–73: the planning experiment with priority to social reforms

The high growth of industrial production during the 'miracle' years 1958–63 was only in part self-sustaining. Imbalances built up to act as a brake in 1963–4. The boom came to a halt as the result both of purely economic factors and of political and social changes. The economic factors can be listed as follows:

(i)   Full employment was reached in critical segments of the labour market, bringing a pressure on wages that had been absent in the 1950s.
(ii) A period of export-led growth—approximately from 1956 to 1961—was followed by an expansion of domestic demand in both consumption and investment; this caused bottlenecks and a worsening of the trade balance; the recession that followed in 1964–5 was in part due to the effect of restrictive monetary and fiscal policies (Forte 1966).
(iii) Fast growth had been made possible by a process of technological imitation which could not last forever. Italian firms were strongly entrenched in the field of intermediate technologies such as highly mechanized spinning and weaving, household appliances, cars and motorcycles, and large areas of mechanical engineering; in order to be successful they did not have to invest heavily in advanced technology, so they were bound to see the end of easy growth when conditions in the labour market changed.

The other relevant factors were:

(i) A resurgence in union power, adversely affecting wages and productivity.

(ii) A change in cultural attitudes towards growth as the social costs of growth in terms of inadequate housing (particularly for migrant families) and public transportation services, and so on, became apparent.

(iii) As a result of East–West détente and of the softening of the Catholic Church's stand against Marxist political parties, a change in the constitution of the government coalition became possible, with the Socialists becoming part of the majority.

The centre-left governments of 1962–72 laid strong emphasis on planning for social purposes: public housing programmes; control of private speculation in urban development; improved schooling; the setting up of a national health service; the switching of resources from private to public transportation; the reform of the tax system to make it more progressive; and the delegation of political power to regional governments.[1]

Most of the measures indicated in the programme of the new coalition were enacted with great delay and difficulty. The regional reform, the health service and the tax reform had to wait until the early 1970s.

Industrial policy was not to the fore except for the much disputed nationalization of the electrical industry in 1962, which had two main effects. First, the balance of power within Confindustria (the employers' confederation) was changed since the old electric utilities had carried great weight there. But it is highly questionable whether the weight of Confindustria itself was reduced. Second, a great opportunity for industrial growth and structural change was created and then thrown away by allowing the old electric corporations to survive and take compensation for the nationalization of their plants in yearly instalments. They were expected to invest the proceeds in new and promising sectors, which by and large they did very badly. Among the old utilities there were two IRI groups. One (SIP) took over the telephone network: this was one way of indirectly financing a public utility with public money and bringing about the unification and rationalization of the system under the IRI. The process was not completed, and an inefficient dualism between the SIP network and the pre-existing state agency for long-distance connections (ASST) persists to this day. The other, the Southern Electric Company (SME), took over all sorts of manufacturing firms with a prevailing interest in the food sector, but completely failed to form an integrated group capable of standing up to international competition. (Italy's weakness in Europe's highly concentrated food industry is striking.) SME was offered for sale to private interests in 1985, but eventually not sold because of political pressure.

The largest private utility, Edison, used compensation funds to take over the biggest Italian chemical firm, Montecatini—then in desperate need of finance—and form Montedison, with disastrous results. Montedison was slow in closing down the numerous old small plants of Montecatini, meanwhile making a number of costly investments in basic chemicals, mainly in the Mezzogiorno. Montedison entered the world chemical crisis of the 1970s in poor technological shape, overburdened by debts, overmanned and specialized only in the old and least profitable sectors of the market.

Equally remarkable are the missed opportunities of nationalization. The electricity business went on much as before, apart from some significant economies from the unification of the network (Zanetti and Fraquelli 1979), some of which would probably have accrued anyway. The nuclear programme, halted by political quarrels in 1961, was not resumed until late in the mid-1960s and then very cautiously. Italy entered the oil crisis of the mid-1970s with the same nuclear electric generating capacity it had had in 1961 and only one nuclear plant under construction.

Apart from the nationalization of electricity, the economic policy of the centre-left governments in the 1960s had some quite unintentional adverse effects on industrial growth, notably in housing and transportation. It was easy to stop the old growth mechanism, but politically difficult to start the new one.

The centre-left's transportation programme was centered on slowing down state expenditure on the motorway network (considered to favour the private sector unduly) while improving the railways and the urban public transportation system. In practice, the negative side of the programme was carried out more effectively than the positive one. The effects on industry have been manifold:

(i) Due to the inadequacy of the railway system, transportation of goods still depends on road rather than rail more than anywhere else in Europe; this tends to have an adverse effect on intra-firm transportation costs for integrated groups with part of their plants located in the Mezzogiorno, and on the access to the North Italian and North European markets of fresh agricultural produce from the South.

(ii) Investment decisions by the State Railways (FS) and by the various local authorities have been so frustrated by financial, political and administrative difficulties as to weaken the transportation equipment sector.

(iii) The poor state of urban commuting systems has reduced the mobility of the labour force and so helped to worsen industrial disputes.

It should be noted that effects (i) and (iii) operate despite a very low fare tariff, which contributes greatly to the deficit of the public sector.

Supply-side measures in the 1950s and 1960s

Though there is not much mention of the term in contemporary records, it would be wrong to argue that Italy had no industrial policy before the 1970s. Action on the supply side is in fact a feature of the Italian tradition. The cultural legacy of fascist corporatism and the great delay in the spread of Keynesian ideas in Italy led to a sceptical attitude towards demand management at a time when it was fashionable elsewhere. The absence of Keynesian thinking highlighted the contrast between a free-market approach with a neo-classical character and a planning approach with an accent on supply-side policies and socialist overtones. Given the initial problems of reconstruction, complicated in the second place by regional inequalities, a straight *laissez-faire* policy was out of the question. Italian economic policy, even in the 1950s, included some degree of state intervention on the supply side as a necessary and natural feature of the market mechanism.

In the early post–war period the scarcity of resources and foreign exchange imposed resource planning. The European Reconstruction Programme (ERP) set targets for basic sectors where there were existing or potential bottlenecks: electricity generation, oil refining, steel, fertilizers. The ERP also set targets for the main industrial sectors of the Italian pre-war economy, engineering and textile. These were necessary to restore some equilibrium in the trade balance.

The 'strategic' sectors were in fact identified with potential bottlenecks. Hence the large expansion programme of the IRI steel plants (the so-called Sinigaglia Plan) and the rapid growth of Mattei's AGIP (later ENI) in the oil and gas business, and thereafter in fertilizers and basic chemicals.

The Vanoni Plan, probably the most Keynesian example of Italian planning, introduced a macro-economic approach with secondary emphasis on sectoral problems. The bulk of public expenditure was to go to infrastructure in the Mezzogiorno in order to initiate a big push for overall growth and thereby reduce unemployment.

Consistently with the Vanoni approach, state intervention in the second half of the 1950s developed mainly in infrastructure and public services such as the motorway network, the telephone system, the setting up of Alitalia. The main efforts in industrial sectors were concentrated on steel, oil and gas, and their by-products. But the inability of the infrastructure policy in isolation to cope with the development of the Mezzogiorno led to a gradual shift towards more direct intervention.

Centre-left blueprints picked up the notion of 'strategic' sectors, but this time with a call for restraint on monopolies (in electricity, steel, cars, basic chemicals, cement, energy and construction), according to the Giolitti Plan of 1964 (Ministero del Bilancio 1967).

In practice, policy in the 1960s brought little anti-monopolistic action beyond the nationalization of electricity. It became clear that the enlargement of the market created by the European Common Market was doing much of the job. Other monopolies were, at least theoretically, broken by the direct intervention of state enterprises (cement, fertilizers), and the problem was then how to control the state enterprises themselves.

The end of the boom and the lowering of the barriers to trade brought to light the first cases calling for a defensive industrial policy after the rescues of the immediate post-war period. Law 1470 of 1961, although scarcely significant in terms of expenditure, was the first example of a rescue policy with little regard for economics and reflecting vested interests. A fund of 5 billion lire was set up to be administered by the public financial institute IMI, to provide soft and long-term loans to small firms in need of restructuring. The fund was refinanced nine times in the following fifteen years, but no satisfactory account of the results of its operations ever appeared, and it is now considered the worst example of state assistance (Amato 1972), despite its financial insignificance. Following the crises of 1965 and 1970, a law to provide for the restructuring and development of the textile industry was approved in 1971. Some rescues were carried out during the 1960s. ENI had entered the engineering sector in the 1950s and the textile sector in the 1960s through the acquisitions of ailing private firms. These rescues were justified by the need to diversify into industries strictly related to the oil and chemical business.

While public attention was paid to basic sectors, to monopolistic sectors and to weak labour-intensive sectors, not much interest was shown in the area of innovation. A significant example of this is the management of the Olivetti crisis in 1964, in the course of which the company sold its computer division to General Electric without attracting any reaction from government, unions or political parties.

Attitudes changed during the 1960s, possibly due to an awakening interest in the sectors of the future throughout Europe (see Servan Schreiber's *Le Défi Americain*, published in Italy in 1967). In 1967 IRI and Fiat merged their aerospace interests and the new Aeritalia company received special grants from the government. In 1968 a public fund was set up to provide soft loans for industrial R & D.

Small businesses were regarded with a benevolent eye throughout the period, possibly for political as well as economic reasons. Legislation in support of small businesses was justified on the grounds of their greater difficulty in securing financial resources. But it is also tempting to see here and in the land reform of 1950 an attempt to reinforce a stable, conservative, economically active class of small capitalists. There was a similarly consistent policy of helping small enterprises in retail trade while inhibiting the growth of large retail companies. For a long time there has been a broad political consensus centering on these ideas in Italy. The large private enterprise raised suspicions both among conservatives, who rather liked to see a large number of small capitalists and not too much concentration of the labour force, and among left-wingers, who were afraid of monopolies and liked to develop cooperative and state enterprises. The cooperative movement always had preferential treatment, being rather evenly divided into a white (Christian Democrat) and a red (Social Communist) branch, with a smaller pink (Social Democrat and Republican) branch trying to take its share. Small business was courted by all political sides: even by the Communists, and with some success, in the 1970s.

The preference for small business was dominant in politics in the 1950s and the early 1960s. For various reasons, a more favourable attitude to the large firm came to be accepted in the second half of the 1960s, in recognition of the fact that economic necessity should prevail over political preferences. Most economists were highly critical of the political preference for small firms and of the gap existing between Italy and other industrialized countries in respect of the size of firms. It was largely held that technical progress, organizational efficiency and hence labour productivity were strongly correlated with firm size: a dualism existed in Italian industry between a progressive sector of larger, more capital-intensive firms and a laggard sector of small, labour-intensive, technologically backward small firms (Lutz 1962).

Industrial managers, for their part, became more and more conscious of the benefits of economies of scale. But in retrospect the complexity of managing large firms was often underestimated. The Fiat policy of concentrating production in a few huge plants led to a concentration of workers that proved very costly in terms of external diseconomies in the 1960s and in terms of industrial relations and organization in the 1970s. A number of large clothing plants built in the 1960s generated significant losses as soon as wages rose and industrial relations became more difficult (some of the largest were rescued by the state-owned GEPI and ENI in the early 1970s).

Nevertheless, the prevalent opinion in the period 1964–70 was that the increasing harshness of international competition had to be met by an increase in the size of both plants and firms, and that the traditional policy of privileging the small firm had to be corrected. This kind of thinking was behind the change introduced in Mezzogiorno incentives through Law 717 of 1965 which provided for more generous investment grants and loans for large plants and firms; it was behind government approval of the Montecatini–Edison merger to the extent of introducing a law that made tax treatment of mergers more favourable; it was behind the favourable attitude of banks and particularly the public-owned long-term financial institutions towards large firms (for instance, the considerable assistance afforded to the SIR chemical group by IMI). Political patronage played its part, but political pressures cannot materialize without some acceptable economic backing.

The drive for size generated the greatest economic disasters in the 1970s. Some economists had overlooked the conflict between sheer size and technological flexibility, between the technology incorporated once-for-all in fixed capital and the scope for continuous innovation. A generally respectable theory was used short-sightedly (to say the least) to justify a wide array of decisions, with little or no recourse to selective analysis. Of course, it can always be argued that the changes in industrial relations and in the international competitive conditions that took place between 1969 and 1973 could hardly be foreseen.

The discovery of industrial policy in the 1970s

The students' upheaval of 1968 quickly spread to the factories. Labour unrest mounted in reaction to the long years of union weakness. The three main labour unions (the Communist-Socialist CGIL, the Catholic CISL, the Socialist-Republican UIL) began to move away from their traditional links with political parties and towards a united labour movement. The renewal of the three-year national contracts for the main industrial sectors in 1969 opened up the longest and toughest confrontation in the history of Italian industrial relations. The government took the workers' side in an attempt to settle the issue and contain social strife. The industrial contracts of 1969–70 were moderately inflationary; much more inflationary were the supplementary contracts signed at the firm and plant level in the following months.

Meanwhile, Parliament approved a Bill of Workers' Rights (Statuto dei Lavoratori), often interpreted with a strong pro-worker bias, which made it very difficult for employers to control absenteeism and lay off workers, even in times of crisis. The rapid rise in labour productivity, needed to absorb the increasing cost of labour, was even more difficult to achieve in these conditions.

Competitiveness declined as Italian inflation rose well above the European average at the beginning of the new decade. Private investment fell in 1970–1, although total investment expenditure was kept high by state enterprises and a few large private companies, mainly chemical, who benefited from generous incentives and built new plants in the Mezzogiorno.

The lira was clearly overvalued at the beginning of 1973, when the Smithsonian agreement on international currencies collapsed. A fluctuating lira depreciated sharply, and in the midst of the following inflationary wave the oil shock hit the Italian economy, which is highly dependent on imported oil. The 1975 recession was deep and yet insufficient to ensure external equilibrium. In February 1976 the lira ran into a new crisis. Exchange transactions were temporarily suspended, and a special tax was imposed on purchases of foreign exchange. But such emergency measures could not prevent a new depreciation.

The problem of industrial adjustment was felt in Italy with a special intensity, for a number of reasons. First, demand management was clearly incapable of reconciling internal and external equilibrium. The effectiveness of devaluation was weakened by the high degree of indexation and the vicious circle linking wages, prices and the exchange rate. Wages in Italy have been indexed to the cost of living since the immediate post-war period. Indexation was established through collective bargaining and periodically reviewed by the parties to the agreement. By the early 1970s the degree of indexation had declined to less than 50 per cent of the average industrial wage, and increasing inflation raised the issue once again. After much strife and bargaining, an agreement was reached in 1975 which increased the average degree of automatic indexation to about 85 per cent, so making it almost impossible to absorb the worsening terms of trade through reduction of real incomes. Moreover, the 1975 agreement established a fixed-sum (rather than proportional) wage adjustment. This was bound to shrink wage differentials, and high inflation produced a greater and faster shrinkage than anybody expected, implying a more than 100 per cent indexation at lower wage levels and feeding some wage drift at higher levels. Following sharp criticism from academic economists, political groups and international institutional creditors of the Italian government such as the IMF and the EEC, the cost-of-living clause was somewhat loosened in 1983 and brought back to a proportional coverage of about 50 per cent in 1984.

Second, the strong investment effort in the heavy sectors such as steel, aluminium and basic chemicals had been geared to an expected trend of consumption growth and stable relative prices; when both trends were sharply reversed, a chain of industrial disasters appeared inevitable.

Third, structural weaknesses such as the high dependence on imported energy and a general specialization in sectors considered backward or obsolescent (textiles, clothing, shoes, traditional engineering) called for intervention in the face of sharper international competition.

Industrial policy became the centre of attention in the mid-1970s (Adams 1985), without ever being properly defined. Important new legislation was announced and debated in and out of Parliament; but it was enacted belatedly and without much effect. The most representative piece of legislation was Law 675 of 1977. It set up a rather complex machinery of sectoral plans, committees of experts, consultation with local authorities and workers' and employers' associations, a Committee of Ministers and a special Parliamentary Commission. The involvement of Parliament in government action reflected the current political climate: a 'national unity' coalition of almost all the parties supported a government formed by only a few of them. The somewhat dirigiste approach reflected the feeling that excessive reliance on market forces and lack of planning had contributed to the crisis.

While new legislation was slow in taking shape, some kind of industrial policy was pursued: important rescues were organized and state enterprises were largely used as an instrument to support the industrial system. The SIR (chemical) group, which had rapidly grown from a small family enterprise into an aggressive concern by means of an extensive recourse to state incentives for new plants in the Mezzogiorno, was technically backrupt and it was only through political pressure that it was rescued by ENI. Italy's largest industrial investment bank, IMI, was so involved in SIR that it had to be heavily refinanced by the Treasury. Another and similar case was that of Liquichimica, where again ENI was called in. ENI took over a number of loss-generating plants and mines from Montedison. IRI took over Fiat's steel plants.

The 'failure' of industrial policies and the swing towards a market-orientated approach in the 1980s

At the beginning of the 1980s the tide turned against labour unions and state intervention.

During the period 1975–9 the slowing down of growth, sectoral crises and the rapid introduction of labour-saving technologies reduced the demand for labour, but in the face of strong union and political pressure, industrial employment did not actually fall until 1981, and the large firms, where union and political pressure were strongest, were in general substantially overmanned by 1979–80.

Mounting unemployment and a general weariness with militancy weakened the unions' position, and participation in strikes fell. An increasing number of workers were put on short time and paid out of a special fund for wage supplements (Cassa Integrazione Guadagni) set up within the national pension administration INPS (Istituto Nazionale per la Previdenza Sociale). In this way compensation for redundancies was quickly transferred from the books of industrial firms to the already ailing general welfare system.

National consensus was abandoned in 1979 with the return of a five-party coalition, including both Liberals on the right and Socialists on the left, but excluding the Communists. There was no sharp change of direction, but tougher monetary and exchange rate policies were established on the linking of the lira to the European Monetary System. At the beginning of the new decade the government made it clear that the reduction of inflation was to be the first target of economic policy, and that exchange rate adjustments would only partially compensate the inflation differential *vis-à-vis* EMS partners. The consequent prospect of a gradual appreciation of the lira in real terms was an invitation to a tough wage policy and to a special effort to improve productivity by slimming the labour force. The leading firms readily conformed, and the general climate of opinion was much less adverse to such a policy than it had been a few years before.

The second oil shock and the dollar shock sent inflation up again to a new peak in 1980. The 1981–3 recession was the longest in thirty years and brought investment in new capacity (though not in productivity measures) to a halt. The new restrictive monetary policy sent interest rates to record high levels all over the world, and in Italy it was applied with great toughness, bringing real interest rates from a negative level in 1979 to positive levels of 5–6 percentage points in the following years. Given the high debt ratios of the large Italian firms, this represented a considerable additional cost.

The results were remarkable. Productivity rose during the recession. Profits recovered gradually, initiating a virtuous circle of increasing self-financing, falling financial debts and falling costs of capital. The recovery was supported by a robust injection of state finance, channelled only partly through the traditional instruments of industrial policy such as subsidized investment and export credits. More important were the income support to laid-off workers, which facilitated workforce reductions, and the recapitalization of the state enterprises, which were charged with the task of rescuing the big losers in Italian industry. State transfers to the state-owned enterprises topped 1.3 per cent of GDP in 1983, by way of delayed compensation for previous disasters. By 1984, even the profit-and-loss accounts of state enterprises began to improve visibly, while a revitalized stock exchange channelled cheap funds to the recovering private enterprises, thus accelerating the virtuous circle.

There were some victims of these policies. Employment in industry, which had fluctuated during the 1970s within a 2 per cent range around the 1970 level, fell by 12 per cent between 1980 and 1985. The unemployment rate rose from 5.4 per cent in 1971 to 7.6 per cent in 1980 and to about 11 per cent in 1985, on the same pattern as elsewhere in Europe; but among the young the rate is now about three times as high as the general rate and twice as high as the corresponding European average rate.

The precarious state of public finance is reflected in a rapid increase of the public debt/GDP ratio from 0.50 in the 1970s to 1.0 in 1986. This is partly due to the direct cost of support for selective industrial restructuring, partly to indirect costs such as the incidence of a tax-based incomes policy to restrain the growth of labour costs.

Foreign-trade earnings were affected by the severe exchange rate policy, by credit restrictions and perhaps by some drying up of government support of export credit and by the increased cost of export insurance as a result of rising financial and political risks in the Third World. Italy's share in OECD manufacturing exports stagnated during the 1980s while import penetration kept rising. Only with the oil price fall of 1986 has the Italian current-account balance been brought back to a surplus after six years of deficits.

The role of industrial policy changed substantially at the turn of the decade as disappointment with the subsidy system of the 1970s spread (CER-IRS 1986; Momigliano 1986). By the early 1980s the policies of the previous decade were being described as a failure. In fact, the sectoral plans as drafted have been quite useless and some subsidies have been paid out too late to provide any help in solving the problems they were supposed to deal with. Nevertheless, the hard path out of a deep crisis, which was social and political as well as economic, was certainly eased by the policy that was followed. A potentially large number of industrial and financial bankruptcies were avoided. A flow of public expenditure was directed to reducing social conflicts and the selective support of exports and R & D.

Whatever may have been the importance of state action for the strengthening of Italian industry, by the mid-1980s a good deal of improvement was apparent and the sense of industrial and financial crisis prevalent in the mid-1970s has disappeared. There is now a wide recognition that the size of the public deficit and public debt, the crisis of the welfare state and the inefficiency of public administrations are the main problems on which public action should now concentrate.

The general climate is much more market-orientated than a few years ago. The reprivatization of Montedison was organized by Mediobanca in 1981 and a 'Report on State Enterprises', published by the Ministry for State Enterprises (De Michelis 1981), has stressed the importance of business criteria, as opposed to macro-economic goals and social responsibility, and advocated a return to the traditional IRI model of mixed private and state shareholding. The opportunity for raising substantial amounts of risk capital and venturing on some privatization of state enterprises came later, with the 1984–6 stock exchange boom.

The main issues in industrial policy in the 1980s are considered to be promotion of innovation and international integration, and it is now appreciated that direct action on industrial firms aimed at raising the general level of employment is likely to backfire (Camera dei Deputati 1982; Rebecchini 1985).

The development of 'internationalization' (a clumsy term which covers the numerous foreign takeovers of Italian firms), the necessity for some Italian acquisitions abroad, and the increasing number of Italian-based multinationals (not only Fiat, Olivetti and Pirelli but also Montedison and Ferruzzi) is making the tight exchange controls on capital movements, introduced during the crisis of 1976, less and less popular. However, the government will insist on having a say in further foreign acquisitions of important Italian firms. Internationalization of industry is now generally understood as requiring integrated capital markets and more outward-looking financial institutions.

5.3 Issues, policies and instruments

In general: allocation of resources

Public transfer payments to industrial firms provide a rough indicator of public effort. These give a good impression of the mounting cost of the defensive industrial policy pursued during the 1970s (Brosio and Silvestri, in Ranci 1983; CER-IRS 1986).

The total amount of state transfer payments to industrial enterprises is estimated at around 1 per cent of GDP in the years 1970–4, growing steadily up to 1983 and then declining following industrial recovery (Table 5.1).

Transfer payments as set out in Row (a) of Table 5.1 include public capital grants for investment projects and for industrial R & D; the subsidy content of various soft loans, including export credits, capital funding of state-owned enterprises and the special reduction in social security charges accorded to Southern enterprises.

Table 5.1. Transfer payments to industry as a percentage of value added in manufacturing, 1970–84

	1970–4	1975–7	1978–9	1980–1	1982	1983	1984
(a)	3.4	4.2	4.9	5.7	8.3	10.0	8.9
(b)	3.4	4.5	5.6	6.3	9.9	13.3	11.9

Sources: Calculated from Brosio and Silvestri in Ranci (1983), Table 2.1, and from Artoni and Ravazzi, in Artoni and Pontarollo (1986), Table 5.

Some tax reliefs, such as the lifting of the corporate profits tax for Southern enterprises, are excluded. Nobody has yet produced an estimate of this but since taxes on profits represent less than 10 per cent of government revenue, and since Southern industry represents still only about 17 per cent of total industry, this is not likely to be a very important omission.

A special incentive to investment was granted in 1977 in the form of a rebate of the value added tax on investment goods; this was granted for twelve months, then extended with certain limitations. Its cost is included in the above estimates.

Row (b) of Table 5.1 includes in addition the net cost to the social security agency (INPS) of the early retirement programmes related to industrial crises and the so-called Cassa Integrazione Guadagni (Gestione Speciale), namely wage supplements to industrial workers laid off or on short time during restructuring or in periods of crisis. The increasing trend of total transfer payments is in part due to these 'social' costs, that have been incurred in the course of economic restructuring.

The other operative item is capital appropriation by the state-owned enterprises. This represented under 20 per cent of total transfers (Row b) in the early 1970s but grew to more than 30 per cent in the period 1977–84. Grants and credits to investment declined over a period of time after initially covering about half of total transfers in the early 1970s, when heavy industry was being established in the Mezzogiorno.

The special rebates on social security contributions for Southern plants have constituted the most important cost in industrial policy for the Mezzogiorno. In making international comparisons it should be noted that the rebates are calculated as the difference between per capita social charges paid out by the employer in the South and the same charges in the North of Italy, where they are higher than in most other industrial countries.

Subsidies to R & D and to industrial innovation form a small, though steadily rising element in total expenditure (Table 5.2).

Export credit support has been growing rapidly in the 1980s, as a subsidy both to interest rates and to insurance against commercial and political risks.

The following paragraphs describe the main areas of public intervention in support of industry. They are presented in four groups:

Table 5.2. Composition of 1984 transfers to industry (%)

	Total	Excluding 'social'
'Social'	25	—
State-owned enterprises	28	37
Investment, R & D, innovation	10	13
Mezzogiorno: reductions in social charges	19	25
Ailing sectors, restructuring	5	7
Export credit	13	17

Source: Calculated from Artoni and Ravazzi, in Artoni and Pontarollo (1986), Table 5.

(i) *Locational*: intervention directed at redressing regional imbalances, particularly in favour of the Mezzogiorno.
(ii) *Structural*: actions with a structural aim, including support of small firms and sectoral measures.
(iii) *Microeconomic*: direct intervention in individual firms, including rescue operations and the whole area of state-owned enterprises.
(iv) *Recent policy instruments*: instruments which have boomed in the crisis years as an effort towards positive adjustment: export credit, support of R & D and public procurement.

Locational intervention

Industrialization of the Mezzogiorno

There have been notable changes in the range of instruments used to facilitate industrial take-off in the Mezzogiorno. These can be summarized over three periods.

(i) 1950–7. The Cassa was set up in 1950 principally to provide social and economic infrastructure facilities. Initially, there was no particular emphasis on industrial development. Some credit and fiscal incentives to small business were introduced, in the hope that this would contribute to the development of existing industry. In fact, this did not happen; indeed, the improved communication system and the growth of Northern industry may have displaced some less efficient Southern industry even in its home market.
(ii) 1956–76. This was a period of twenty years of policy-induced industrialization with an accent on local small firms in the first decade and on large investments by Northern large firms in the second decade. From 1951 to 1961 total migration from the Mezzogiorno amounted to 2 million people (plus a considerable internal migration from inland areas

to the coast and particularly to the larger towns): it was clear that agriculture would never provide adequate employment. In 1957 Law 634 provided for capital grants and soft loans towards the investment cost of new industrial activities, and established a number of *aree di sviluppo industriale*, where it was hoped that some external economies might result from the local grouping of industries. The existing requirement for the public administration to buy 30 per cent of its supplies from firms located in the Mezzogiorno was further supplemented: public concerns (including the public utilities) were required to direct their 40 per cent of investments to the Mezzogiorno. A similar obligation was imposed on state enterprises in respect of 40 per cent of their total investments and 60 per cent of their investments in new plants. Since these requirements could be met most easily by locating a few capital intensive plants in the South, to balance essential maintenance and improvement investments in existing Northern plants, they introduced a sectoral bias in the overall growth of the state industrial holdings.

Private industry was attracted by the incentives, which were related to capital expenditure and therefore apt to create the same kind of bias. The whole philosophy of industrialization was shifted in the mid-1960s from the primary aim of promoting a gradual growth of existing industry to a strategy of investments imported mainly from the North of Italy but also in a few cases from abroad. In the planning period of the mid-1960s the government tried to exert moral pressure on the major industrial groups to invest in the South, using the small discretionary power it possessed to offer incentives.

The clearest example of such arm-twisting was the call for investments in central Sardinia as part of a programme to uproot the *banditismo*. Two synthetic fibre projects were developed: one by SIR was never completed; the other, by Montedison and ANIC (ENI) jointly, proved a disaster in all the years up to 1985.

Some initiatives were better prepared and had a happier outcome, for instance, the Fiat plants in the Mezzogiorno are considered to be usually efficient, and Olivetti has successfully developed a numerically controlled machine-tool plant near Naples.

In fact, partly as a result of full employment in the North, there was a significant wave of industrial investments in the Mezzogiorno between 1958 and the early 1970s. The productivity of such investments has been on average rather low. The Mezzogiorno's share of total investments in manufacturing rose from 17 per cent in 1951–63 to over 30 per cent in 1963–73 to decline a little during the 1970s; the corresponding share of manufacturing value added rose from only 12.2 per cent in 1951–63 to 13 per cent in 1963–73 and to 14 per cent in the 1970s, while the Southern share in manufacturing employment oscillated slightly around 18 per cent without any apparent growth trend.

(iii) After 1976. Sharp criticism arose of large, capital-intensive, often inefficient investments, the 'cathedrals in the desert'. In some cases the
decision to locate an industrial plant in a particular region has attracted
many more people away from agriculture and other traditional activities
than the plant can possibly employ permanently, so creating simul-
taneously unemployment, migration and a degree of overmanning in the
plant itself, in response to local pressures on management to undertake
unnecessary hiring.

In successive pieces of legislation in the 1970s—the most important being
Law 183 of 1976–the bias towards capital-intensive activities was balanced
by gradually introducing (from 1968 onwards) an exemption from the very
high social security charges, corresponding to a reduction in the cost of
labour by nearly 30 per cent.

A number of publicly owned financial institutions were created to help
small firms to grow or to overcome transitional difficulties: the most
important being RIME (Finanziaria Meridionale, owned by the Cassa) and
INSUD (part of the EFIM state holding). The existing institution GEPI,
which had been set up in 1972 with the purpose of taking shares in restructuring firms, and which had become *de facto* a fourth state holding, was
prevented from expanding its activities outside the Mezzogiorno.

New incentives were introduced to facilitate the creation of research
centres and laboratories in the Mezzogiorno. This was part of an effort to
upgrade the industrial apparatus of the South (which is conspicuously
dependent upon decisions taken elsewhere and on imported technology) to a
point where some self-fuelling of growth might start.

The crisis of the 1970s hit Southern industry, highly specialized in the
heavy sectors, particularly hard. A number of plants had to be closed down,
some construction had to be halted, some new plants never started production, and the first victims were the most adventurous initiatives like the basic
chemicals plants of SIR and Liquichimica. IRI has found excess capacity in
steel an almost intractable problem, since it is socially unacceptable to close
down the old Naples plant (which was rebuilt in the very middle of a
demand crisis) and both socially and economically inadvisable to abandon
the newer Taranto plant.

Law 183 covered the period up to 1981. It was then extended and refinanced for successive short periods while a comprehensive reform was
under consideration. New Legislation (Law 64) was only approved in March
1986: the Cassa per il Mezzogiorno is now being transformed into a financial
agency while public works are the responsibility of regional governments
with a central government department handling general planning and coordination. A parallel Law (number 44 of 1986) granted generous financial
support to new small firms set up by young people in the Mezzogiorno, in
manufacturing, services and agriculture.

Sectoral problems and administrative inefficiency notwithstanding, industry in the Mezzogiorno has made some progress in the last fifteen years. Between the 1971 and 1981 censuses, manufacturing employment grew by 25 per cent; 77 per cent of these new jobs are in plants with less than 100 workers, about 50 per cent in firms owned by local people. Moreover, overall indicators of net growth fail to reflect the gross level of new industrial expansion in the Mezzogiorno, for many productive units in traditional sectors were wiped out by the growth of inter-regional trade and imported manufactures. Output per worker in Southern industry is now 60 per cent of that in Northern industry, as compared with 50 per cent in 1960. The percentage difference in per capita production between North and South shrank from forty-six in 1950 to thirty-eight in 1983.

Massive migration in the 1950s and 1960s improved the indicators. The Mezzogiorno's GDP grew 2.6 times while the population increased by about a million. In the North-Centre, GDP grew 2.9 times but population was swelled by immigration and rose by 6 million. During the 1970s migration stopped altogether, and GDP and the population grew at the same rate in both areas, halting the catching up process.

A new breed of Southern entrepreneurs is now growing, with particular concentration along the Adriatic coast. That there is self-sustaining growth in the Mezzogiorno is now beyond question; the question is how far this is the result of state action, and whether it makes any sense to go on treating the Mezzogiorno as one special area while geographical distances shrink in general and differences between regions in the Mezzogiorno grow.

At any rate, the degree of self-sustaining industrial growth that can be envisaged in the Mezzogiorno is clearly insufficient to bridge the employment gap as the labour supply increases through the 1990s. Public intervention to reduce unemployment, which is expected to increase beyond the present level, is now generally considered necessary, and the new Law 64 provides for annual appropriations of the order of 2 per cent of GDP over the next ten years for this purpose.

Other influences on the regional distribution of industry

The following factors combined to foster the spread of industry which developed in the 1960s and 1970s:

(i) state subventions towards medium and long term loans to stimulate the concentration of industry in the depressed areas of Northern and Central Italy (Law 634 of 1957);

(ii) legislation favouring small enterprises according to geographical location;

(iii) the spontaneous radiation of industry from the heavily industrialized Turin–Milan–Genoa triangle into neighbouring areas of Lombardy, Veneto and Central Italy in response to saturation inside the triangle combined with the availability of cheap labour outside it.

The fast-growing area in the North East and Centre of the peninsula has become known as the 'third Italy'. Fuà (1983) sees a special new model of industry developing based on the small firm in a favourable environment of diffused urbanization, part-time farming, home ownership, small town solidarity and cultural traditions which favour expertise in businesses such as fashion clothing, leather goods and furniture.

There has also been special treatment for designated areas with idiosyncratic ethnic and cultural characteristics, the *regioni a statuto speciale* (Friuli-Venezia Giulia, Valle d'Aosta, Sicily, Sardinia and the autonomous provinces of Trento and Bolzano).

Incentive schemes set up by Northern regional governments have led to some conflict with national policy and with Southern interests, who feared a damaging competition in the granting of incentives. Law 183 of 1976 put a ceiling on these regional incentives.

Special legislation was passed for Venice, providing incentives to the Mestre-Marghera industrial area to stop the loss of jobs and population. Similar legislation also helped localities hit by natural disasters with incentives for the reconstruction and growth of industry. The instruments generally used were state subventions for medium- and long-term loans, direct funding of soft loans through such public financial institutions as Mediocredito Centrale, or straight grants to investment.

Structural intervention

Small firm support and general problems of credit subsidies

It has been a commonplace over the last forty years in Italy that the small enterprise is essential to economic prosperity and growth and needs some special public support, but there has been controversy about implementation.

Law 623 of 1959 provided for soft loans for investments by small and medium-sized industrial enterprises, with a state contribution graduated in accordance with regional conditions. It was refinanced several times up to 1976.

The Mediocredito Centrale, financed by a Treasury grant and capital raised through bond issues, was established to refinance local institutions providing soft loans for small enterprises. A network of Mediocrediti Regionali was gradually set up by the numerous local savings banks (Casse di Risparmio) to operate on the long- and medium-term market, which ordinary commercial and savings banks are prevented from entering by the 1936 Banking Law. The integrated system of Mediocrediti Regionali and Mediocredito Centrale has been quite effective in channelling funds to small industry; in several cases the availability of subsidized rates has been secondary to the basic service of providing credit and some advisory help to the small entrepreneur. Firms often asked for Mediocredito finance while also applying for the more favourable but slower state subsidy under Law 623. This double channel ensured continuity and a hedge against periodic interruptions in the supply of subsidized credit under Law 623. In fact, new appropriations in the state budget were often delayed until after funds previously appropriated had been exhausted.

In 1976–7 a new legal framework was introduced to provide both support for small firms and incentives for the industrialization of backward areas. Law 183 of 1976, which has been described above, not only provided for subsidies for investment in the South (graduated by region, firm size, plant size, sector) but also laid down general instructions for the extension of similar subsidies to the North and Centre, so as to assure a consistent, graduated set of incentives. Provisions for the North and Centre were enacted in Decree 902 of 1977, which replaced Law 623 with a similar system of subsidized credits through the new Fondo Nazionale, administered by the Ministry of Industry.

Normally, a small firm buys machinery and equipment, even of an advanced type, one piece at a time so the system set up by Decree 902, which requires credit applications to be submitted as detailed investment programmes, has proved unduly cumbersome. Some help is, however, provided to firms buying machine tools and similar types of machinery through Law 1329 of 1965 which is still in operation: payment is made by the buyer through issuing a special promissory note which can be discounted by the seller at any bank, and rediscounted at Mediocredito Centrale at a low rate. The mechanism is fast, automatic and convenient for both seller and buyer. It was supplemented, between 1983 and 1986, by a temporary system of straight grants and tax rebates to machinery acquisitions by small firms (Law 696).

Restructuring and reconversion

After the oil shock it was generally felt that a new effort was needed to help industry out of severe financial crisis. The resulting Law 675 provided for credit incentives for the restructuring of (mainly large) firms within the context of sectoral plans. But it failed to get a single plan beyond the blueprint state. The plans were simply treated as a legal cover for the granting of credits and never updated nor in fact taken seriously.

The provision of sectoral subsidies was at first considered by the EEC Commission to infringe Articles 92 and 93 of the Treaty of Rome because it altered the conditions of competition among firms. Consequent negotiations between Rome and Brussels delayed the grant of the first credits until ten years after the oil shock that had been at the origin of the crisis—well after the firms had found a way out of their difficulties.

Law 675 appropriated about 5 trillion lire for the Fondo per la Ristrutturazione e Riconversione. A further appropriation of equal amount was sanctioned in 1983, right at the very end of the Fondo's life. About three-quarters of the total has been allocated to subsidize back credits or provide direct Treasury Credit (and straight grants in the Mezzogiorno) towards restructuring programmes. The actual disbursement has thus been spread out over a long period so that by 1985 only about 500 billion lire had been disbursed.

The use of the Fondo has been heavily concentrated on large firms in the 'mature' sectors: 30 per cent of the subsidies have been allocated to the steel industry, 32 per cent to the automotive industry, and 18 per cent to basic chemicals. The remaining 2.5 trillion lire have been used to finance a number of special programmes such as a fund for manpower mobility, a fund for guaranteeing loans to small enterprises and other incentives described in other sections of this chapter.

Financial restructuring

The other instrument of succour proposed for Italian groups to cushion the effect of high and rising interest rates on firms with high debt–equity ratios. The 1936 Banking Law prevented direct intervention but in 1975 and 1976 some proposals were put forward by the former Governor of the Bank of Italy, Guido Carli, for the takeover of industrial firms by the banking system in exceptional circumstances.

Law 787 of 1978 was the belated and tiny fruit of these ambitious proposals. It provided fiscal advantages to banks consolidating the debts of industrial firms or joining in special consortia to convert credits into equity. Credit consolidation, which was left to the individual banks' initiative, had a fairly widespread application: in the period 1978–83, consolidations approved under Law 787 totalled 1,600 billion lire. On the other hand, Consortia, requiring agreement between different banks, were much more difficult to organize: only four were set up, one of which (SIR chemicals) immediately required new special legislation, absorbed special subsidies and eventually found itself compelled to hand over all SIR's basic chemicals plants over to ENI. In fact, the main problem with Law 787 was that, while industry was only averagely undercapitalized overall, there were a few large firms whose superficial financial difficulties concealed a state of deep economic crisis, and in some cases like SIR, outright bankruptcy.

Micro-economic intervention

Rescuing ailing firms

Apart from instruments specifically designed for restructuring, rescue operations were performed by GEPI, a special corporation owned by IMI and the three public industrial holdings—IRI, ENI, and EFIM—set up in 1972 to help industrial enterprises in temporary difficulty.

GEPI bought shares in ailing firms, usually in partnership with private entrepreneurs who directed operations and eventually took over a major share of the business. The formula worked in a number of cases, such as

Maserati (cars), but more often intervention was applied to really hopeless cases, mainly in response to political pressure on GEPI's management and even under specific parliamentary direction. GEPI was thus compelled to take over lame ducks and try to diversify their operations while keeping workers in disguised unemployment. GEPI's workforce is now about 30,000. Half of these have no prospect of profitable employment in the near future.

The reaction against excessive public expenditure on rescues induced Parliament to limit GEPI's new acquisitions in the late 1970s. Under Law 95 of 1979 (known as the *Legge Prodi* after the then Minister of Industry) insolvent firms can be placed under an *amministrazione straordinaria* by the Ministry of Industry for up to four years and administered by a *commissario* under the surveillance of a judge. Some large groups (Maraldi steelworks and sugar plants, Monti refineries, Liquichimica), a publisher (Einaudi) and 250 other firms have been so administered. Some rescues have been successful, others have failed to show results and there is a widespread view, shared by Prodi himself, in favour of dropping Law 95 and revising the ordinary bankruptcy procedure instead, to give judges greater power to take into account such immaterial assets as technological knowhow, goodwill, organization and skilled personnel in the course of insolvency enquiries.

Public ownership of industrial firms·

The existence of a relatively large public sector in industry can be seen both as an instrument of industrial policy and as one element in the economic and political system that has to be taken into account in the making of any strategy. The active role of state enterprises in the decades of growth has been reviewed in the previous chapter.

Several problems have arisen during the 1970s, transforming what used to be looked at as an efficient player in the Italian industrial team into an industrial problem itself. It is not quite a joke to say that after twenty years of growth through investments (the 1950s and the 1960s) and ten years of growth through rescues, state-owned enterprises (SOEs) had to be rescued themselves.

The difficulties facing the whole of Italian industry in the 1970s were particularly pronounced in the public sector. It had a large stake in the heavy industries which were worst hit by the world crisis, such as steel, shipyards and petrochemicals. It was up against union militancy and was at the same time under political pressure to settle labour disputes promptly in a manner favourable to the workers. It faced almost insuperable union and political opposition to workforce reductions.

Some of the failures have been blamed on the worsening quality of management and on its diminished autonomy due to increasing interference by politicians. The theoretical division of labour between politicians setting the strategies and management choosing the tactics (Holland 1972) has been sometimes reversed, with SOE management taking the place of weak governments in setting the general priorities and political parties interfering with appointments at intermediate levels or decisions affecting key constituencies. In fact, little attention was paid to innovation and a number of loss-making activities were kept running without any substantial decisions being taken. There has been little or no development abroad and few joint ventures with private and foreign companies, even in areas where this was necessary to achieve competitiveness in world markets.

The utilities suffered from a government pricing policy that had to take account of social implications and the inflationary impact of price rises, but which was not supported by any clear policy of state financing.

The financing of the mixed system fell into deep crisis as private capital fled from loss-making enterprises while the SOEs' management seemed to make little effort to raise private risk-capital or arrange long-term loans, devoting its energies to pressing for direct capital underwritings from the state.

There was a clear turnaround in 1983–4, under new management. ENI's deficit was eliminated by 1984 and ENI made a profit in 1985, while its chemical devision, Enichem, was reorganized and moved towards breaking even. IRI cut its deficit by one-third in 1984, halved it in 1985, and aims at break-even in 1986.

Some reduction of debt and of interest costs has arisen from a few public enterprises reverting to the issue of shares or selling off non-voting stock. Large privatizations, involving loss of public control over firms, have been attempted by the new management, but sometimes have been blocked by political pressure.

Public procurement

Only recently has public procurement been considered as a potentially powerful instrument of industrial policy. Public procurement is certainly important, but estimates vary widely about what is considered the public industrial sector. A Parliamentary Commission estimated direct purchases from the central administration to be 5 per cent of GDP in 1984; the employers' confederation, Confindustria, reported to the same Commission that total demand from the whole of the public sector amounted to 14 per cent of GDP (Artoni and Pontarollo 1986, p. 102).

This of course includes minute purchases of consumption goods and office material; on the other side, it excludes a large part of the telecommunications business, where the monopsonistic purchaser is the STET group, owned by IRI and thus by the state, but as a public company with private shareholders as well. The Italian telecommunications market has greatly increased recently. Annual investment runs between 4 and 5 billion dollars and is steadily rising. It is a largely captive market: the largest Italian manufacturer, Italtel, is owned by STET.

The legal framework and the established procedures do not favour an active use of public procurement. In some cases, producers are organized as a group and influence the public administration in a way that guarantees fairly constant levels of sales to each firm. Pressure from the Commission of the European Community in favour of a more open approach is beginning to concern Italian public administrators and major suppliers.

Main recent policy instruments

By the mid-1970s it was becoming clear that the industrial crisis could not be met via cash grants to firms that were restructuring or simply ailing and that a solution could only be found through greater industrial export capacity and by accelerating innovation within industry. A statement to this effect was clearly set in Ministero dell'Industria (1977), which was an official document on how to handle subsidies for restructuring under Law 675. But the contents of this law called for a different approach. Two traditional instruments, which had been somewhat neglected of late, were rediscovered and reinforced: trade policy and public support of industrial R & D.

External trade policy

Trade policy had generally been considered in terms of import protection. Post-war trade liberalization, by way of both tariff reduction and quota elimination, was carried out smoothly during the 1950s and early 1960s.

Italy's tariff—and for the most part non-tariff—protection is now determined by European Community rules. Few exceptions remain, perhaps the most significant being a quota virtually barring all car imports from Japan (thanks to a bilateral agreement signed in the 1950s at the insistence of the Japanese, who were at the time afraid of Fiat's possible penetration of their market). Motorcycle imports from Japan are also subject to quantitative restrictions, although these are not as strict as for cars.

Grilli and La Noce (1983), estimating effective protection in 1975, found a large sectoral variability; tariff protection correlated with the penetration of non-EEC exports into the EEC market, suggesting a response to EEC-wide rather than national demands for protection.

EEC protection for consumer goods subject to Third World competition, such as textiles and clothing, is particularly important for a large producer such as Italy, and the three successive Multifibre Agreements negotiated by the EEC Commission introduced a considerable diversion of trade in favour of Italian producers.

Export credit facilities were relatively modest in Italy until 1976, when new legislation was triggered by the adjustment difficulties of the post-oil-shock years. Law 227 of 1976 provided for funds and administrative facilities, particularly aimed at developing exports of investment goods to Third World and socialist countries. The network of Italian commercial offices abroad was strengthened. Support of exports applies now to about 6 per cent of exports; the same level applies to France and Britain, while figures for

Japan are slightly lower and for Germany and the United States much lower (Delli Gatti, in Onida 1986).

Subsidized credit has contributed to the performance of Italian exports of investment goods, although exports of consumer goods have done even better without support. Some embarassing bad debts in such countries as Iran have been an undesired outcome of this policy.

Support for R & D and industrial innovation

The public financing of R & D projects run by private enterprises was first authorized by Parliament in 1968 to be administered by a special section of IMI, the Fondo per la Ricerca Applicata (later placed under the supervision of a new Ministry of Scientific Research). The Fondo is authorized to grant easy credits up to 90 per cent of the project cost, or a combination of straight subsidy and easy credit. The Fondo's operations have been subject to the usual interruptions due to lack of appropriations or changes in procedures, and often a grant officially attached to a project already under way is used to initiate new, and possibly unrelated, projects. The Fondo's operations were greatly increased by Law 675 of 1977.

In 1982 Law 46, besides reinforcing the Fondo of IMI, introduced a new 'Fondo per l'Innovazione', administered by the Ministry of Industry. It was designed to extend public support to those phases of development immediately preceding full production. It largely paralleled the existing Fondo and was set up in response to demands by some sectors of industry (mainly automobile) and also to restore the balance of power between the two ministries. The combined effect was a substantial increase in state expenditure for industrial research.

Basic and applied research is also carried on by universities and by a network of research centres such as those responding to the Consiglio Nazionale delle Ricerche (CNR — National Research Council). These public institutions operate with various degrees of efficiency (better in theoretical physics than in applied chemistry, for example). Their relations with industry have generally been unsatisfactory. Some large research projects, funded by the government and enacted through cooperation between public research institutions and private industry are under way, but with a long delay after they were first established in principle in 1977.

5.4 Conclusions

Italy's industrial policy is an example of government action lacking a comprehensive design. Important and courageous choices were made in the early post-war years, when the protectionist apparatus was quickly dismantled and Italy actively favoured European integration. A second important choice, though less explicit and conscious, was the build-up of national productive capacity in steel and energy by state firms. Only one further choice of equal importance was made in the following three decades: the effort to bring manufacturing industry to the Mezzogiorno through incentives and direct operations by state enterprises.

In addition, a number of new instruments were resorted to, mainly using different types of subsidies. New goals were set, such as the promotion of industrial R & D, not, however, with very great effect. The most visible and costly development was the use of state-owned enterprises in the crisis decade of the 1970s to rescue parts of the private sector. An established tradition was followed: that the public area in industry expands in response to ideological preferences and to the practical requirements of rescue. The trend was reversed in the 1980s, again underlining an ideological turnaround, as well as a change in conditions affecting profitability.

Has the 'weak state' then not been a decisive impediment to reasonably effective industrial policy? Critics of Italian economic policy usually maintain that it has, and stress the lack of coordination among legislative acts and between different public bodies as an example of failure. Many suggest a comparison with the French or even the Japanese model to argue that strong, highly centralized action, capable of directing sectoral choices and picking the winners to make national champions, is necessary to industrial policy.

Such statements are far from self-evident. It is by no means clear that an economic policy concerned with industrial development should be of the strong, centralized type. Yet shortcomings in legislation and administrative action are evident in Italy, and any observer must agree that a great deal more coordination and organization in the public sphere is required to run any economic policy, even a *laissez-faire* policy, in a satisfactory way. Legislation must be more consistent and timely, public administration should be more competent and reliable. The state is not only weak but also unpredictable and inaccurate.

The weakness of public action is certainly costly for industrial development. Low levels of public R & D expenditure, a poor system of technical schools and higher education, inefficient public services in transportation and communications, and a housing problem that reduces labour mobility are the most evident and lamented aspects of the problem. In some cases the impact on industrial costs is direct and immediate: social security charges are the highest among large industrial countries, while the pension system and health and welfare services are no better than average.

Italy presents a mix of high and low levels of regulation. Prices charged by public services are rigidly regulated so that enterprises (public and private) running them have practically no freedom in their pricing policies. Even in the case of contracts for electricity supply to the largest industrial users, ENEL is bound to apply the general tariff set by government. Price controls are one way or another extended to cover a number of private goods and services such as fresh milk, newspapers, bread, petrol, haircuts and bar services. Yet no anti-trust legislation has ever been introduced; public regulation of stock market operations is very weak and there is no restriction on insider trading; pharmaceuticals were exempt from any patent regime until a few years ago, when a court judgment, not government or parliamentary action, determined the introduction of patent regulation.

This is in part the outcome of a legislative system overburdened with detail and scarcely able to choose priorities. The Italian Parliament produces several hundred legislative Acts each year, minutely defining minor matters, and each of these requires separate approval by two chambers, often preceded by multiple examination in several parliamentary commissions. Important laws may thus languish for years before being adopted.

The other important factor of discontinuity and weakness stems from the nature of the political system itself. Stable majority coalitions break up from time to time and produce a series of unstable governments, while no alternative majority has emerged in forty years.

The administrative apparatus is weak and slow, yet periodic attempts are made by political decision-makers to push controls to lengths that would tax the resources of any bureaucracy. The consequence is evasion of regulations and the reduced effectiveness of incentives. Rent control is very rigid and has contributed to slowing down residential construction; yet it is increasingly evaded. The tax system is highly complicated so that most individuals need a consultant to complete their tax returns, while tax avoidance through legal loopholes and straight evasion are widespread. Minute controls on capital movements imply a harassment of travellers and tourists, as well as additional costs to exporters; they are being partially dismantled as Italy complies with European Community directives. Subsidies to investors in the Mezzogiorno are subject to numerous requirements and controls, and are paid out so slowly that up to a third of the benefit has been calculated to be lost through interest costs; yet it is clear that large and badly planned handouts have contributed to some industrial disasters, and it is widely suspected that some subsidies intended to promote sound industrial activity have in fact enlarged the profits from economic crime. The distance between high goals and low or devious performance increases the perception of a weak state.

It is usual in Italy, as well as elsewhere, to contrast the general inefficiency of the public sector with the vitality of private firms. In Italy the contrast has been large and inefficient organizations, whether private or public, versus small (and beautiful) ones. This was probably more appropriate in the 1970s than either before or since: the crisis of large firms belongs to a period of acute social strife and cultural transition. Even though the crisis of large firms is over, industrial development is certainly more dependent on dynamic small business in Italy than elsewhere. The impressive export performance of such sectors as clothing and the whole 'fashion system' is largely the outcome of such dynamism. The Italian case has been well illustrated in Piore and Sabel's analysis (1984). Italian small firms often proliferate in industrial districts where the individual firm is highly specialized and remains small, yet the area as a whole achieves economies of scale and highly integrated production and offers a very wide supply of goods which attracts large buyers and supports sophisticated commercial structures (the most notable examples are Prato in woollen textiles, Carpi in knitwear and Como in silk). Such areas are characterized not only by external economies but also by the development of voluntary cooperation in services.

In recent years, though, large-scale private enterprise has staged an impressive comeback and the stock exchange is at last showing an increasing volume of activity with a variety of operations and participants.

Even the 'spontaneous' development of private enterprise is not entirely unrelated to government policy. The success of the small firm can be attributed less to a positive policy of easy credit than to a sort of negative industrial policy characterized by relatively mild regulation and some relaxation of rules (such as in labour legislation), plain tolerance of evasion, or inability to enforce the law (as in fiscal matters).

The positive turnaround of large-scale private industry is connected with the great rescue operations of the government and with positive political action. The most visible and yet least important side of this is the special legislation granting subsidies for restructuring and innovative investment. The greatest help has come from special labour legislation providing for the subsidization of early retirement and temporary layoffs. On the financial side, the recent introduction of institutional investors greatly helped the stock exchange boom of 1985–6, while the gradual introduction since 1974 of accounting rules, balance-sheet certification and regulation of the stock exchange by a new agency, CONSOB (Commissione Nazionale per le Societa' e la Borsa), has imported greater reliability and stability into stock exchange operations.

State enterprises come between large private firms and public bodies: regarded as highly efficient in the 1950s and 1960s, they went through a deep crisis in the 1970s, both for economic reasons and because of an excess of political interference, but are now heading towards greater stability.

Industrial policy was burdened with two heavy tasks during the adjustment crisis of the 1970s; though never clearly defined, it was expected to produce the improvement in the unemployment/inflation/external-deficit trade-off, which macro-economic policy was incapable of bringing about. In fact, it was implemented in the form of an array of subsidies directed primarily to the defence of existing firms and jobs. It obviously failed to live up to these expectations.

The strong position of trade unions and in general the prevalence of social rather than economic values in the 1970s, has been thought responsible for the slow pace of Italian adjustment. There is some truth in this argument, although the left-wing wave was itself a reaction to some properties of the previous growth model, particularly the disproportion between a rapid growth of industry and a slow development of social structures, services and controls. It is not clear whether the return of capitalist values in the mid-

1980s is accompanied by a better understanding of the medium-term implications of industrial growth or is set to reproduce the pattern of a short-sighted profit boom followed by a destructive reaction.

Note

1. The main planning lines were laid down in 1962 in a short document by the then Budget Minister, Ugo La Malfa ('Nota Aggiuntiva', in Ministero del Bilancio 1967, Vol. 2). A commission for drafting a national programme was set up and handed in a majority report in 1973 (the so-called Saraceno Report, in Ministero del Bilancio 1967, Vol. 2). A minority view of great interest and subsequent influence was developed into a booklet by Fuá and Sylos Labini (1963). Finally, a national programme was drafted for the period 1965–9 (Piano Giolitti, Ministero del Bilancio 1967, Vol. 3) and successively updated (Piano Pieraccini for the period 1966–70, in Ministero del Bilancio 1967, Vol. 3).

References

Adams, P. (1985), 'Government–industry relations in Italy: the case of industrial policy, unpublished PhD dissertation, Yale University.

Amato, G. (1972), *Il Governo dell' Industria in Italia*, Bologna, Il Mulino.

Artoni, R. and Pontarollo, E. (1986), *Trasferimenti, Domanda Pubblica e Sistema Industriale*, Bologna, Il Mulino.

Bollino, C.A. (1983), 'Industrial policy in Italy: a survey', in F.G. Adams and L.R. Klein, eds., *Industrial Policies for Growth and Competitiveness*, Lexington, Mass., Lexington Books.

Brosio, G. and Silvestri, G. (1983), 'Uno Sguardo d'Assieme', in Ranci (1983).

Camera dei Deputati (1982), *Relazione sulla Politica Industriale: i Problemi della Innovazione*, Commissione Industria, Rome.

CER-IRS (1986), *Quale Strategia per l'Industria? Rapporto sull' Industria e la Politica Industriale Italiana*, Bologna, Il Mulino.

De Michelis, G. (1981), *Rapporto sulle Partecipazioni Statali*, Milan, F. Angeli.

Forte, F. (1966), *La Congiuntura in Italia 1960–1965*, Turin, Einaudi.

Fuá, G. (1983), 'L'Industrializzazione del Nord-Est e del Centro', in G. Fuá and C. Zaccia, eds., *Industrializzazione senza Fratture*, Bologna, Il Mulino.

Fuá, G. and Sylos Labini, P. (1963), *Idee per la Programmazione Economica*, Bari, Laterza.

Grilli, E. and La Noce, M. (1983), 'The political economy of protection in Italy: some empirical evidence', *Banca Nazionale del Lavoro Quarterly Review*, June.

Graziani, A., ed. (1979), *L'Economia Italiana: 1945–1970*, Bologna, Il Mulino.

Holland, S., ed. (1972), *The State as Entrepreneur: New Dimensions for Public Enterprise: The IRI State Shareholding Formula*, London, Weidenfeld & Nicolson.

La Palombara, J. (1966), *Italy: The Politics of Planning*, Syracuse, Syracuse University Press.

Lutz, V. (1962), *Italy: A Study in Economic Development*, Oxford, Oxford University Press.

Ministero del Bilancio (1967), *La Programmazione Economica in Italia*, 5 vols., Rome.

Ministero dell'Industria (1977), *Relazione sullo Stato dell'Industria Italiana*, Rome.

Momigliano, F., ed. (1986), *Le Leggi della Politica Industriale in Italia*, Bologna, Il Mulino.

Onida, F. (1986), 'Vincolo Estero, Competitività, Fattori di Forza e di Debolezza Strutturale: Uno Sguardo di Sintesi', in F. Onida, ed., *L'Integrazione Internazionale e le Politiche per il Commercio Estero*, Bologna, Il Mulino.

Pavitt, K. (1984), 'Sectoral patterns of technical change: towards a taxonomy and a theory', *Research Policy*, No. 6.

Piore, M. and Sabel, C. (1984), *The Second Industrial Divide: Possibilities for Prosperity*, New York, Basic Books.

Ranci, P. ed. (1983), *I Trasferimenti dello Stato alle Imprese Industriali negli Anni Settanta*, Bologna, Il Mulino.

Rebecchini, F. (1985), 'Indagine Conoscitiva sulla Politica Industriale', Commissione Industria del Senato, Rome, mimeo.

Zanetti, G. and Fraquelli, G. (1979), *Una Nazionalizzazione al Buio: L'Enel dal 1963 al 1978*, Bologna, Il Mulino.

6 United Kingdom: a resistance to change

Geoffrey Shepherd

Our industrial policy was reminiscent of a bull in the ring charging in different directions at unattainable objectives and always perishing at the last.[1]

6.1 British manufacturing performance

At the end of the nineteenth century the UK accounted for one-third of the exports of the industrial nations. By 1983, the year when the value of maufactured imports first exceeded that of manufactured exports, this share had been reduced to one-thirteenth. Of course, the economy has continued to grow and the country remains affluent. Of course, the catching-up process by other countries was inevitable. But the UK has clearly been overtaken by many countries: from 1870 to 1978 British GDP per worker grew by a factor of little more than three, while the equivalent factors for the United States, Germany and Japan were seven, ten and over fifty respectively.[2]

The UK's relative decline proved surprisingly bearable. In the 1950s and 1960s the country had genuinely 'never had it so good', with full employment and a welfare state sharing the fruits of growth more evenly than before. In this period signs of discomfort arose from 'stop–go' growth, and relative industrial decline was to become less bearable in the 1970s as world growth slowed, the UK became more exposed to international competition and redistributing the cake became more painful. From 1973 to 1982 annual inflation was not below 8 per cent, while unemployment had risen to 6 per cent by 1976 and 13 per cent by 1983.

A number of events have focused pressures on one sector, manufacturing. As the main tradables sector it has had to bear the brunt of belated British integration into the EEC, but under doubly adverse conditions. On the one hand, it has faced the two deepest recessions since the war (1973–6 and 1979–82). On the other, supplies of North Sea oil shifted British comparative advantage away from manufacturing: from 1977 to 1981 unit costs in manufacturing soared compared to those of the UK's competitors (macroeconomic policies, especially from 1979, did not help in this).

It would be wrong to talk simply of a failure to adjust. Statistical measures of movements of resources between industries show that, while the UK was slower than its Western European competitors in shifting from old to new industries in the 1960s, its performance moved nearer the average in the 1970s (Sharp and Shepherd, forthcoming, Ch. 2). But changes occurring *within* sectors—innovation in processes and product—are probably more important sources of growth than shifts *between* sectors. The UK reached barely 60 per cent of the level of labour productivity—a rough proxy for process innovation—of its EEC partners in 1973. By 1981 this figure had fallen to about 50 per cent (Roy 1982, Table 8). A useful, if proximate, indicator of the degree of product sophistication, hence of product innovation, can sometimes be obtained by comparing unit values from international trade statistics. One study of the engineering industry found that German unit values for exports were consistently higher than British and that the gap grew in the period 1963–75; French unit values were also higher, but less consistently so (Saunders 1978).

In the earlier post-war years the UK exported far more manufactures than it imported, broadly exchanging more sophisticated manufactures for raw materials and semi-manufactures. Its pattern of trade was far less European than that of other European countries. But its Commonwealth trading links progressively weakened and, particularly from the late 1960s, it had to adjust to a new division of labour with the industrialized countries, notably the EEC. This involved a rapid increase in the extent of intra-industry trade—the exchange of similar or complementary products within a narrowly defined industry or product group. The UK has progressively caught up on its European partners in this form of trade and has become increasingly integrated into the complex division of labour of the Western European market.

In some senses, British industry has adapted considerably, over some two decades, to the fundamental change in its position in the international division of labour. Yet, while doing so, it has consistently failed to upgrade relative product quality and performance. This comparative advantage in older, less dynamic product areas pushes the UK towards direct competition with the newly industrializing countries of Asia and the new Southern European members of the EEC.

Outline of this chapter

This chapter traces the post-war development of the policies that have sought to deal with manufacturing industry, placing them in the context of the economic institutions that characterize the British industrial system. The view taken is that British industrial decline above all reflects a deep-seated institutional conservatism—a resistance to change—with historical roots in the industrial and imperial successes of the nineteenth century. This conservatism was reinforced after World War II—until the 1970s at least—by a strong political consensus favouring policies of full employment and social welfare. The macro-economic difficulties that resulted from the imposition of these policies on a weak economy further removed attention from the micro-economic problems of the industrial sector. Moreover, the consensus helped reinforce vested interests opposed to industrial change. None the less, a combination of growing exposure to international competition and resistance to this exposure has led since the 1960s to the *ad hoc* development of a host of selective industrial policies—policies targeted at specific sectors, sub-sectors or firms that have come to be known collectively as 'industrial policy'.

The institutional background to Britain's post-war industrial system is sketched out in section 6.2. This provides the context for section 6.3, which describes the post-war evolution of the perceptions and policies important in influencing the climate for change in British industry. The discussion touches on several areas, including macro-economic, industrial relations, and trade and competition policies, in addition to selective policies. (Education policies are a regrettable omission in this chapter.) The historical picture that emerges is confusing because policies are often contradictory, changeable and unclear. The concluding section of this chapter looks for order in this confusion, but given the deep-seated institutional problems that selective policies were unable to address, the confusion is perhaps inevitable.

6.2 The institutional environment

Modern capitalist economies are characterized by certain dominant institutional features which may replace, undermine or complement the competitive process. Such features typically derive from the characteristics of the large corporation, trade unions, governments, the financial system and the education and training system. The UK's institutions are not as well suited to industrial growth as those of its competitors. Many of these institutional weaknesses are rooted in the historical experience of early industrial capitalism in Britain.

Historical developments

Textbook capitalism—approximating that of nineteenth-century Britain—is characterized by well-functioning markets and perfect competition. However, the institutional developments in national variants of modern capitalism have somewhat changed the model (see sect. 1.2, pp. 11–15). Among the most important changes are the evolution of the large, multi-divisional corporation, the union organization of the labour force, the growth in the span of government activities and the corporatist and oligopolistic forms in which these large organizations have cooperated with each other. Such cooperation in a sense replaces the competitive process, but it does so only partially: the degree of oligopolistic behaviour in the competitive process has been somewhat tempered by the growth of international competition.

Our characterization of the deficiencies in British institutions does not do justice to the controversies in the economic history literature, but it draws in part on the main arguments in a recent collection of papers edited by Elbaum and Lazonick (1986, Ch. 1).

(i) Large, well-integrated modern capitalist firms were slow to emerge in the UK.
(ii) Powerful trade unions continued to pre-empt (weak) managers' ability to manage.
(iii) Governments continued to maintain a distance from industry and its problems.
(iv) Since the end of the last century the financial system has been little integrated with industry.
(v) The educational system and institutional research have also been poorly integrated with industry.

There is much controversy over the causes of declining British industrial performance from around 1870, after more than a century of undisputed leadership in the industrial revolution. For instance, some have stressed the economic disadvantages, others the social, of being the firstcomer; there is also an argument over the rationality and capability of British entrepreneurs (see, for instance, Aldcroft and Richardson 1969, sect. B; Elbaum and Lazonick 1986, Ch. 1).

That changes over time have not been greater reflects the accidents of history in two particular respects. First, the evident beginnings of British industrial decline in the late nineteenth century coincided with the apogee of empire, and British industry could to an extent take refuge in imperial markets. In 1932 this refuge was formalized by the introduction of imperial preferences. During the 1930s not only did the government introduce import protection for industry for the first time, but it also permitted, indeed encouraged, the participation of firms in domestic and international cartels. While protection and cartels appear to have allowed the UK to recover relatively rapidly from recession in the 1930s, they also helped postpone the need to deal with the problem of competitiveness.

The second accident of history was the political continuity and stability the UK has continued to enjoy. In particular, it was the only Western European belligerent to be on the winning side and to avoid enemy occupation in the two great wars of the twentieth century, and this too helped postpone the pressure to deal with economic problems.

The major institutional features

The firm

There is much discussion of the 'poor' quality of British management (for a review of the evidence, see Caves 1980). However, assuming the fault does not lie in British genes, such evidence raises more questions than it answers. A more historical view of the evolution of large British firms might suggest that this poor management in part reflects the lateness and incompleteness of the transformation to the modern corporation in the UK.

The firms at the centre of British industrial success in the nineteenth century tended to be small, horizontally and vertically specialized, orientated to production rather than selling, family-owned and internally financed. Markets were very competitive, and the buying–selling function was institutionalized through merchants (and through markets such as the Manchester Cotton Exchange). Such firms were resistant to the modern corporate form developing in competitor countries from the end of the century (Elbaum and Lazonick 1986, Ch. 1; Hannah 1977). If mergers and amalgamations did take place, they often remained incomplete, managers of the constituent parts often insisting on maintaining autonomy. The reasons appear largely social: entrepreneurs were individualistic—a reflection of the individualism inherent in the philosophy of *laissez-faire*; they were also conservative—resting, perhaps, on the laurels of British achievement—and suspicious of newer, more scientific approaches to management. These kinds of social explanations appear, with others, in the economic history literature; see, for example, the support that Aldcroft and Richardson (1969, Sect. B) give to such explanations. More recently Wiener (1981) has argued that the emergent entrepreneurial culture of the nineteenth century was absorbed and destroyed by the dominant aristocratic culture.

The sociological barriers to transformation notwithstanding, the growth of producers' cartels in the 1930s represented an important development in inter-firm cooperation, though one designed to impede competition. After the war, these cartels were progressively broken up by anti-trust legislation (see sect. 6.3 below). But this development has to be set against the long-term growth in industrial concentration, particularly since World War II. This growth was particularly strong from the late 1950s; by the early 1970s, the concentration process appears to have ceased (see Sharp and Shepherd, forthcoming, Ch. 4). The driving force in this process appears to have been mergers rather than organic firm growth (Hannah and Kay 1977). Mergers may have been favoured in the post-war period for several reasons: they were a defensive response to decartelization; there was a financial motive, given the advantageous tax treatment accorded to debt capital in the early 1970s (Prais 1976, Ch. 5); and the government actively promoted mergers in the late 1960s. There is also evidence that the increase in aggregate company concentration by the end of the 1960s led to an expansion of multi-plant operations, with too little rationalization at the plant level; moreover, mergers have often failed to result in better profitability (Sharp and Shepherd, forthcoming, Ch. 4).

This particular form of concentration process has led to several distinct characteristics in Britain's industrial structure. First, the UK appears to have a more concentrated industrial structure—including fewer small firms—than Germany, France or Italy (see, for instance, Tables 6.3 and 6.4 of Prais 1976). Second, inasmuch as post-merger rationalization has been weak, primacy must be given to financial and market-power motives in explaining the merger process. Thus giant firms have emerged without the unequivocal corporate transformation that we discussed earlier.

However, the 1960s represent a watershed in many ways: mergers were only partially successful in replacing domestic cartels as instruments to restrict competition; countervailing power became important; for instance, concentration in production and retailing often went in parallel, and competition from imports increased as trade liberalization measures began to take effect. From the 1970s onwards there have been signs, albeit not systematic, of a minor corporate revolution as firms have faced up to international competition for the first time in many decades (see, for instance, the qualitative evidence from textiles, consumer electronics and motor cars reviewed in Ch. 3 of Sharp and Shepherd, forthcoming).

Industrial finance

The industrial and financial communities in the UK have developed somewhat separately. In the 'market-based' financial systems of the UK and the United States, industrial investment tends to have been primarily financed by equity; in the 'bank-based' systems of France, Germany and Japan by loans, often accompanied by a closer relationship between banks and industry (Zysman 1983). Over time the share held in British equity by institutional investors (pension funds, insurance companies and unit trusts) has grown at the expense of individual investors, but these institutional investors have not sought closer ties with their investments. The government does not have sufficiently close ties with the financial system to be able to use it, should it want to, to channel credit to industry in a discretionary fashion.

Some see the relations between industry and finance as a fundamental part of the British industrial problem (see, for instance, Zysman 1983; this position is also central to current Labour Party thinking); others question the extent to which banks play a leading role in 'directing' industry in other countries where the relationship is closer. In any case, there is reported to be an increasing reliance in UK industry on term lending and an increasing involvement of the clearing banks in industrial affairs (Vittas 1986).

The unions and industrial relations[3]

British unions are notable for their industrial and political strength and their basically defensive objectives. They have proven as conservative as their bargaining counterparts, industrial management; yet, like the managers, have also shown signs of flexibility more recently. The strength and conservatism of the labour movement have their roots in the trauma of early industrialization, when *laissez-faire* liberalism and fears of a revolution on the French model were replacing paternalism with repressive legislation seeking to ban all organizations and combinations. Corelli Barnett remarks that this crude opposition of class interests explains 'why Britain is almost alone in Europe in having a "cloth cap" work-force instead of a bourgeois one' (Barnett 1975, p. 9).

Three factors appear to underlie the strength of the union movement. First, it is strongly linked to the Labour Party. Indeed, perceiving the hostility of the courts to its cause, the union movement originally set up the Labour Representation Committee—the forerunner of the Labour Party—to defend its interests in Parliament. The unions are the major financial backers of Labour and have a large vote in some of the party's institutional decision-making. However, beyond the defence of their immediate interests—securing wage rises, better working conditions, and job security—the unions have not sought a leading role in politics, nor have they generally advocated radical political or economic policies.

Second, the unions have a large membership (which grew from 39 per cent of the labour force in 1945 to 52 per cent in 1976; Crouch 1979, pp. 213–14). They are also well funded and thus able—unlike the French unions, for instance—to contemplate prolonged industrial action. Third, individual trade unions are predominantly organized along occupational lines (formerly craft lines), and these unions and their members have, through custom, in many cases acquired the 'ownership' of certain designated tasks, or 'job territories', in firms where more than one union is represented (see Ch. 7, below). What this means is that firms and unions have agreed that a specific union has the right to fill specific jobs in a firm. This custom originates in coinciding interests of workers and employers: the workers to be given a measure of job security, the employers to avoid inter-union disputes over 'who does what'.

British labour relations are further characterized by specific organizational features. First, unions and employers have strongly preferred the flexibility of voluntarism and custom to the inflexibility of the law in guiding their relations. In spite of this, industrial relations have been increasingly affected by the law since the 1960s (see sect. 6.3, below). Second, industrial relations can be somewhat fragmented: there is a relatively large number of unions (even if a few giant unions dominate); vertical control—by the Trades Union Congress or by individual unions—often proves difficult to enforce; there is often more than one union in any one plant, and squabbles about 'who does what' are endemic. Third, and related to the second point, the level of collective bargaining is often decentralized, partly because this is the most practical level at which to deal with problems of inter-union rivalry.

The sources of union strength and the organizational features of industrial relations described above have combined to create a specific impact on the process of industrial adjustment in the UK. First, many believe that the decentralized and non-coordinated process of collective bargaining in the UK has been inflationary: individual groups of workers are obliged to bargain to maintain their differentials *vis-à-vis* other groups, even if they know that the overall process is inflationary. Successive governments since the 1950s have been preoccupied with wage bargaining as a source of inflation.

Second, the emphasis of individual unions on defending 'job territories' in multi-union plants makes the negotiation of technical change—which often involves changing or eliminating tasks, hence invading 'job territories'— extremely painful. Moreover, union decentralization and rivalry make it difficult for the union leadership to influence the conduct of bargaining about the introduction of technical change at lower levels.

It is important not to lose perspective on British labour relations. First, they are not as rigid and chaotic as they are sometimes painted. In terms of job security, for instance, British employers have recently appeared freer to make workers redundant than their continental colleagues. Moreover, in recent years—and no doubt under the pressure of recession—unions have shown substantial flexibility in industries such as cars, where industrial relations were in the past notoriously difficult. Second, the present state of labour relations is the creation of both employers and unions, betraying a historical conservatism on both sides (and, in many ways, a curious abdication by employers—in search of a quiet life—of the right to manage). Both sides have disdained the idea of any real measure of industrial democracy.

Nevertheless, labour relations have continued to pose fundamental problems to the British industrial economy: in the narrow they have led to industrial disruption and put a brake on technical change; in the broad they have helped concentrate the collective British mind on issues of income redistribution, while making consensus on policy towards industry very difficult.

Government and politics

Government economic policy and government's relations with industry have been characterized by ambiguity, about both the legitimacy and nature of intervention. This very ambiguity has impeded effective government policies, whether interventionist or non-interventionist.

At the root of the problem of the legitimacy of intervention is a strong philosophical tradition of the state as keeper of order and guarantor of the liberty of individuals and not, as in the French tradition, some incarnation of the nation's collective will. However much dirigisme has entered the British system, it is accepted with difficulty: industry and government still do not see each other as natural partners. This separation is probably accentuated by features of the permanent bureaucracy that provides continuity in government. Senior civil servants are generalists, rather than technicians, and tend to belong to a different elite from the industrialists (and prevalent social values afford lower status to industrial than 'professional' occupations). It is not surprising that there is little career movement between industry and the civil service.

Economic policy has, of course, been the subject of intense debate between the two dominant political parties. Labour has governed the country for some seventeen years of the four post-war decades (five of these years in coalition with the small Liberal Party), a period of left-wing government substantially longer than in Germany, France or Italy. Until the mid-1970s the dominant economic ideology was that of a mixed economy where Keynesian demand-management would assure full employment and a suitable growth climate to encourage industrial investment. This ideology was the basis for a *de facto* economic consensus between the parties. But both major parties had a radical alternative ready to present when the consensus ideology was seen to be wanting. The social-democratic centre-right of the Labour Party has always cohabited—but never easily—with a more radical left demanding both planning and greater state control over key parts of the economy. While the left has been allowed a hand in preparing election manifestos, the centre-right has always been dominant in government. The centre-left of the Conservative Party has been characterized by 'one-Nation Toryism'—in practice, a tendency towards populist, interventionist and corporatist policies. The Conservative right-wing is the inheritor of the 'liberal-conservative/ tradition of free trade and *laissez-faire*. Unlike Labour's radicals, the Conservative right-wing has shared in government—in the early 1950s, in 1970–2 (the first two years of the Heath administration) and since 1979.

Several points can be made about the pattern of economic ideology. First, the arguments occur as much within as across parties. Second, much has been made of the disconcerting effects of policy changes introduced by new governments (the nationalization—denationalization—renationalization of steel being an obvious example). Yet it is equally valid to see these kinds of changes as a consequence rather than a cause of economic failure. Moreover, it has been suggested that there has been greater continuity in policy than is at first obvious. (It is ironic that a conservative government was the first to introduce a form of longer-term planning, in 1962, while Labour governments were the first to introduce an anti-trust policy, in 1948, a statutory incomes policy, in 1966, and a form of monetary policy, in 1976.) Third, as Wilks (1986) argues, the real effect of ideological differences is not so much to create actual policy discontinuities as to force politicians and parties into rigid doctrinal positions that preclude constructive discussion of practical solutions. Fourth, the two major parties remain class-based in spite of the objective erosion of class perceptions and the rise of a new, less politically captive white-collar class; in this context the role of economic ideology is more to mobilize traditional electorates than to affect practical economic policies.

Industrial corporatism has been growing since World War I (Middlemas 1979). This growth has been facilitated by the (relative) cohesion of the trade-union movement, the growth of large firms and the growth of public economic activity. Moreover, Labour and Conservative have a 'natural' alliance, respectively with the unions and business. Among the post-war vehicles of this corporatism have been the Social Contract between Labour and the unions (1974–9) and the tripartite economic coordination exercises of the National Development Council (NEDC), but many other tripartite bodies have existed at various levels, particularly since the development of tripartite habits during World War II. The corporatist consensus favoured a Keynesian-redistributive policy. This reflected public views and, behind this, the experience of unemployment and deprivation of the 1930s. For all the historical continuity the UK has enjoyed, this consensus represented an important shift from the *laissez-faire* and free trade of the nineteenth century.

The Thatcher government entered office a declared enemy of corporatism and it has vigorously attacked one leg of tripartism, the trade unions. In this sense the Thatcher government—with its design to move society back to an entrepreneurial rather than redistributive culture—represents the first truly radical break with the pattern of post-war economic politics. This challenge reflects, more or less, the end of the period—say, the first six decades of the twentieth century—during which the UK economy was able partially to insulate itself against the world changes that had been overtaking it.

6.3 The development of policies toward industry, 1945–85

1945–51: post-war recovery under the Labour government

By 1950 the British economy had more or less returned to normal and some of the characteristic themes of the post-war economy had become established. First, full employment and redistribution had become central political objectives. Second, the role the UK sought as a world power and its reliance on the United States led to obligations: to liberalize trade and payments, to support a major reserve currency, and to run a large defence budget, all of which put a heavy strain on the economy manifested by inflation and recurrent balance-of-payments crises. In consequence, and in the light of a relatively rapid post-war recovery, government and industry continued to give little priority to the problems of industrial productivity and competitiveness. Things got off to a very different start after the war in the rest of Western Europe.

Redistributive policies

The key to the post-war era is found in the searing experience of unemployment and social deprivation in the 1930s. After the high level of cooperation between labour, business and government in the war effort, the British population, in victory, nursed high expectations of social and economic change (Pollard 1983, Ch. 2). In the public eye the Conservative Party was associated with the disasters of the 1930s and, in the election of 1945, the mandate for change was given to the Labour Party. Even though Labour had retained a programme of socialism through planning and public ownership, this mandate was for full employment, enlarged welfare provisions and broader educational opportunities, all objectives that had been agreed by the wartime coalition of both parties.

From 1945 major legislation created a universal system of national insurance (covering unemployment, sickness and other benefits), universal family allowances, and a National Health Service (Calvocoressi 1979, Ch. 2).

A strong post-war consensus developed on the use of Keynesian policies to maintain full employment. Deflation had come to be viewed as a major cause of the problems of the 1930s. In fact, full employment had been achieved during the war, and pent-up wartime demand and foreign demand meant that the problem of the 1940s was one of 'excess' rather than 'deficient' demand.

Full employment boosted trade-union membership and influence. Until 1949 labour relations were generally good, and in practice the unions did informally restrain wage rises, but this restraint collapsed after a large 1949 devaluation (Pollard 1983, Ch. 6).

External trade and payment policies

Victory left the British Empire intact (even if the process of decolonization was soon to get going) and left the UK as the strongest Western ally of the United States. This imposed a high defence budget and involved UK support of the external trade and payments policies sought by the United States, entailing many problems for the war-weakened British economy in the short term.

The UK responded to US desires for convertibility far faster than any other European country. A first post-war US loan in 1946 was conditional on British removal of foreign-exchange controls on sterling (still an important currency reserve) in July 1947. This liberalization led to such a run on sterling that controls had to be restored almost immediately. From 1948 the UK then benefited, like the rest of Western Europe, from Marshall Aid. At the end of 1948, foreign-exchange controls were again relaxed, and another run on the pound led to a massive devaluation (from $4.03 to $2.80) in September 1949. By 1950 most of the remaining foreign-exchange controls had been removed.

US influence also helps to explain the UK's role in championing the GATT trading system, eventually committing it to abandoning the imperial preference system of 1937. The commitment to the United States and the Commonwealth explains why the UK rejected the offer of closer European links in coal and steel offered by the Schuman Plan of 1950. As with the

UK's eventual entry into the Common Market, the GATT commitment was an implicit, partly unrecognized industrial policy arising from largely political considerations.

Policies aimed at industry

The Labour government inherited a commitment to planning, encouraged by its wartime experience of a more closely and more successfully planned economy than any of the other belligerents. But planning was never a first priority. The government had only been prepared to enlist consent, rather than compulsion, in the execution of plans, and a majority view began to prevail that full employment and redistribution could be achieved through demand management (Budd 1978, Ch. 4).

Public ownership of industry was probably an even more important inherited socialist philosophy than planning. Again, the Labour government proved pragmatic, nationalizing parts of the economy on an *ad hoc* basis and with a rationale more to do with extending a traditional role for government than with seeking to direct the whole economy from the 'commanding heights'. The major industrial nationalizations were in coal (1948), electricity (1947), transport (1947), gas (1948) and iron and steel (1949) (Pollard 1983, Ch. 6).

The Monopolies and Restrictive Practices Act was passed in 1948 (Gribbin 1978)—a cautious piece of legislation: cartels were innocent until proven guilty—but it started a process that would largely destroy the cartels by the 1960s.

It would be unfair to say that after the war there was *no* realization in the UK of the underlying micro-economic problem of low productivity and poor international competitiveness. But it was so easy for British industry to export to war-damaged Europe, and the sense of complacency generated within industry lasted well into the 1950s. Working parties and councils formed at the end of the 1940s to look at some of these industrial problems, were stifled by the general opposition of industry (Pollard 1983, Ch. 6).

The 1950s: Conservative government, stop–go and laissez-faire

The 1950s were carried along by unprecedented affluence. Nevertheless, inflation and balance-of-payments difficulties and the stop–go management of the economy that sought to deal with them, caused increasing concern. Wage demands and the reserve currency role of sterling were variously identified as the culprits, while the underlying weaknesses of the economy received relatively little consideration.

The Conservatives, returned to office in 1951, had become as committed as Labour to full employment (Shonfield 1965, p. 99). They removed most controls, eschewed any incomes policy, and reversed the iron and steel nationalization of 1949, relying on a 'Keynesian' belief that demand management could effect a controlled trade-off between unemployment and inflation (the Philips curve relationship) and that the private sector would take care of growth. They intervened less than any other post-war government, including the 1979 Conservative government.

The 1950s are retrospectively renowned for the stop-go cycle of growth in which expansion of the economy, largely induced by fiscal measures, was followed by inflation and balance-of-payments crises and deflationary measures. These crises were habitually attributed to the sterling problem, but it now seems more likely that the weakness of sterling was the result of trying to keep the rate of unemployment (which varied from 2 to 2.5 per cent in the 1950s) too low. At the same time, the government was coming to see wage demands as a major source of inflationary pressures. Public opinion was turning against striking unions, and this may have helped the government to win the election of 1959.

The stop–go cycle helped promote a growing, if faint, awareness in the second half of the decade of the UK's competitive problems. Beyond public expenditure on military and civil nuclear technologies, few specific industrial policies were introduced in the 1950s. In 1954 investment allowances were introduced (in addition to existing depreciation allowances introduced after the war). In 1959 several developments presaged the more interventionist 1960s: a Minister of Science was appointed; the Cotton Industry Act provided funds for rationalization to counter the effect of Asian imports, and the government sponsored various mergers in the aircraft industry.

The Restrictive Trade Practices Act of 1956 was probably the most important piece of industrial-policy legislation in the decade. Cartels were now to be guilty till proven innocent.

The direction of British manufacturing trade was beginning to shift from the Commonwealth to Western Europe, but the UK withdrew from Common Market negotiations in 1956. To counter the resulting discrimination it went for the negotiation of tariff cuts in GATT (as a means of reducing the Common Market's common external tariff) and promoted the creation of the European Free Trade Area (EFTA) in 1959.

There were significant developments in the political background in the 1950s (Budd 1978, Ch. 5). 'Keynesian' consensus and relative affluence encouraged the erosion of a blue-collar class loyal to Labour and the emergence of a new white-collar/professional middle class less politically attached to any one party. At the same time, the long-standing divisions within each party resurfaced. Dissatisfaction with the *laissez-faire* of the liberal-conservative strain in the party led to the re-emergence of the Tory strain of 'One Nation' conservatism more favourable to intervention and corporatism. Harold Macmillan personified this tendency and his leadership of the party from 1957 presaged the developments of the early 1960s. The big internal debate of Labour in exile was between the revisionists (led by Gaitskell and Crosland), who broadly believed that capitalism had been tamed since the war, and the Socialists, who wished to extend public owner-ship. At the end of the decade the party was advocating the reintroduction of planning and the creation of a National Investment Bank.

1960–4: the Conservatives and planning and incomes policies

In the 1960s direct intervention at the level of the firm began to appear as an identifiable constituent of industrial policy. But experiments continued to counter the problems of inflation and the balance of payments, coupled with an ominous deterioration in industrial relations. Thus the 1960–4 Conserva-tive government sought to develop an incomes policy and to introduce French-style indicative planning. An attempt at voluntary wage restraint through a National Incomes Commission (1961) failed in the face of union opposition (Crouch 1979, Ch. 2).

It was a general recognition of the UK's failure to match the economic performance of the Continent that turned attention to French planning. (Why, Alan Budd has asked, did people not turn to the German model, with an even more impressive growth? The answer, he suggests, is British cultural ties with France and the then-government's penchant for intervention; Budd 1978, p. 87). The trade unions were at first reticent on planning, fearing that it could interfere with free collective bargaining. They were not entirely wrong, for planning *à la* Macmillan appears to have been as much an exercise in corporate consensus-making specifically directed at an incomes policy as it was a technical exercise in indicative planning. It was also no doubt an exercise in stealing Labour's thunder.

The National Economic Development Council (NEDC) with its secre-tariat (NEDO), a tripartite body bringing government, business and unions together, was founded in 1961 (Middlemas 1983). It relied solely on persua-sion (and has survived as today's only major tripartite—and relatively apolitical—body). The tripartite, sector-specific Economic Development Committees attached to NEDC formed the political and technical basis for the development over time of NEDC/NEDO's more sector-specific approach to industrial problems (especially from 1975).

NEDC's low-key indicative planning was consistent and well-informed at the sub-sectoral level. Its 1963 plan, *Growth in the United Kingdom Econ-omy to 1966*, was well received and influential at first. But independently of the plan, the government embarked in 1963 on a 'dash for growth' with an expansionary budget intended to break the vicious circle of low growth and release the underlying constraints. The consequence was a balance-of-payments crisis in 1964, followed by a deflationary budget.

1964–70: Labour and the growth of selective intervention

Harold Wilson's Labour government (1964–70) brought with it, as the compromise of the warring Labour factions in exile, a programme with more emphasis on planning than public ownership, even if steel was renationalized in 1966. As with the Conservatives, Labour's plan was as much an incomes policy as it was an industrial policy, and it was rapidly overtaken by economic crisis and a marked deterioration in labour relations. It was from the emphasis Wilson put on scale and technology to face increasing American and European competition rather than from mainstream Labour ideology that industrial policy developed—a policy of special support for manufacturing, assistance for the regions and distressed sectors, and the encouragement of large, leading firms (national champions).

Planning and labour relations

The new government created in 1964 a Department of Economic Affairs (DEA), of greater political weight than NEDC but still relying only on persuasion. The National Plan it produced in 1966 was killed off by another sterling crisis, and in 1967 Wilson was forced to devalue the pound (from 2.8 to 2.4 dollars). In 1968 the government produced a consultative document, well short of a plan, *The Task Ahead*, but in fact indicative planning has been dead ever since 1966.

The 1966 sterling crisis led the government, however, to introduce, for the first time a statutory incomes policy (a six-month wage freeze followed by severe restraint). While the TUC continued reluctantly to cooperate, this further pressure on the previously voluntaristic and consensual pattern of labour relations proved too much for several unions and many union members. 1968–9 were years of much labour unrest.

Industrial policy

This developed through a series of *ad hoc* legislative measures, and with a proliferation of institutions. Meanwhile, pro-market industrial policies continued. In 1964 the Resale Prices Act ended price-fixing by producers. Previous legislation had virtually eliminated cartels from manufacturing by the middle of the 1960s (Gribbin 1978). Firms responded by seeking other forms of market dominance, and this partly explains the merger boom of the 1960s and the growth of concentration in manufacturing, though these were also an international phenomenon. The 1965 Monopolies and Mergers Act brought mergers within the scope of competition policy, but monopoly legislation remains relatively tolerant in respect of the trade-off of the benefits of size and the costs of concentration and does not appear to have affected industrial structure decisively.

As a consequence of the Dillon and Kennedy rounds in GATT, the opening to trade was greater in this decade than in the 1950s. In the period 1960–70 the ratio of manufacturing imports to manufacturing production grew from 7 to 12 per cent, while the equivalent export ratios grew from 15 to 18 per cent.

The growth of a specific industrial policy according priority to manufacturing can be considered under the three headings of general, regional and (firm- or sector-) selective policies.[4] The government introduced two major measures of *general policy*: the Selective Employment Tax of 1965 (lasting till 1970), which discriminated against service employment; and the introduction through the Industrial Development Act, 1966 (and lasting till 1970), of investment grants (cash grants of 20 per cent of the cost of plant and machinery), which supplemented a variety of existing tax allowance schemes.

Regional policy

Regional policy has a history going back to the 1930s, but the Wilson government stepped it up in two principal ways. The Industrial Development Act of 1966 offered investment grants for development areas of 40 per cent on plant and equipment and 25 per cent on buildings. From 1967 the Regional Employment Premium was introduced as a labour subsidy in development areas. Grant (1982, pp. 56–9) has argued that regional aid was highly politicized and related to marginal parliamentary seats.

Selective policy

The Science and Technology, and the Development of Inventions Acts, both of 1965, increased public R & D funding available to industry. The Industrial Reorganization Corporation (IRC) was created in 1966. The Industrial Expansion Act of 1968 gave the government general powers to intervene less restrictive than those binding the IRC. It used these to back two major aluminium projects and to support the merger of the four main British computer firms to create ICL in 1968–9.

The IRC was the first manifestation of various forms of public investment bank that have become a part of Labour's industrial philosophy, partially replacing public ownership. During its brief life (1966–70) it was involved in over fifty merger proposals, and in share purchases, and loans and paid out 120 million pounds in total. Its most famous interventions were to help create British Leyland in 1968 and to back GEC's takeover of Associated Electrical Industries in 1968. It also showed a preference for 'national' solutions. The IRC and the Industrial Expansion Act thus became the first instruments to promote 'national champions'.

A number of sectors were singled out for special support by various means, most notably textiles, shipbuilding, machine tools and aircraft. The major motivation for government intervention was to maintain employment, and there is not much evidence that public money helped improve productivity.

Aid to the aircraft industry had a venerable pedigree and cost considerably more than other sectoral support. By 1960 the shift of defence requirements from aircraft to guilded missiles and the escalating development and launch costs of new civil aircraft convinced the government of the need to rationalize the industry, a policy which helped reduce the number of units from twenty-two in 1958 to three by the end of the 1960s. The development of the supersonic Concorde was particularly expensive.

The minor explosion of selective and non-selective policy instruments caused something of an institutional crisis. The Ministry of Science, created in 1964, at first started with a narrow science-based brief and gradually acquired responsibility for aircraft and energy research, for the IRC, and for a growing number of assistance schemes and services.

What were the origins of this new selective form of industrial policy? It does not figure in mainstream Labour ideology, while the emphasis on scale and national champions, became a concern at the same time in France and Germany. The 1960s was the decade when trade liberalization within GATT and the EEC was posing new competitive challenges to all countries. In this light much of Britain's new selective intervention, whether in 'high' or 'low' technology, can be seen as trying to bolster once-strong or threatened firms or sectors.

1970–4: Conservative disengagement and U-turn

In opposition the Conservative Party had reacted to the failures of planning and incomes policies in the 1960s by turning back to the disengagement philosophy of its conservative-liberal wing and adopting a policy to control the unions through legal measures. Once in office the new Edward Heath government acted vigorously on both fronts. Yet it spectacularly reversed its disengagement policy in 1972 as part of a desperate bid to reflate the economy as inflation and unemployment grew. Thus industrial policy more obviously became a part of broader policies to combat recession.

As to disengagement, the National Board on Prices and Incomes was wound up; so was the IRC; regional development grants were discontinued; selective intervention was pruned; and, in the case of R & D support, public expenditure criteria were considerably sharpened; investment grants were terminated. There were some minor denationalizations. But NEDC survived intact and the Ministry of Technology, the Department of Economic Affairs and the Board of Trade were merged into a giant Department of Trade and Industry.

The Conservative government was now set on confrontation with the unions. The government broke most previous channels of communication and made little attempt to conciliate in a series of major strikes in 1971–2. In August 1971 it introduced legislation designed to reform industrial relations with a new legal framework limiting union power and inhibiting strikes. This exacerbated and politicized government–labour relations.

In 1972 came the famous U-turn. (Already in 1970–1 the government's disengagement philosophy had been dented by a political obligation to save first Rolls Royce then Upper Clyde Shipbuilders from bankruptcy, at a combined cost of well over 200 million pounds.) As unemployment rose, the government undertook another 'dash for growth' through expansionary fiscal policies, floating the exchange rate in June 1972 in order to try to avoid the balance-of-payments consequences. In 1972 it also introduced an interventionist Industry Act. Failing to get cooperation from the unions, it imposed unilaterally a severe incomes policy, starting with a three-month pay freeze and followed by a further two stages, the last of which contained an indexation provision. Pay restraint proved successful in 1973, but imported inflation continued apace and, with the advent of the oil crisis in late 1973, the miners then went on a full strike. Heath called an election for February 1974, which was fought on the issue of 'Who governs Britain: the unions or the government?' After a fairly evenly balanced result between the two major parties, the Labour Party formed a government with Liberal help.

The 1972 Industry Act remains the most comprehensive piece of industrial legislation to have been passed in the UK. Its corporatist philosophy fitted in well not only with the post-1972 Heath approach but also with that of subsequent Labour leaders (Grant 1982, p. 50). Section 7 of the Act offered regional grants over and above non-discretionary regional aid (which was reintroduced in 1972), and Section 8 provided assistance for wool textiles, offshore supplies for oil installations, shipbuilding, machine tools, computers and motorcycles. In addition, the government returned in 1972 to a system of generous investment allowances, allowing 100 per cent initial-year allowances for plant and equipment and 40 per cent for buildings.

Somewhat incongruously amid the turmoil of 1970–4, the government was finally able in 1972 to negotiate British entry into the European Community. Since the late 1960s the pace of import penetration had begun to quicken as the Kennedy Round cuts worked through: from 1970 to 1974 the ratio of imports to production rose from 12 to 18 per cent, and of exports to production from 18 to 21 per cent.

The Conservatives legislated the 1972 Industry Act as part of a reflationary policy, thus linking macro-economic and micro-economic policy. The Act was also an instrument *par excellence* for politically motivated rescue operations in the face of rapidly rising and regionally concentrated unemployment, but the Conservative government did not have long to use its new industrial policy instrument.

1974–9: Labour government and the growth of industrial policy

The centrepiece of the economic strategy of the new Labour government was an incomes policy based on a 'social contract' with the unions. This broke down after 1977 when the government was forced to adopt a tighter control of the money supply and a new period of conflictual labour relations was ushered in. Labour's industrial policies, though secondary to and little connected with its central economic strategy, represent the high-watermark of industrial policy since 1945. Born of socialist ideology (in 1970–4), industrial policy quickly became an instrument of crisis reaction to the recession once Labour got into office, then evolved from around 1976 towards a combined instrument of crisis reaction and structural change. This evolution towards 'positive adjustment' policies reflected both a new budget stringency and a growing appreciation in government of international competitive pressures in a period combining recession and rapid technological change.

External Adjustment Pressures

From the early- to mid-1970s new pressures intruded from outside the national political arena. There was the world recession, while the rise in commodity prices affected the UK's terms of trade more adversely than those of any other members of the OECD. These pressures and the slowdown in export markets came soon after the government's reflationary measures of 1972–3. Inflation shot up from 9 per cent in 1973 to 24 per cent in 1975 and unemployment from 3.2 per cent in 1973 to 6.0 per cent in 1976 (considerably worse than the OECD average). Not only did the UK quite suddenly realize that it had to adjust to a new world of 'stagflation', but the whole shock helped bear in on the country the extent to which it had fallen behind in international competitiveness and the consequent need for structural adjustment and technical development.

Following the shock of the recession and the experience of political confrontation in 1970–4, the public appeared to want to draw back from the brink and re-establish some form of consensus: this, at any rate, is one interpretation of the inconclusive results of the February 1974 election (Crouch 1979, p. 101).

Macro-economic difficulties and the social contract

Labour came into office under conditions more difficult than for any new government since 1945, facing enormous political pressure for subsidies to maintain jobs and output, and a confident and politically strong trade-union movement. Negotiations between the unions and the Labour Party culminated in what came to be known as the 'Social Contract'. The TUC and Labour agreed common general social and economic policies: in return for a Labour government generally restoring the rights of unions and workers lost under the last government, the unions would voluntarily take into account overall economic conditions when they made pay claims (Crouch 1979, pp. 89–90). This agreement laid the basis—until 1976–7 at least—for a return to a corporatist form of economic consensus. In addition, legislation in 1974–5 substantially restored, and in many respects substantially strengthened, the position of unions and workers.

In 1976, as the economy's external position worsened, the government sought a more formal wage restraint offering tax cuts as a *quid pro quo*. It possessed quite powerful weapons of wage restraint through the control of public-sector settlements and the insertion of pay-restraint clauses in contracts it had with private firms. This power and the cooperation of the TUC appear to have been successful, in the short-term of 1976–7 at least, in the first two phases of wage and price restraint. This was the high-point of the Social Contract. However, a sterling crisis in autumn 1976 led to an IMF loan with very stiff conditions attached, and the government's economic (and industrial) policy fundamentally changed (James Callaghan became Prime Minister in 1976). The major policy aim became to control the money supply (and public expenditure). A consequence of this was the re-emergence of large-scale industrial action from 1977. In the famous 1978–9 'winter of discontent' the level of industrial action was sufficient to topple the government in the April 1979 election.

Industrial policy

The Labour administration represents a high-point in industrial policy, in terms both of interventionist intent and of levels of expenditure (though expenditure cuts by the subsequent Conservative government were not apparent until after 1981/2). A number of stages in the development of Labour's industrial policy in the 1970s can be identified: the formulation of a radical industrial policy while still in opposition; the formulation of a more watered-down, none the less strong (by historical standards) industrial policy on assuming office (the 1975 Industry Act); the 1974–5 period of implementation, a period of 'lame duck' interventions; the 1975–6 period of implementation—a narrowing of priorities. True to historical form, once the Labour Party was in office, the right-wing reasserted itself over the left-wing.

The Labour Party, in opposition from 1970 to 1974, reacting against the perceived failures of Wilsonian social democracy in 1964–70, again turned towards more socialist solutions for industry. In particular, it saw multi-national corporations as failing to act in the national interest. Specific proposals were for a state holding company, planning agreements (a hybrid marrying the French growth-contract approach with imposed measures of industrial democracy), and a major extension of nationalization in order to curb the MNCs and encourage industrial regeneration.

The 1975 Industry Act created the National Enterprise Broad (NEB), made provision for negotiating planning agreements, established measures to control inward foreign investment, and required companies to disclose certain information to government. The inward investment provision was never invoked because, on the contrary, it became Departmental policy to *promote* inward investment. Company information disclosure was not implemented for fear of antagonizing business (Grant 1982, p. 50). Moreover, only one Planning Agreement, with the ailing US motor car firm Chrysler, was ever concluded. In fact, the major legislation on which the subsequent expansion of industrial policy was based was the Conservatives' 1972 Industry Act and Labour's 1965 Science and Technology Act.

The NEB was the one lasting achievement of the Act, even surviving in reduced form the Conservative government of 1979. It was, however, constrained by an external borrowing limit of 700 million pounds and it was also required to earn an 'adequate' return on its capital, which proved difficult as the government soon turned it into a 'hospital for lame ducks' by requiring it to oversee the management of firms such as BL (cars), Rolls Royce (aero-engines), Ferranti (data processing) and Alfred Herbert (machine tools)—all rescued from imminent bankruptcy. Nevertheless, the NEB managed as a sideline to pursue what later came to be regarded as its central function—acting as a catalyst to new high-technology start-ups, notably in micro-electronics, office automation and, latterly, biotechnology.

The government also moved to fulfil election pledges to extend public ownership. British Aerospace and the remains of the shipbuilding industry (renamed British Shipbuilders) were nationalized in 1977, but this fell well short of many expectations of the left of the Labour Party.

The mid-1975 referendum favouring continued British membership of the European Community (after a renegotiation of terms in 1975) was a defeat for Labour's left-wing (and the TUC). It signalled a retreat from Socialist industrial policy to a different animal called the 'Industrial Strategy', launched in late 1975. This was meant to be a self-analytical form of planning, strategic and sectoral rather than quantitative and aggregative, looking for growth points and bottlenecks. It fitted in with the government's growing interest in a supply-side approach (Grant 1982, p. 63). Its main vehicle was to be thirty-nine Sector Working Parties (SWPs) created to cover a variety of sectors. Like the EDCs, which they partly replaced, partly supplemented, they were tripartite and reflected a corporatist approach. The industry and unions were meant to be the guiding forces in the exercise, government little more than the ringmaster.

The SWPs have survived and contributed to a better government understanding by the end of the 1970s of the problems facing British industry and the crucial importance of technological developments to long-run competitiveness. What they have achieved in practice is harder to determine. They were, however, influential in promoting a number of sectoral schemes (introduced in 1975–7 under Section 8 of the 1972 Industry Act) reinforcing the Industrial Strategy approach. These schemes were small, but some of them have been credited with giving a useful stimulus to innovation.

Industrial policy priorities were clearly refocused from around 1976. This may have two evident origins. First, the belt-tightening after the 1976 sterling crisis and the IMF intervention inhibited public spending. Second, rising unemployment was a country-wide problem and this undermined the traditional rationale for regional aid (Grant 1982, p. 54). As a result, there was a marked switch, around 1975–7, from regional aid to employment-support programmes such as the Temporary Employment Subsidy (1975–9) and the Short-Time Working Subsidy (1978–9).

Selective aid itself clearly switched emphasis around 1977 from sector-specific schemes and firm rescues to discretionary schemes promoting innovation (for instance, the Product and Process Development Scheme of 1977, the Micro-electronics Industry Support Programme and Micro-electronics Applications Programme of 1978). This tendency was also mirrored in NEB's reorientation towards promoting catalyst developments.

Somewhat apart from the mainstream of industrial policy, an important element in public industrial expenditure from 1973/4 onwards was the interest subsidies provided by the Export Credit Guarantee Department to offer favourable export-credit packages.

Disengagement under the New Conservatives, 1979–85

Margaret Thatcher's Conservative government has sought the most fundamental changes in the rules of the economic game since 1945. With the formal adoption of monetarist doctrine, deflation has replaced full employment as the prime economic objective. The power of the trade unions and imperfections in the labour market have been attacked through rising unemployment, labour legislation and policy on public-sector salaries. The problems of nationalized industry have been tackled through a large programme of privatization and the imposition of spending limits on corporations still in the government sector.

Potentially at least, these measures constitute a powerful implicit industrial policy of reinforcing the operation of the market: 'Mrs Thatcher and her colleagues may have had a vision of the kind of society that they would like to construct—a cross between nineteenth-century Birmingham and contemporary Hong Kong, located in Esher' (Riddell 1985, p. 165). On the other hand, conventional industrial policy has not broken so radically with the policies of past governments. Industrial policies have been narrowed in the direction of high technology and, to an extent, small business; and since 1981 the cost of direct support to industry has fallen. Nevertheless, industrial intervention is alive and well; on the foreign trade front in particular, the government has shown little propensity to retreat from inherited mercantilist policies. If industrial policies have been at odds with the radicalism of other Conservative policies, this also reflects the continuing tensions between the reformist urge of government leaders and the inertia or special interests they have found below them within the government.

As far as can be judged, the record of policy achievement on the industrial front, as in other economic areas, is mixed. The 'cold shower' of monetarism has led to apparent improvements in industrial management and performance, but it is difficult to perceive a large-scale burgeoning of a new entrepreneurial culture.

Monetarism and recession

After their last election defeat of 1974, the Conservatives rapidly swung back to radical economic prescriptions under the intellectual leadership of Margaret Thatcher and Keith Joseph. Monetary control has played a significant part in reducing inflation from 18 per cent in 1980 to 5 per cent by 1983. The control of inflation was accorded a significantly higher priority than reducing unemployment. Indeed, monetarism sees initially rising unemployment as a necessary step in the cure of inflation.

A policy of high interest rates at a time when the UK was enjoying a growing trade surplus in petroleum products contributed to large revaluation of the pound. The combined effect of this revaluation and movements in British prices and labour productivity relative to those of other industrial countries was that from 1977 to 1981 the UK's relative unit labour costs rose by an unprecedented 59 per cent (Sharp and Shepherd, forthcoming, Ch. 2). This collapse in cost-competitiveness combined with the post-1979 world recession and the deflationary effects of monetarism at home to induce the most severe industrial recession since 1922: from 1979 to 1982 UK manufacturing output declined by 15 per cent and employment by over 20 per cent. Unemployment steadily rose from 5 per cent in 1979 to almost 13 per cent by 1983, the highest in the OECD except for Belgium and Spain. Most of the direct job losses appear to have been in manufacturing.

Labour markets

In the Employment Acts of 1980 and 1982 and the Trade Union Act of 1984, the government took steps to introduce democratic procedures and remove some of the unions' legal immunities (Riddell 1985, pp. 186–8), leaving it generally to employers to pursue their new legal rights through the courts. A case law is now slowly building up.

Most of the major industrial relations disputes of the Thatcher era—both on wage and job-security issues—have been in the public sector. These have included steel (1980), the civil service (1981) and the National Health Service (1982), but most importantly the miners. The government won a resounding victory in the 1984–5 miners' strike, with the aid of its new legislation and of general (but by no means complete) public support, and also because it had been preparing for this essentially political confrontation (notably through building up coal stocks).

From early on the unions put up a united front of wholesale opposition to the new legislation, but this unity has gradually been eroded in a period when the unions have probably reached their lowest level of political power for half a century. There is substantial disagreement among unions and unionists, but there is perceptible feeling in much of the movement that some of the legal changes are here to stay.[5] Indeed, the most right-wing unions have been pursuing strategies of cooperation with employers, through no-strike agreements for instance.[6]

While these changes in industrial relations are potentially far-reaching, it is still too early to assess how effective they will prove or how easily reversed under another government.

Public ownership

The government's privatization policies involve both denationalization and, through the reduction of statutory monopolies, liberalization of markets. In the event, Conservative achievements in this area have far outstripped the promises of their 1979 election manifesto (which were deliberately low-key). In their first term of office the Conservatives privatized a number of concerns, including British Aerospace and the British National Oil Corporation. In their second term (from July 1983) privatization has become even more important. In 1984 British Telecom, accounting for over 10 per cent of total employment in public corporations, was sold off. British Gas followed in 1986. Indeed, the only major nationalized industry not an announced candidate for privatization is the National Coal Board (Steel and Heald, 1985, p. 69).

Kay and Silberston (1984), among others, have pointed out that denationalization and liberalization are often in conflict since a loss of statutory monopoly both makes the firm less financially attractive to sell and creates opposition from the firm's management. Both the privatization of British Telecom—accompanied by only a limited diminution of its statutory monopoly—and British Airways' successful resistance to more complete airline deregulation suggest that the government has been prepared to compromise on liberalization in order to achieve its principal political goal of denationalization.

For those publicly owned industries not (or not yet) profitable enough to be sold off, the government has prescribed spending limits ('cash limits') which have significantly reduced the amount of public aid going to the British Steel Corporation, British Leyland and British Shipbuilding. The Competition Act of 1980 brought public industries within the ambit of the Monopolies Commission.

Industrial policy

Conventional industrial policy clearly occupies a less important position than the policies we have so far described. (On such policy since 1979 see Grant 1982, pp. 78–99; Wilks 1985; Riddell 1985, pp. 166–9.)

From 1979 to around 1981, under Sir Keith Joseph, the Department of Industry pursued a somewhat rudderless industrial policy combining a continuation, more or less, of past policies with a rhetoric of disengagement. The NEB was retained, though with a reduced brief to act as catalyst in starting up high-technology ventures. (The NEB was merged in 1981 with the National Research and Development Corporation to form the British Technology Group.) NEDO was left more or less intact (losing seven of its sixty-one Economic Development Committees or Sector Working Parties), but there was no more talk of the Industrial Strategy. The government was also forced into injecting large amounts of money into ailing large firms in the recessionary conditions of 1980–1, notably British Steel Corporation, British Leyland and Rolls Royce in the public sector and ICL (computers) in the private sector. On the other hand, the conditions attached to regional and selective aid were tightened. Among the few major initiatives of industrial policy in this period were the provision of some effective schemes to aid small-scale industry: the Loan Guarantee and Business Start Up schemes of 1981, introduced by the Treasury and the introduction in 1981 of fourteen tax-free Enterprise Zones (a number that has now grown, with the success of these first zones, to twenty-five).

The Department of Industry appeared to regain a measure of direction from around 1981, switching emphasis from capital formation to training, management and advanced technology (Wilks 1985, p. 135). One of the major outcomes of this new coherence was the Alvey Programme, set up in 1982–3, to foster pre-competitive research cooperation on fifth-generation computing.

The government has been reluctant to abandon policies, developed in the 1970s, of non-tariff protection of imports or subsidization of some exports (though the level of subsidy to exports was significantly reduced by agreement within the OECD). Indeed, there was some talk in the early 1980s of using public procurement (of British goods) as a more positive tool of industrial policy, though little came of this.

There was arguably a broad continuity in selective industrial policy—as well as in trade policy—between the Labour government of the later 1970s and its Conservative successor, but there was an important disengagement in terms of expenditure. In 1980/1 and 1981/2 public expenditure in support of industry had reached its highest ever level, thanks largely to the cost of corporate rescues. After this, the general level began to decline for the first time since the 1960s (see sect. 6.4, below) despite the fact that support for various high-technology and R & D programmes actually grew. (In 1984 the government also abolished the accelerated-depreciation system of investment allowances which had favoured industrial investment, in favour of a more neutral system and a lower corporate tax rate.)

Monetarism as industrial policy

The Conservative government's macro-economic policy has contained a good deal of implicit industrial policy. There is the no doubt intended policy of seeking to correct labour market distortions through unemployment. On the other hand, and less intended, was the 'cold-shower' effect of severe recession. Whatever the merits of pursuing deflation through flexible exchange rates and effective revaluation, it is difficult to describe policies contributing to the loss of international competitiveness that British industry experienced from 1977 to 1981 as anything but anti-industrial policies.

On the other hand, there is anecdotal evidence about the 'cold shower' effecting minor revolutions in managerial attitudes, industrial relations and industrial performance. Since 1981 corporate profits have regained the levels they last enjoyed in the early 1970s. But the statistical increase in productivity (from an average of 2.2 per cent in 1970–80 to 5 per cent per annum in 1980–4) must be set against a general and massive decline in output when much low-productive capacity was shut down.

The 1979–82 recession and Conservative policies have further polarized positions in the debate on British industry. Broadly, three camps in the debate remain (right, left and centre), but there have been some important shifts. First, the right has perhaps a coherence and strength it has not had before. Second, the centre is more monetarist that it was (see Cobham 1984). Third, the left, following the development of ideas by the Cambridge Economic Policy Group during the 1970s, is more thoroughly wedded to the idea that a Keynesian solution must proceed via import controls. What is more, the polarization of left and right led to the creation of a new political force in the centre, the Alliance, formed in 1981 from an electoral coalition of the newly formed Social Democratic Party and the Liberals. The continuing growth in unemployment as the country approaches another general election now set for June 1987 has led to growing demands from the Tory side of the Conservative Party for a more interventionist industrial policy.

6.4 Conclusions: the post-war policy environment for industry

We have taken the view in this chapter that the poor performance of British manufacturing industry above all reflects deep-seated institutional problems. There is a conservatism in British economic institutions that is an inheritance of the nineteenth century. In particular, we suggested that the modern capitalist corporation had been slow to emerge in this country, that poor labour relations and the structure of the unions have impeded industrial change, and that the historical continuity of the political system has reinforced this conservatism.

This conservatism in industrial society seems to have grown out of the complacency of early industrial and imperial achievement, though the conservatism of labour also has important roots in the harsh conditions that workers faced in nineteenth-century Britain. The country has enjoyed substantial political continuity compared to the other countries of Europe, and there have been few dramatic occurrences to disturb this complacency. Industry could avoid some of the pressures of foreign competition by taking refuge in colonial markets for much of the twentieth century.

In many ways, World War II reinforced industrial conservatism. There was a strong post-war consensus on a redistributive economic mechanism, with Keynesian policies and a welfare state as the instruments of this. Over time there were increasing arguments about redistribution, expressed in the form of growing tensions in industrial relations. None the less, the basic consensus on full employment and public social welfare programmes lasted until well into the 1970s. In effect, the country tried to live beyond its means and the immediate price it paid was the stop–go cycle of inflation and deflation.

There were several elements that combined to conceal the micro-economic nature of the problems of British manufacturing and the institutional weaknesses underlying these problems. First, the speed of the UK's post-war recovery, compared to its continental neighbours, led to an export boom which made these problems easy to forget until well into the 1950s. Second, and more enduring, the major preoccupation of policy-makers was with distributional questions and macro-economic problems. In this way the malfunctioning of individual parts of the economy was not taken into account. But the failure to address some of the core problems of the economy must also have been in part deliberate: the consensus favouring redistribution came, of course, to reflect special interests — both of labour and of business — in preserving the *status quo*. These interests would have been threatened by a more dynamic economy.

Policy towards industry

The various policies towards industry fall under three sets: macro-economic and industrial relations policies; competition and trade policies; and selective industrial policies.

Macro-economic policy and industrial relations

There has been a considerable stop–go cyclicality in post-war inflation, exchange rate movements, and production costs compared to those of the UK's competitors. Over the long term labour relations have become increasingly confrontational, though the degree of confrontation has varied, depending on the complexion of the government of the day. Macro-economic instability and deteriorating labour relations have helped create adverse expectations in industry and discouraged investment. It is debatable how far industrial relations can be changed by policy — the experience of the present government may throw light on this — but certainly successive governments have placed too little emphasis on the adverse industrial environment created by macro-economic instability.

Competition and trade policies

Of the three policy sets, policies to increase domestic competition through legal measures to break up cartels and monopolies and through improving the access of foreign producers have proven by far the most consistent. This consistency has been achieved in spite of the timidity of British competition policy—compared, say to the United States—precisely because tariff cutting and European economic integration have been working in the same direction. Policy consistency in this area is threatened by the growth of non-tariff barriers and export subsidies since the 1970s.

The consistency of this policy set is not unconnected with the fact that it has not, or not yet, become party-politicized. In many ways it is surprising that, with the interventionist industrial policy that has developed in other areas, the logical connection with trade policy has not been made more thoroughly (except, perhaps, by the Labour left). The international experience of the 1930s still appears to exert its influence on British trade policies, but the bipartisan policy consensus also has other political origins. The consensus against anti-competitive practices was forged as a result of the British experience of cartels in the 1930s. British adherence to free trade, into the 1970s at least, can largely be explained as a political commitment to the United States—the price for the UK's own world-power status after that war and a commitment made in spite of a growing British penchant for protectionism in the twentieth century.

Selective industrial policies

These clearly grew in importance from the 1960s to the early 1980s. Superficially at least, there have been broad guiding themes to such policies and changes in such themes over time. In the 1950s selective policies largely operated in areas where there was an established public role, nuclear power and defence. Selective policies began to infiltrate the private sector from the mid-1960s around the theme of structural policy to create large, flag-bearing firms to compete internationally. With recession in the 1970s the theme turned more squarely to the rescue of ailing firms and sectors and direct income support. Then gradually—starting around the mid-1970s—there was a shift in the weight of policies towards 'positive adjustment', with a greater emphasis on horizontal policies (i.e. cross-sectoral policies aimed at specific bottlenecks such as the supply of high technology or of finance to small firms). By the mid-1980s there had been a marked 'disengagement' from some of the more defensive policies of the 1970s.

This broad sweep of selective industrial policies has its origins more in economic expediency than in ideology, whatever the tenor of the national debate on industrial policy. Moreover, the development of these policies was part of a Western European phenomenon. 'Big is beautiful' also became a policy fashion in France, Germany and Italy at the same time as international competition became more severe as a consequence of European integration and GATT tariff cuts. The crisis reaction to recession in the 1970s was also defensive in much of Western Europe. Finally, disengagement also seems to have been a common reaction of the 1980s to the crisis measures taken in the 1970s.

The value of industrial subsidies can provide a crude measure of the evolution and composition of selective industrial policies (see the Appendix to Ch. 6 of Sharp and Shepherd, forthcoming). The effective subsidy ratio is defined as the percentage ratio of identifiable direct industrial subsidies to manufacturing GDP. A series of ratios has been calculated for regional aid, trade support (largely export interest subsidies), civilian industry and energy R & D, support for nationalized industries, and miscellaneous selective policies (which also include a number of 'high technology' schemes). These are reproduced in Figure 6.1. Several points can be made from this series:

(i) The aggregate effective subsidy ratio for all categories except national-ized industries grew through most of the period, from almost 2 per cent in 1969/70 (the first year for which we have a measure) to over 5 per cent in 1981/2; this growth was common to all categories except R & D subsidies.

(ii) In a clear reversal of the historical trend the aggregate ratio fell by half from 1981/2 to 1984/5; this decline was, again, common to all categories except R & D subsidies, whose ratio actually grew.

(iii) Within these overall trends, there was a clear counter-cyclical pattern to the subsidy which rose significantly in two sub-periods, from 2 per cent in 1979/80 to over 5 per cent in 1981/2; this behaviour was common to all categories except—once more—R & D subsidies (the information on nationalized industries is incomplete).

The above presentation of broad trends risks overstating the degree of consistency in selective industrial policies and may mislead as to their true objectives. A particular source of confusion arises from the difference between policy declarations and policy actions. For instance, measures to promote small business may have become a major declared objective since 1979, but the level of subsidy to small business was far inferior to the level of continuing support for the civilian aerospace industry. Moreover, however tilted the policy declarations might be towards 'positive adjustment', it would seem that a great deal of selective intervention has been defensive, even if defence can be dressed in the guise of 'renewed infant industry' arguments. This is most obviously suggested by the counter-cyclical pattern of subsidy that we observed above. In this sense, selective industrial policies can be seen as an arm of the redistributional policies which, we have argued, characterized post-war Britain.

In addition, selective industrial policies have tended to sow confusion and create adverse expectations in the private sector. Examples of inconsistencies over time in policy action are regional aid, where levels of subsidy have been stepped up and down and aid criteria changed; public ownership; and broad support to manufacturing investment, which changed from grants to tax allowance and then was eliminated. But the adverse expectations created by the ideological debate between the two governing parties has proven far worse. The debate on selective industrial policy has become politicized in the same way as the debate on macro-economic policy and labour rela-tions—quite contrary to the debate on competition and trade policy. This

Figure 6.1.   Ratio of subsidies to manufacturing GDP, 1969–70 to 1984–5 (%)

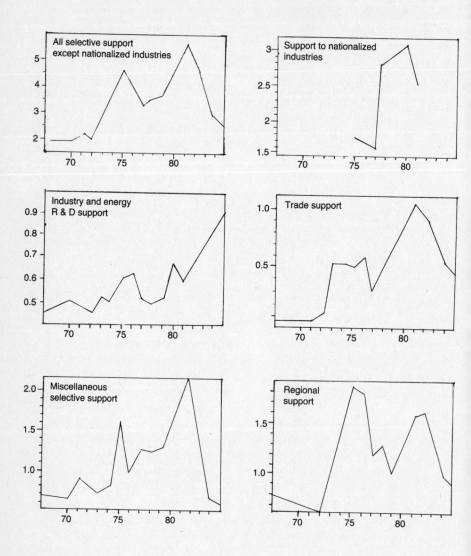

Source: Ratios for 1969/70 to 1981/2 are taken directly from Sharp and Shepherd (forthcoming), Table 35; ratios for 1982/3 to 1984/5 have been estimated by adjusting ratios from Table 36 of *ibid*. (a different but comparable series) to a common basis in 1981/2 for both series; given this, the chart is more useful for indicating directions of change in ratios, rather than absolute levels.

politicization makes constructive dialogue and effective, sustained policy unlikely.

If selective policies have in general created uncertainties, it is not clear that, where they have been applied, there are many large success stories. There have of course been some successes, associated, for instance, with the IRC, the NEB or the work of NEDO. In some cases jobs may have been saved, usually at a large cost, but these policies have not succeeded in pointing many firms or sectors in new directions. On the contrary, candidate sectors for selective intervention such as textiles, steel, shipbuilding and motor cars, have often become long-term 'patients' partially isolated in semi-permanence from the discipline of the market.

In sum, it is unlikely that selective industrial policies have contributed much to improving the environment for industry in Britain. These policies have often been *ad hoc*, defensive and not particularly effective in their specific objectives, while in general they have tended, like macro-economic policy, to destabilize expectations. The curiosity is that, so far at least, competition and trade policies have provided a partial antidote by working in a different direction emphasizing market signals and clear, simple rules. However, the growth of non-tariff import barriers threatens to bring trade policy into line with selective industrial policy.

Even though the present government has done little to dismantle the apparatus of non-tariff protection, it has somewhat succeeded in rationalizing selective industrial policy. More generally, it has tried harder than its predecessor governments to move towards an 'enterprise culture'. But it is not at all clear that a great deal of progress has been made in reversing the 'institutional' habits that Britain has developed since the last century.

Notes

1. In a letter from Eric Midgley.
2. Calculated from Figure 3.1 of Jones (1981). For a more detailed account of British manufacturing performance see Chapter 2 of Sharp and Shepherd (forthcoming).
3. See also Chapter 7, below, by David Marsden, as well as Marsden (forthcoming).
4. On the development of such policies in the 1960s, see Mottershead (1978) and Silberston (1981).
5. See *Financial Times*, 20 March 1986.
6. See *Financial Times*, 31 January 1986, on the electronics union, the EETPU.

References

Aldcroft, D.H. and Richardson, H.W. (1969), *The British Economy 1870–1939*, London and Basingstoke, Macmillan.

Barnett, C. (1975), *The Human Factor and British Industrial Decline: An Historical Perspective*, London, a 'Working Together' Publication.

Budd, A. (1978), *The Politics of Economic Planning*, London, Fontana/Collins.

Calvocoressi, P. (1979), *The British Experience 1945–75*, Harmondsworth, Penguin.

Caves, R.E. (1980), 'Productivity differences among industries', in R.E. Caves and L.B. Krause, eds., *Britain's Economic Performance*, Washington, DC, Brookings Institution.

Chandler, A. (1977), *The Visible Hand*, Cambridge, Mass., Harvard University Press.

Cobham, D. (1984), 'Popular political strategies for the UK economy', *Three Banks Review*, No. 143, September, pp. 17–36.

Crouch, C. (1979), *The Politics of Industrial Relations*, London, Fontana/Collins.

Elbaum, B. and Lazonick, W. eds., (1986), *The Decline of the British Economy*, Oxford, Clarendon Press.

Grant, W. (1982), *The Political Economy of Industrial Policy*, London, Butterworths.

Gribbin, J.D. (1978), *The Post-war Revival of Competition as Industrial Policy*, Government Economic Service Working Paper No. 19, Price Commission, London.

Hannah, L. (1977), *The Rise of the Corporate Economy*, London, Methuen.

Hannah, L. and Kay, J.A. (1977), *Concentration in Modern Industry: Theory, Measurement and the UK Experience*, London and Basingstoke, Macmillan.

Jones, D.T. (1981), 'Industrial Development and Economic Divergence', in M. Hodges and W. Wallace, eds., *Economic Divergence in the European Community*, London, Allen & Unwin.

Kay, J.A., and Silberston, Z.A. (1984), 'The New Industrial Policy—Privatisation and Competition', *Midland Bank Review*, Spring, pp. 8–16.

Marsden, D. (forthcoming), 'Labour and the adjustment process: collective bargaining', in Sharp and Shepherd (forthcoming).

Middlemas, K. (1979), *Politics in Industrial Society: The Experience of the British System since 1911*, London, André Deutsch.

—— (1983), *Industry, Unions and Government: Twenty-One Years of NEDC*, London and Basingstoke, Macmillan.

Mottershead, P. (1978), 'Industrial policy', in F.T. Blackaby, ed., *British Economic Policy 1960–74*, Cambridge, Cambridge University Press.

Pollard, S. (1983), *The Development of the British Economy: 1914–1980*, 3rd edn, London, Edward Arnold.

Prais, S.J. (1976), *The Evolution of the Giant Firm*, Cambridge, Cambridge University Press.

Riddell, P. (1985), *The Thatcher Government*, rev. edn, Oxford, Blackwell.

Roy, A.D. (1982), 'Labour productivity in 1980: an international comparison', *National Institute Economic Review*, August.

Saunders, C. (1978), *Engineering in Britain, West Germany and France: Some Statistical Comparisons*, Sussex European Papers No. 3, Brighton, Sussex European Research Centre.

Sharp, M., and G. Shepherd (forthcoming), *Managing Change in British Industry*, Geneva, ILO.

Shonfield, A. (1965), *Modern Capitalism: The Changing Balance of Public and Private Power*, London, Oxford University Press.

Silberston, A. (1981), 'Industrial policies in Britain 1960–80', in C. Carter, ed., *Industrial Policy and Innovation*, London, Heinemann.

Steel, D. and D. Heald (1985), 'The privatization of public enterprises 1979–83', in P. Jackson, ed., *Implementing Government Policy Initiatives: The Thatcher Administration 1979–1983*, London, Royal Institute of Public Administration.

Vittas, D. (1986), 'Banks' relations with industry: an international survey', *National Westminster Bank Quarterly Review*, February.

Wiener, M.J. (1981), *English Culture and the Decline of the Industrial Spirit, 1850–1980*, Cambridge, Cambridge University Press.

Wilks, S. (1985), 'Conservative industrial policy 1979–83', in P. Jackson, ed., *Implementing Government Policy Initiatives: The Thatcher Administration 1979–1983*, London, Royal Institute of Public Administration.

—— (1986), 'Has the state abandoned industry?', *Parliamentary Affairs*, Vol. 39, No. 1, January, pp. 31–46.

Zysman, J. (1983), *Governments, Markets, and Growth: Financial Systems and the Politics of Industrial Change*, Ithaca and London, Cornell University Press.

7 Collective bargaining and industrial adjustment in Britain, France, Italy and West Germany

David Marsden*

7.1 Introduction

In the 1950s and 1960s, it was possible to discuss policies for economic growth and industrial change without paying much attention to the constraints of collective bargaining. Among the most important reasons for this were the existence in many countries of a considerable reserve of labour in agriculture, the greater weakness of organized labour, and the faster rate of growth then that gave employers more leeway with which to pay for changes in work methods, and gave workers displaced from one industry a much better chance of finding alternative employment in another.

From the late 1960s a number of major changes occurred in labour markets which mean that even if unemployment increases further, a return to the conditions of the earlier years is unlikely. The first has been the drying-up of a number of sources of labour in declining sectors, for example with the decline of agricultural employment, or with the big reduction in the number of women not working, with the consequent tightening of labour markets. Many such workers had little previous experience of industrial and trade-union organization. The second has been the big advances in social legislation and in collective bargaining in the late 1960s and early 1970s in both the field of individual and collective employment rights (e.g. over dismissal and redundancy), and in the range of subjects effectively covered by collective bargaining. These have been only partially revised in the 1980s. Some have argued that these institutional changes have considerably reduced the ability of companies to adjust to changed economic circumstances. A third factor has been the end of a period of 'easy growth' when buoyant profits and the expectation of growth gave companies the wherewithal to pay for the cooperation of their workforce. In the present economic climate

* An earlier version of this paper was presented at the Centre for Labour Economics' Unemployment Seminar at the LSE. I should like to thank members of the seminar for their comments, and also to thank W. Sengenberger, G. Shepherd and J.J. Silvestre for extensive comments. This chapter was originally based on research funded by the OECD, see Marsden (1981a), and I should also like to thank OECD staff who commented on it, especially Oliver Clarks and John Martin.

companies have to deal with a much stronger and more organized workforce which is backed up by recent legislative changes in employment law, but at the same time have much less to put on the bargaining table.

This chapter examines labour market adjustment and the role of collective bargaining, especially as it affects company internal labour markets in the four largest EEC countries, namely Britain, France, Italy and West Germany. The general strategy will be to look at the allocative role of wage structures and the evidence concerning their role in labour market adjustment. Against a background of fairly rigid wage structures (or at least of wage structures which change as much in response to non-market considerations), it will be suggested that much adaptation takes place by quantitative and qualitative changes rather than price changes. A problem then arises if recent changes in job protection legislation and collective agreements inhibit quantitative adjustments as between firms or industries as this will shift the burden of the adjustment to the economy as a whole. The extent to which recent changes inhibit employers' ability to adjust their level and structure of employment is easily exaggerated, partly because of the existence of a form of *de facto* job security for firms' core workforces which is associated with internal labour markets and the development of certain types of skills. Internal labour markets play a central role in qualitative adjustments of the labour force on account of the extent of training, redeployment between jobs, and even of job respecification which takes place within internal labour markets.

Finally, it will be argued that while the structure and organization of unions and employers' associations at the national level has an important influence on the ability of different countries to adopt a concerted approach to industrial adjustment, of equal importance are the arrangements for consultation and collective bargaining at the plant and company level for adjustment within internal labour markets. Thus the emphasis will be shifted from the question of the 'rigidity' or 'flexibility' of labour market institutions in different countries to the type of flexibility that the pattern of labour market organization and each industrial relations system provides.

7.2 Patterns of adjustment

Broadly speaking, two forms of labour force adjustment may be distinguished: mobility between firms or industries moving from less to more productive areas, and adjustment within firms. The latter is particularly important for adjustment to incremental change in technology and product design which requires changes in working practices, and retraining. Industrial relations and the structure of institutional labour markets influence the way in which such questions are handled and the range of options open.

In the four countries, labour mobility has contributed to economic growth in recent years, although, as will be shown later, within manufacturing its contribution to productivity growth has been smaller than might be expected. In France and Italy a greater part of the growth in industrial employment in the 1950s and 1960s has been fed by the decline of the agricultural labour (ECE 1979). This has applied less in West Germany, and even less in Britain. In all four countries the services sector has greatly expanded in the post-war period, fed in particular by the expansion in women's employment.

Within manufacturing, the main branches with declining or stagnant shares of employment have been textiles, clothing, leather, wood and basic metals, while the expanding branches have been in chemicals and engineering industries. On the whole, particularly in the 1970s, with the expansion of sales from Third World producers in the lower-value-added branches, there has been a shift towards industries with higher-value-added and higher-skill contents, the shift being rather slower in Britain than the other three countries. Of major importance then is the efficiency of the labour market in inducing movements of labour towards these higher-value-added industries, and the extent to which this is favoured or impeded by the growth of legislation and collective bargaining from the mid-1960s related to 'job security'.

In the 1960s and 1970s the expanding industries within manufacturing have been fed to a greater extent by labour released from other branches of manufacturing in West Germany and, particularly in Britain, as compared with France and Italy. Because of its greater extent in manufacturing, collective bargaining may have a greater effect upon adjustment through labour mobility in Britain and Germany (see Table 7.1) than in France and Italy, where the decline of the agricultural labour force contributed most to expanding branches within industry in the 1950s and 1960s. In the 1970s this was less marked, and in the future, shifts between branches within manufacturing are likely to play an increasingly important role in these countries also. Thus the influence of collective bargaining on labour mobility between industries is likely to continue.

According to the Economic Commission for Europe (1981, p. 197), structural change in employment in manufacturing industries was greater in all four countries in the 1960s than in the 1970s. In the 1970s the gap between Britain and the other three countries widened markedly, suggesting that employment was not moving as much between industries. While the structure of output in constant prices changed by a similar amount in Britain compared with her neighbours, the smaller change when measured in current prices suggests that Britain was less successful in moving from those branches the price of whose output fell most during the 1970s—a further indicator that Britain has been slower than the other countries in moving into the higher-value-added branches.

Equally important to the labour force adjustments between industries are those which take place within industries and within firms, required for productivity growth. Salter (1969) showed that while the average level of

Table 7.1. Sources of the absolute rise in employment in the labour-'absorbing' branches of manufacturing industry 1958–60 to 1968–70 (%)

	From textiles, clothing and leather	*From other manufacturing branches*	*From outside the manufacturing sector*
United Kingdom	48.6	32.6	18.8
West Germany	32.3	25.6	42.1
France	31.1	4.2	64.4
Italy	4.0	0.9	95.1

Source: ECE 1977, p. 93.

productivity growth was maintained in the pre-war period by the exceptional performance of a few industries, in the post-war period, productivity growth was more evenly spread and occurred also in many of the less prosperous branches. This was confirmed for a later period by Wragg and Robertson (1978). Tight labour markets in the post-war period may have reduced the opportunity for firms to rely on cheap labour as a substitute for new investment. This continued through the 1960s and the 1970s, and in all four countries there were relatively fast rates of productivity growth even in the branches which were reducing employment, hence the relatively small contribution, in statistical terms, of labour mobility to aggregate productivity growth found by the ECE (1977) and by the OECD (1979). A second feature is that the differences between the four countries in productivity growth in manufacturing as a whole broadly reflect differences between the four countries within individual branches. This was most pronounced in Britain, where the ECE found that in the 1960s, in seventeen out of eighteen, and in the 1970s, thirteen out of eighteen manufacturing branches, Britain had the lowest rate of productivity growth (ECE 1979, Table A. 13; 1981, Table 1.1.36). At the other extreme, in the 1960s Italy had the highest average rate of productivity growth, as well as the highest rate in nine out of eighteen branches. Hence, to assess the possible impact of collective bargaining upon adjustments at the 'micro-micro' level which may affect the rate of productivity growth, it is necessary to look at factors affecting many individual branches.

In the past, labour market specialists have concentrated on the ability of the labour market's price mechanism, wage differentials, to attract workers from less productive to more productive areas of employment. It is to this and evidence relating to its effectiveness that we now turn.

7.3 Wage structure and labour market adjustment

Introduction

During the 1960s and 1970s governments and trade unions influenced wage structure in a number of ways, including equal-pay legislation for women in Britain, and incomes and wages policies designed to favour lower-paid and less-skilled groups. In addition, the growth of collective bargaining, particularly in Italy, has given greater scope for non-labour market considerations in the determination of pay structure, and a good deal of concern has been expressed that this may inhibit the role of wage structure in bringing about labour market adjustment.

The significance of such changes depends upon the extent to which the competitive model of labour market adjustment is an adequate reflection of the underlying processes in the labour market. This will be examined in two stages: first, a short discussion of empirical evidence on the role of wage structure in promoting labour mobility, and then a discussion of the main recent changes in industrial and occupational wage structure. In view of the broad stability of wage structures, the clearer the influence of government action and bargaining policies upon these, the less likely it is that wage structures are responding to changing labour market conditions. It will be argued that changes in wage differentials across the labour market play only a limited part in promoting adjustment, and that consequently, other forms of adjustment assume an enhanced role.

Industrial wage structure and adjustment

In theory, in competitive labour markets, wage differentials provide the chief mechanism for adapting labour supply to demand, so that flexibility in the wage structure is important for reallocating labour between firms. In the Marshallian long-run one would expect differences in relative wages between industries to reflect their skill mix and working conditions, so that long-run changes in relative pay would not be correlated with long-run changes in an industry's level of employment. But they might be related in the short-run, and possibly the medium-run.

There are two main situations in which a rise in an industry's demand for labour should lead to an increase in its relative wage. First, where industries are concentrated in a limited number of local labour markets, a short-run increase in their recruitment is likely to attract workers away from other employers, or require an expansion of training facilities, both of which imply an upward-sloping short-run supply curve of labour to those industries. In addition, relative wages should also be more sensitive to increases in an industry's demand for labour in periods of low unemployment. In an economy in which money wages are not easily reduced, relative pay in industries seeking to reduce their workforces may decline in periods of inflation as they give smaller-than-average pay increases or because of longer-term adjustments such as adapting production methods so that a less qualified labour force can be used.

A second reason is that firms with a strong demand for their product are penalized (through loss of market share) if they cannot meet this demand fast enough. As a result, they pay higher wages in order to reduce turnover and to fill vacancies more quickly. Firms with a sluggish demand can afford to fill vacancies more slowly. Hence flexibility in the inter-firm and inter-industry wage structure may promote adjustment either by increasing the supply of labour to a particular firm, or industry, or by enabling vacancies to be filled more quickly (Phelps 1971; Pissarides 1976; Hicks 1955, Appendix).

In practice, many firms prefer not to use relative pay in order to attract additional labour. It is often hard to raise the wage for new recruits without doing likewise for all a firm's employees. Less costly methods such as additional training for current staff, changes in working practices, and special incentives to reduce wastage are commonly used (Thomas and Deaton 1977; Hunter 1978).

Evidence on the role of wages in labour mobility

In the mid-1960s the OECD (1965) carried out a major study of the relationship between wages and labour mobility, including a thorough review of existing studies. Their statistical analysis consisted mostly of correlations between year-to-year changes in relative earnings of individual industries and changes in their share of employment. On the whole, they found little evidence of a relationship between increases in an industry's relative earnings, and increases in its labour force, and in those four cases in which it held at the more aggregated two-digit level, it was greatly diminished or disappeared at the more disaggregated three-digit level. In the British case, Reddaway (1959) suggested that if wages were fixed at the industry level, labout demand would affect the pay of bargaining groups at this (two-digit) level, and consequently wages would be relatively insensitive to localized changes in labour demand. However, it is ironic that this view should have been put forward in a period during which wage bargaining in many industries was being decentralized to the plant and company level.

The OECD's findings are broadly supported by a number of labour market studies in Britain, notably by Mackay *et al*. (1971) and Robinson (1970). These revealed persistent large differences in wage levels for the same occupation between firms on the same local labour market, without any clear tendency for workers to move from the lower- to higher-paid firms, and without any tendency for the dispersion of wage levels to be any smaller in tight than in slack local labour markets. Similar findings were reported for

France by J.J. Silvestre (1973). An alternative approach was adopted by Pissarides (1978) using quarterly data on employment, relative wages, vacancies and unemployment for fourteen sectors in British manufacturing industry. In his model, firms signal their demand for labour to the labour market by changes in relative wages, and by announcing vacancies. He found that relative wages did play a significant role in promoting mobility between industries, and that in the five sectors for which the comparison could be made, a 1 per cent change in relative wages would produce a much larger increase in employment than an equivalent increase in vacancies.

It may be possible to reconcile Pissarides' study with evidence from the earlier studies by examining the quality of the labour mobility underlying changes in employment between branches. Certain occupations, such as maintenance crafts, and certain groups, such as young workers and the unskilled, have distinct wastage patterns as compared with most other groups of workers, many of whom are locked into internal labour markets. Pissarides' study may reflect the mobility of the former categories and so may be quite consistent with the absence of effective labour mobility for the other groups.

Changes in industry differentials and adjustment

Over the last fifteen years the inter-industry wage structure (for manual men workers in about thirty industries in mining, manufacturing and construction) in Britain, France, Italy and West Germany has shown a great deal of stability in the rank order of average earnings levels between industries, although there have been some exceptions, and there have been changes in the spread of earnings levels between industries. For France, Italy and West Germany the rank correlations between average earnings by industry between October 1966 and October 1977 were 0.90, 0.82 and 0.87, respectively, and the averages of the year-on-year rank correlations were 0.97, 0.96 and 0.96, respectively. Data for Britain over the shorter period between 1972 and 1977 reveal a similar overall stability of rank order (Marsden 1980, 1981b).

The small difference between the average of the year-on-year correlations and those between 1966 and 1977 indicate some gradual changes in industry ranking, but overall there has been a great deal of stability despite shifting economic fortunes and employment levels of individual industries. The two most notable changes which occurred in Britain were the decline of the car industry from top of the league in 1972, and the rise of the coal industry from the middle to the top of the league by the middle of the 1970s. Both industries illustrate better the OECD's (1965) 'prosperity thesis' (that workers in industries with expanding markets are better able to bargain for higher pay) than the short-run 'competitive hypothesis' (where changes in relative wages are the main instrument for adjustment).

Figure 7.1.   Industry differentials in the United Kingdom, Germany, France and Italy, October 1966 to October 1983: manual men average gross hourly earnings (unweighted coefficient of variation over about thirty industries in mining, manufacturing and construction)

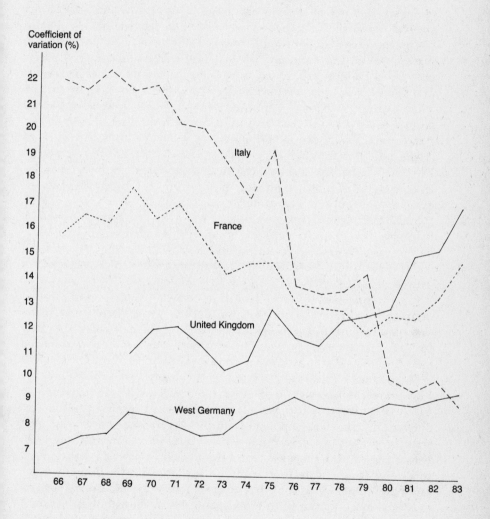

Sources: Eurostat (hourly earnings and hours of work) and Department of Employment October earnings survey (earnings of manual workers).

Changes in the dispersion of pay levels between industries may also have contributed to labour redeployment, an increased dispersion encouraging moves to higher-paid industries. Figure 7.1 summarizes changes in the unweighted coefficient of variation of earnings between industries (again manual men in about thirty industries in mining, manufacturing, and construction). There has been a major compression of industry differentials in France, and even more so in Italy from the late 1960s, until about 1980, when in France they increased again, and in Italy the long decline more or less ceased. There has been some indication of a counter-cyclical pattern in Britain, and in West Germany, where industry differentials appear to have been increasing slowly. One way of assessing how far these changes are part of the adjustment process is to examine some of their causes. Those changes which can be shown to result from government or union policies are, *prima facie*, unlikely to form part of price adjustment mechanism, unless they coincide with labour demand pressures.[1]

The most dramatic changes have taken place in Italy, and these appear to be strongly related to a simplification of wage bargaining at the industry level with the progressive phasing out of regional differentials, and the merging of a number of occupational grades in industry-level agreements by about 1973–4. In the same period there was strong rank-and-file pressure for a reduction of pay inequalities. From 1975, and particularly after 1977, introduction of flat-rate compensation for increases in the cost of living under the reformed 'Scala Mobile' further reduced differentials, especially between unskilled and other workers.

It is puzzling that the inter-industry coefficient of variation of earnings decreased so little in 1978 and 1979, since the system of flat-rate indexation came into full force in 1977. This may be partly explained by the particularly large fall in relative pay (without changing rank order) of the highest paying industries, notably the extraction and refining of oil and natural gas, up to 1976, and their partial recovery in pay in 1978 and 1979.

In France, too, changes in the system of collective bargaining appear to have exerted some, although perhaps rather less, influence upon industry differentials. The most important factor has been changes in the minimum wage, which was raised by 35 per cent as part of its reform after May 1968. Before then it had been linked to changes in the cost of living, and during a period of rising real incomes it had fallen progressively behind average earnings. The new provisions were designed to take account also of increases in general living standards. In 1968 it rose from about half of male manual average earnings to about 60 per cent so that the change had relatively little effect upon differentials, particularly among adult men. The 12 per cent increase introduced in the adjustment of July 1973 had a more pronounced effect. It took the SMIC from 69 and 63 per cent to 87 and 78 per cent, respectively, of the hourly wage rate of unskilled adult men in food and textiles, and in engineering industries. The SMIC was also boosted when the Socialist and Communist government came to power in 1981. The compressive effect has usually been partially offset as other workers have attempted to use the SMIC as a benchmark for other wage increases, although French employers have always strongly opposed moves to use the SMIC's indexation as part of a more general indexation of wage scales. However, as in Italy, the decline in the relative pay (again without much change in rank order) of the highest paid industries also reduced the dispersion between industries and was largely responsible for the small increase in 1982 and 1983. These included oil refining, as in Italy, but also some branches of engineering, which had contributed greatly to French growth in the 1960s. In contrast, France has not shared the Italian moves for greater equality, and the only incomes policy provision to restrict the increases for the higher paid, which came in M. Barre's austerity package in November 1976, applied to only a small proportion of high-paid earners. Anticipating somewhat, it might be argued that the smaller changes in industry differentials in Britain and West Germany owe something to the stronger pay linkages between industries arising from stronger occupational labour markets in these two countries.

Cyclical fluctuations in the spread of inter-industry pay levels, falling in periods of a tight labour market as lower-paid industries have to bid harder to retain their workforces, and to call forth new sources of labour supply, and rising in a slack labour market, might be taken as evidence of the wage structure working to redistribute labour between activities. In both West Germany and Britain, inter-industry differentials appear to decrease during the European-wide boom of the early 1970s, to rise again with the advent of the first oil crisis of 1973, to level off or fall after the recovery and then to rise again as unemployment increased in the early 1980s, especially in Britain. However,the correspondence is not very close (and there appears to be no such pattern in either France or Italy). Moreover, the changes in Britain also coincide with periods of incomes policy, with an increase in industry differentials after the break-down of the incomes policy of the late 1960s; a decrease with the introduction of Heath's policy and an increase with its subsequent break-down; and a new period of decrease with the most effective part of the Labour government's Social Contract, followed by an increase as the favourable provisions for the lower paid were removed. Bigger increases for the lower paid were a feature of incomes policies both of Mr Heath and Mr Wilson during the 1970s.

Thus changes in industry differentials in the four countries over the last fifteen years suggest that changes in the wage structure are not to be explained entirely by changes in government and union policies, and that wage structure between industries may play some role in labour market adjustment. But the extent of this role is limited on account of the overall stability, the rank order of industry pay levels, and the pressure of other forces which create other types of change. This conclusion is consistent with that of the OECD's (1965) study of wages and labour mobility which argued that the evidence for a relationship between changes in relative wages and changes in employment is weak, and thus that the wage structure was only partially effective in bringing about labour market adjustment.

Changes in occupational differentials and adjustment

Economic theory attributes an important role to occupational differentials in determining the supply of labour to different occupations, but statistical evidence shows that these too display long periods of stability despite changes in labour market conditions. Consequently, a number of writers have argued that social custom is a more important determinant of occupational differentials, and changes in social custom or government, union or employer policies are a more important cause of changes in differentials than market forces. The main changes in occupational differentials have been a decline in the relative pay of managerial staff in all four countries, and except in West Germany, a decline in the relative pay of non-manual workers. The decline of the relative pay of managers appears to have started earliest in West Germany, running throughout the 1960s until the late 1970s, but to have started later in France (after some increase through the mid-1960s) and in Italy (apparent in salary rates for middle management after 1968 and in earnings for middle and some higher managers according to data for 1974 and 1977). Routh's (1980) data for Britain show a similar decline in the relative pay of 'managers and administrators' over the period between 1955–6 and 1978. A good deal of this long-term decline in relative pay appears to be associated with an increase in the proportion of workers in these occupations. This is probably not an indication of any failure of the price mechanism so much as the result of a change in the nature of the occupation, as managerial jobs only exist within managerial hierarchies, and in the supply of trained staff for managerial support functions, which have also grown considerably over the period.

By and large, managerial occupations are still mostly outside the scope of collective bargaining. Except when incomes policies seek to restrict pay increases for the higher paid, which has happened in Britain and France, and in Italy (with the suspension of indexation for the higher paid in 1977), employers usually give their managers similar increases to those conceded to other employees in collective bargaining. The main exception to this has been the effect of flat-rate indexation in Italy since the mid-1970s, which according to Italian employers, has had a considerable effect upon pay hierarchies within the firm.

Skill differentials are much more open to the influence of wage-bargaining policies. When they have occurred, changes in skill differentials in the four countries over the last fifteen years appear to be so closely linked to incomes policies, systems of indexation or union wage policies, that it is hard to detect the working of a flexible price mechanism. In a recent study Marsden (1985) using the overall unemployment rate as an indicator of shifts in the relative demand for skilled and unskilled labour—as suggested by Reder (1955) and Oi (1965)—found little systematic relation between changes in skill differentials and changes in unemployment during the 1960s, and into the 1980s, for a number of OECD countries, including those covered in this chapter. The main changes in Britain appear to stem from incomes policy (Brown 1976) and in Italy from union policies (dell'Aringa 1975; Santi 1981), and the working of the Scala Mobile indexation. Skill differentials displayed much less change in France and Germany.

Wage structure and adjustment: conclusions

To summarize so far, it appears that changes in the wage structure play only a limited role in labour market adjustment as is indicated by its long-term stability and the fact that many of the changes were closely related to union and government wage policies. This is not to say that the wage structure has no effect upon firms' employment decisions, or upon the general functioning of the labour market. However, if price adjustments are made difficult because of the variety of institutional factors shaping pay structures, quantity adjustments in the pattern of employment may still take place. Indeed, part of the philosophy of the Swedish 'Solidaristic wage policy' and the West German unions' policy of small inter-industry and small inter-regional differentials, has been that quantity adjustments, through shifts of employment between industries or occupations backed up by an active labour market policy, are to be preferred to price adjustments through changes in relative pay. Provided the quantity adjustments (and the accompanying quality adjustments) can take place, stability of wage structures need not mean that the economy is unable to adapt to a changing environment. However, some of the recent changes in legislation and collective agreements on job security have led some to ask whether these will hinder the quantity adjustments which are doubly necessary if wage structures are fairly unresponsive. It is to these that we now turn.

7.4 Job-security provisions and industrial adjustment

Introduction

From the mid-1960s there have been a number of collective agreements and laws passed relating to redundancies, setting out the provisions for consultation with the employers, and sometimes also with the local employment offices, and for compensation to individual workers. There have also been increased legal rights concerning individual dismissals in a number of countries, and increased employee influence over questions such as training and redeployment within the enterprise. It has often been argued that the improved provision for job security has increased the problems of labour force adjustment within firms and that because job-security rights are not transferable, they discourage workers from seeking better jobs in other firms.

This section reviews recent changes in provisions relating to job security in the four countries, arguing that in most cases the actual provisions are not very generous and the administrative obligations not as restrictive as sometimes supposed. It is then argued that the effect of such provisions upon labour force adjustment also depends upon the extent to which adjustments normally take place within firms' internal labour markets, which themselves necessitate a degree of job security. To some extent there is a trade-off between labour force adjustment through the use of internal and of occupational labour markets. These two strategies in labour management represent alternatives, each with certain advantages and disadvantages depending on the nature of the adjustments that economic circumstances require. There is no suggestion that one form is inherently superior to the other.

Job-security agreements and legislation in the four countries

The most long-standing collective agreements relating to redundancy are to be found in France and Italy originating in the agreements of 1969 in France and 1965 in Italy. These were framework agreements negotiated at the highest level between the national employers' confederations and the main union confederations in each country.[2] In the 1960s a number of rationalization agreements were negotiated in West Germany, but there was no general agreement on redundancies. As in Britain, regulation of minimum conditions for redundancies was left to the legal process with the West German Protection Against Dismissal Act of 1969 (amended 1978) and the British Redundancy Payments Act of 1965 and the subsequent Employment Protection Acts. In Britain, unions have long been reluctant to negotiate general agreements on redundancies, preferring to leave negotiation until the moment of crisis rather than give general recognition to the legitimacy of such measures. Similar sentiments, no doubt, exist among French and Italian unions, but because of the greater importance of internal labour markets, and the consequent reduced transferability of skills, in these two countries (as will be argued below), there has been greater concern with job protection.

Lesser reliance upon occupational labour markets for skilled labour in France and Italy may also help to explain why the network of legal and collective regulation of redundancy is greater and more complex in these two countries. In France, before the 1969 national agreement (and the 1969 agreement in the Lorraine steel industry, which established a model for it), the main provisions concerning redundancies had been that the employer should give the enterprise committee (*comité d'enterprise*) adequate notice of intended reductions in manpower (Delamotte 1969; Reynaud 1969; Camer-lynk and Lyon-Caen 1978). The 1969 agreement, which was supplemented by a further agreement in 1974, and the subsequent legislation of 1973 and 1975 which extended and generalized the agreements, extended consultation. It obliged the employer to establish a *plan social* with the enterprise committee, setting out the plans for the reduction of employment, and using redeployment as far as possible as an alternative to redundancy. If agreement is not reached on the social plan, the question is referred to the local joint employment committee (*comité paritaire d'emploi*, established under the 1969 agreement) or to the relevant union and employers' association. Thus there is implicit pressure to turn consultation into collective bargaining if agreement cannot be reached at an early stage. In addition, major redundancies required authorization from the labour market authorities, which gives the unions a chance to use their political influence. This provision was repealed by the new Chirac government in 1986. Overall, these provisions encourage employers to seek alternatives to large-scale redundancies.

The agreement and subsequent legislation in France came in the aftermath of the 'Events' of May 1968, when the strength of organized labour had greatly increased. In contrast, the framework agreement in Italy, still in force, was negotiated four years before the Hot Autumn, and gave powers of consultation to the 'internal commissions' (*commissione interne*), plant-level consultative bodies set up by collective agreement in the 1950s. During the events of the Hot Autumn much more powerful factory councils emerged (*consigli di fabbrica*) which in many cases have developed full bargaining powers over a wide range of issues. It is therefore hard to assess the full effectiveness of the agreement. In addition, the unions have pressed employers and government to facilitate labour mobility without intervening periods of unemployment. First the bipartite local placement boards, envisaged in the 1970 *Statuto dei Lavoratori*, maintain a list of job candidates. Employers have to notify the boards of all vacancies, and accept the candidate sent along by the board, unless there are good reasons for doing otherwise. Recently, these provisions have been relaxed somewhat (Garonna 1986). In any case, their effectiveness was often undermined by some ingenious ways of hiring new labour.

Secondly, the short-term layoff fund, the Cassa Integrazione Guadagni (CIG), has been used to maintain workers' earnings at 80 to 90 per cent of their level in the event of short-time working and of layoffs, and there is no break in the continuity of employment. Use of the CIG for layoffs is intended to facilitate the redeployment of labour between firms, and to shift to the state the wage costs of firms in sectors declared to be 'in crisis'. In principle, such periods should not last more than twelve months. In a study of four firms in the Turin area, Bulgarelli (1980) illustrates how firms use the CIG in periods of crisis, and the way agreement is reached with the local employment office, the factory council and the unions on use of the CIG and on redeployment and retraining for staff already with the firm. The agreement also includes a restructuring and investment plan. Fiat made extensive use of the CIG in its restructuring in the early 1980s (Becchi and Negrelli 1984).

Although the 1965 agreement provided that compensation for those made redundant should be negotiated at lower levels of bargaining, and that they should continue for a period on full pay, the latter function appears to have been taken over by the CIG. This reduces the burden on employers shedding labour, but the cost of the scheme is partly financed by the high levels of social charges paid by Italian employers (abour 50 per cent of total labour costs). In addition,the enhanced role of the factory council increases the likelihood of negotiation over work reorganization accompanying restructuring.

Neither West Germany nor Britain has economy-wide agreements on job security. The West German rationalization agreements of the 1960s were mainly concerned with redeployment and retraining of staff in adjustments which did not require major changes in the level of employment in the company (Delamotte 1969; Gennard 1979). Redundancy provisions applied only to older workers. After the 1973 oil crisis there followed a new wave of agreements with the emphasis on employment adjustments for economic reasons.

In West Germany there is no general legal provision for redundancies beyond provisions for notice, although the legislation on co-determination, particularly the 1972 Works Constitution Act, gives considerable powers of consultation and co-determination on redundancies, redeployment and retraining of personnel. For redundancies, the employer has to obtain the agreement of the works council on a 'social plan' detailing measures of redeployment, retraining and compensation for those laid off. Although considerable, these powers are perhaps less extensive than those conferred by the French legislation because the works council's negotiations with the employer are subject to a peace obligation.

In Britain a floor of rights on redundancy is provided by the Employment Protection Consolidation Act of 1978, which replaced and extended the provisions of the 1965 Redundancy Payments Act. Since 1980, some of the provisions have been relaxed for small firms. These Acts stipulate certain conditions for notice, consultation and for compensation in the event of redundancies, but contain no pressure towards negotiation as in France and Italy, nor to co-determination as in West Germany. The general pattern in Britain, especially in the private sector, has been to rely upon negotiation at the company level when the need for redundancies is declared. Employers have feared that a general agreement worked out beforehand would merely serve as the floor for new negotiations when the time came. Employers in Britain do not appear to have experienced the difficulties of some of their continental European counterparts in obtaining redundancies. Unions have frequently complained of the eagerness with which many of their members accept redundancy pay rather than press for alternative measures. Indeed, many British employers have used relatively generous redundancy terms as a way of negotiating changes in working practices among those workers who remain (Marsden and Silvestre 1986). This may change if high levels of unemployment persist. Again, the greater reliance upon occupational labour markets in Britain, to be dealt with later, may be a factor both in the acceptance of redundancy and the potentially greater difficulty to obtain adjustment by redeployment of existing staff between jobs within the company.

Factors reducing the effectiveness and cost of job-security measures

The areas in which job protection measures are likely to have an effect upon the ease of adjustment may be considered to be the following:

(i) The advance warning required for workers' representatives, and for individual workers affected, although not that great, might prolong the period over which a company has to pay for sections of its labour force which it no longer needs. However, such periods rarely exceed a few weeks, so that in most cases forward planning could greatly reduce such costs.

(ii) The cost of laying people off, in terms of the legal minima for redundancy payments, in both Britain and France, mostly falls far short of the sums sometimes accorded to long-service workers, for example, in the steel industry. In addition, it is subject to a minimum length of service of two years, which excludes a high proportion of women and a significant proportion of men. On the basis of the legal minima, workers made redundant after ten years would, in France, be entitled to about one month's pay, or if they were over 41, to fifteen weeks' pay. Moreover, a proportion of these amounts is paid out of a special redundancy fund to which all employers contribute. This is confirmed by a survey of redundancy provisions carried out for the British Department of Employment and the Manpower Services Commission in January 1981. This found that, in Britain, only about one-third of all those made redundant (and three-fifths of all those eligible) received any pay over and above their minimum statutory entitlement (Anderson 1981). Thirty-five per cent of all those made redundant received nothing, and only 4 per cent received more than £5,000. The main reason for non-eligibility for redundancy payments was insufficient service, which accounted for two-thirds of those made redundant but who were not eligible for payments.

(iii) The cost may be enhanced by additional compensation conceded in collective agreements. But one has to set against this the ability to obtain consent to manpower reductions. Part of the philosophy of those who drew up the British 1965 Redundancy Payments Act was that financial compensation should ease the burden which fell on individual workers, and thus increase their readiness to cooperate in restructuring.

(iv) In addition to the cost of layoff, the pressure on companies, particularly in France and Italy, to minimize redundancies by redeployment and retraining may increase the cost to individual employers of major adjustments. In all countries, workers who are laid off and then need retraining are helped by public retraining facilities. However, retraining of remaining employees may be costly to the individual company. Again, there are certain compensating advantages, of which the most important are lower selection costs and the lower wastage among longer-service employees.

(v) In most cases, criteria for laying off particular workers have to be agreed with worker representatives, and this may reduce the extent to which the employer may use redundancies to 'shake out' less efficient staff. It is, however, impossible to quantify this cost.

(vi) One of the least discussed costs arises out of the linking of redundancy provisions to length of service. This increases the cost of job changing to individual workers, and may thus reduce labour mobility, although the overall effect clearly depends upon the force of such provisions.

(vii) Intervention by the public authorities in France and Italy may have delayed workforce reductions and provided unions with another means for opposing redundancies. But as the restructuring at Fiat in 1980–1 showed, state involvement and subsidy through the CIG can sometimes ease this process (Becchi and Negrelli 1984). Union interest in such intervention itself may stem from the importance of internal labour markets in these countries.

Job security and the 'trade-off' between reliance upon internal and occupational labour markets

The extent to which all these costs might affect industrial adjustment depends very much on the structure of labour markets. In labour markets resembling those of competitive theory, which rely upon labour mobility between firms as the chief adjustment mechanism, the implications are fairly serious. This is particularly so if wage structures change only very slowly in response to changes in labour demand, and often move in the opposite direction to that required on grounds of economic efficiency.

However, the widespread existence of internal labour markets alters this picture considerably. Internal labour markets are usually based upon skills which are more specific to the requirements of a particular employer, and which are therefore less transferable than apprenticeship-based skills, such as can be found in Britain and West Germany. Because the external market for the former skills is fairly limited, a firm seeking to expand the number of appropriately skilled workers in its labour force has to organize the training, and the development of suitable work experience itself. One of the most economical ways of doing this is to organize job hierarchies or career structures which people may move along as their training or experience increases. It also has the advantage of reducing wastage (a major cost of training). This represents an investment by the firm in its employees, but employees also invest in this process, usually by taking a lower wage rate than could be obtained in alternative employment in the initial stages, and by devoting the period of their lives in which they are most easily trained (or thought by employers to be so) to acquiring a non-transferable skill. This process requires some *de facto* job security. It can be argued that, in many cases, the legislation and the collective agreements on job security only add additional costs to the employer in so far as they increase such *de facto* job security where it already exists, and by extending it to other areas of employment.

The balance between transferable and non-transferable skills can have a profound effect upon patterns of adjustment. Where non-transferable skills are an important component of a worker's package of skills, redeployment and the accompanying retraining within the enterprise are an extension of existing patterns within the firm's internal labour market. On the other hand, workers whose chief skills are transferable have less incentive to accept redeployment and internal retraining because they stand to lose some of the bargaining advantages that arise from having transferable skills. Accepting piecemeal adaptations of their skills to the needs of an individual company, they will have less opportunity to maintain their transferable skills by constant practice. Moreover, career structures, and thus future earnings opportunities, will probably be more limited in the case of piecemeal adaptation than in more fully developed sections of the company's internal labour market. Thus, to some extent, internal labour markets involve different adjustment principles to those of occupational labour markets, and the two forms of adjustment cannot easily be combined. There appears to be a 'trade-off' between external mobility between companies, which involves a greater degree of rigidity of occupational boundaries within the company, and the reduced external mobility, but greater flexibility of occupational boundaries within the firm.

Finally, although in both Britain and West Germany occupational markets are open mostly to skilled rather than semi-skilled workers, their existence greatly restricts upgrading opportunities for the semi-skilled with the result that employers' ability to organize internal labour markets for this category is considerably less than in France or Italy. As a result, British and West German semi-skilled workers also have a smaller investment in, and are less tied to, their current employers than their counterparts in France and Italy. In this respect, occupational markets dominate other forms of labour market organization in British and German industry.

Clearly, the job-security measures discussed above are more likely to have a bad effect upon labour markets where the occupational model is dominant, and less effect where internal labour market structures predominate. The next section will discuss some of the evidence relating to the extent and structure of internal labour markets in the four countries.

7.5 Internal labour markets in Britain, France, Italy and West Germany

The question of whether greater use is made of internal labour markets in one country than another is one of degree. Even within countries there is a good deal of variation between sectors, sections of the workforce within companies, and between segments of the labour market within particular activities. For example, in large public and private organizations with highly developed internal labour markets, there is frequently a section of the labour force, often women, engaged on jobs which offer poor career prospects and have a high rate of turnover. Subcontracting between large firms with highly developed internal labour markets and small ones whose existence is much more precarious, is another example.

Nevertheless, there is evidence of greater reliance upon internal labour markets among manual workers in industry in France and Italy than in either Britain or West Germany. Some statistical evidence, drawn from a recent comparative study of pay structure in Western Europe (Saunders and Marsden 1981) will be discussed first, followed by material from other comparative studies.

Apprenticeships give rise to skills which are readily transferable from one employer to another, and so are associated with occupational labour markets more than internal labour markets. Using data on apprenticeships in Britain for 1974 and the 1973 Eurostat survey of vocational training, Saunders and Marsden (1981) argue that apprenticeships are the most important source of manual skills in West Germany and, despite their present state of crisis, have been, to a slightly lesser extent, in Britain. In contrast, apprenticeships have played a much smaller role in French and Italian industry.[3] As it is unlikely that French and Italian workers, in similar industries to those in Britain and Germany, are any less skilled, and as the difference does not appear to be made up by formal vocational training in schools, it is fair to suppose that the main form of training for skilled labour in France and Italy consists of work experience and training organized by individual employers. This may be similar in technical quality to apprenticeship training, but it is likely to be more closely tailored to the individual employers' requirements, and therefore less transferable than equivalent skills in Britain or West Germany. This receives some support from case studies carried out in French and German manufacturing industries (Maurice, Sellier and Silvestre 1982).

Second, where apprenticeships form the basis of training, one would expect earnings to increase during training and then level off after its completion. Thus earnings would not increase with length of service, there being no corresponding increase in skill. On the other hand, where employers organize their own training, in order to reduce the costs of wastage and to minimize training costs, they are likely to do so on an incremental basis fitting increased skill into a grade structure. In order to retain staff, but also to match individual employment costs to productivity, employers are likely to increase pay with training and experience, and thus with length of service. Hence, as Britain and Germany make greatest use of apprenticeships, one would expect a weaker relationship between earnings and length of service in these countries than in France or Italy, which is in fact the case.

A third piece of evidence can be gleaned from age distributions of workers of different skill grades. In Britain and Germany the age distributions of skilled workers are fairly flat or decline after the 21–24 age range, while in France and Italy they continue to rise until the 35–45 age range. This is consistent with the argument that Britain and Germany rely upon apprenticeships which are completed by workers in their late teens and early twenties, while France and Italy rely much more upon incremental training and upgrading which can continue into a much later range.

A fourth piece of evidence comes from the pattern of inter-industry differentials for workers with different lengths of service. Where incremental training and internal labour markets play the dominant role, one would expect workers to become less easily substitutable one for another as experience, and thus length of service, increases. Hence, the competitive pressures of the labour market would be most keenly felt among short-service workers who have not yet been differentiated by incremental training, and to be weakest among long-service workers. Thus earnings differentials between industries should be smallest for short-service workers and greatest for the high length of service ranges. This is in fact borne out. In France and Italy the unweighted coefficient of variation of average hourly earnings between industries increases with length of service, whereas in Britain and West Germany it does not.

Although each of these pieces of evidence taken individually might appear rather shaky, taken together they provide reasonable evidence that greater reliance is placed upon internal labour markets for manual workers in industry in France and Italy than in Britain and Germany. This contrast also receives support from the company case studies carried out in France and Germany by Maurice, Sellier and Silvestre (1982), and by Maurice, Sorge and Warner (1979), who extend some of the case study material to Britain. Moreover, these studies suggest that a number of these inter-country differences extend to the non-manual workforce in industry.

The greater reliance upon occupational labour markets in industry in Britain and Germany and on internal labour markets in France and Italy, may explain why French and Italian unions have pressed for greater protection from redundancy than their British or German counterparts.

7.6 The regulation of internal labour markets and adjustment

Introduction

Reliance upon internal or upon occupational labour markets may be seen as alternative methods for firms to adjust their labour forces in response to changes in demand or in technology. Redeployment between jobs within the firm often entails a degree of retraining, or at least of developing a new kind of work experience. Because of differences between firms, it is unlikely that the mix of skills thus developed by individual workers will correspond to that required by jobs in other firms on the same local labour market. Although this may pose little problem for workers already established on internal labour markets and whose mix of skills is not easily transferable, the position is very different for workers with transferable skills. For such people, movement to a different type of work or to work which differs significantly will involve the addition of new skills to their existing transferable skill 'portfolio'. The resulting mix may not itself be transferable, in the sense that it improves their earnings opportunities elsewhere, because they do not keep their initial skills in a state of continuous practice. Moreover, workers with transferable skills derive much of their bargaining power from their potential mobility, so it is often not in their interest to accept redeployment if it jeopardizes this transferability. Thus on *a priori* grounds one would expect adjustment to involve a greater degree of inter-firm mobility in Britain and Germany, and a greater degree of intra-firm mobility in France and Italy. Unfortunately, direct tests of this proposition on published data are extremely difficult.

Nevertheless, some evidence for these different patterns of labour force adjustment is provided by the short-term employment functions in manufacturing industry estimated by the ECE (1981) for the period 1960 to 1979. The form of the equation estimated was:

$$\log E_t = a + b \log Q_t + c \log E_{t-1} + d.t$$

where E refers to employment, Q to output, and t to time. The coefficient b on the output term shows the sensitivity of employment to output changes, and the coefficient c on the lagged employment variable shows the speed with which employment is adjusting to output levels (the closer it is to unity, the slower, in aggregate, firms adjust their labour input). The values of the b were higher in West Germany and Britain (0.451 and 0.291, respectively) than in France and Italy (0.197 and 0.103, respectively), indicating greater sensitivity of employment to output changes in West Germany and Britain. Likewise, the values of c were lower in West Germany and Britain (0.284 and 0.345, respectively) than in France and Italy (0.734 and 0.682, respectively), indicating a faster adjustment of employment to output levels in West Germany and Britain. This lends further support to the idea of greater adjustment through occupational labour markets in West Germany and Britain, and through internal labour markets in France and Italy.[4]

Before discussing the impact of internal labour markets upon adjustment, particularly in the sense of qualitative adjustments, as opposed to the price or quantity adjustments discussed so far, it is necessary to examine the role of collective bargaining in the four countries, and the way this affects the working of internal labour markets and plant level adjustments. It will be argued that despite the similarities between Britain and West Germany in the reliance upon apprenticeships as the predominant form of industrial training, there are major differences in their nature between the two countries, and in the way they are regulated through collective bargaining. It will be argued that these have an important effect upon the flexibility of the two systems.

Britain and West Germany

A system of vocational training is concerned with a great deal more than simply communicating skills from one generation of workers to another. Control over training has long been the main way of regulating growth in the supply of a particular skill, and thus the relative wages of skilled workers and their bargaining power relative to other groups and to the employer. Restriction of entry into an occupation was cited by Sidney and Beatrice Webb (1920) as one of the three economic devices open to a union. They also argued that an important feature of 'scientific management' consisted of an attack upon the position of skilled workers, using the simplification of job contents in order to make their jobs more accessible to unskilled and semi-skilled workers, and thus wresting control over the supply of skilled labour from the skilled workers.

The demand for skilled workers is also affected by the greater or lesser ease with which less skilled workers and trainees can be employed as substitutes. Many skilled jobs contain tasks which can be undertaken by other workers, and many can be simplified and divided up in such a way that less training is required of each individual worker. This is one of the reasons for demarcation, or 'who does what' rules.

Both of these methods, of regulation of apprenticeship and of job demarcation, were an integral part of methods of job regulation of craft unionism in nineteenth-century Britain. Despite the great decline of craft unions and their absorption into general unions, they have provided British unions with an organizational model particularly with regard to patterns of job regulation. Even among white-collar workers today there are strong tendencies to organize on occupational rather than industrial lines, and in times of pressure on jobs, to defend occupational boundaries.

To put the point in a rather extreme fashion, one might say that in many areas of British industry skilled jobs are defined in terms of the set of tasks which have been grouped into these jobs rather than in terms of the level of technical competence required to carry them out. This is not to say that skilled workers in Britain are technically any less competent than their counterparts in other countries, but that technical competence, although a necessary condition for undertaking such tasks, does not itself define skilled work. This is defined in terms of sets of tasks which form the 'job territory' of a particular group of workers who have, in terms of collective bargaining rules, the exclusive right to carry out these tasks. In an enterprise, once one group of workers has begun to appropriate a set of tasks out of the total to be performed, it is then natural for other groups to seek to establish a similar form of property right over other sets of tasks. Thus, as new groups organize, they have a strong incentive to adopt similar methods of job regulation. Hence the continued importance of this form of regulation despite the decline of craft unions as such. The effect on economic mechanisms is perhaps best seen in comparison with skilled labour in West Germany.

Craft unionism was never a strong force in the development of the German labour movement. The main reason would appear to be Germany's more rapid transition from artisan to large-scale factory production. British craft unionism grew at a time when few employers were large enough to undertake the organization of their own training provisions, and when the scale of production was increasing slowly enough to permit the established system of vocational training to adapt.

The very rapid changes which took place in Germany placed too great a strain on the traditional methods of apprenticeship, so that many large private employers, such as Krupp, often established their own apprenticeship schools, and as a result acquired a great deal more control over the training process than had employers in Britain. This employer control over training removed the basis on which craft unionism could have developed in Germany. As a result, the apprenticeship system in Germany does not have the same historical links with control over the supply and demand for skilled labour, and is not today associated with a system of job territories. Because skilled workers have not adopted such methods of job regulation, the incentive for other groups to do so has been less. Thus apprenticeship training in West Germany is more closely associated with the acquisition of a defined level of technical competence assessed by examination (in contrast to the usual absence of any passing out test in Britain where time-serving has been the rule).

A second factor lies in the comparative centralization of job regulation in the enterprise in Germany by means of the works councils, which have considerable powers within the enterprise in vocational training career development and deployment of the labour force. Moreover, their influence on the methods used by German unions extends back to their formation in 1919 and their activity during the Weimar Republic. In works councils, interest representation is based more on the concept of membership of the enterprise which defines the electoral constituency than in equivalent institutions in Britain, where it is often based on the job, the work group or the occupation. This does not prevent skilled workers in West Germany from dominating most works councils, but the defence of their interests can be pursued by other means than the protection of 'job property rights'.

The greater centralization of workplace bargaining in the works council, which is made possible by the more abstract basis of job regulation, appears to be more favourable to adapting to incremental technical change. When skilled jobs are defined in terms of a set of tasks as in Britain, relatively small technical changes can disturb job contents and thus the distribution of tasks between different groups. Consequently, the threshold at which such changes trigger off bargaining is much lower than it would be when skill is defined by technical competence. To handle detailed matters of job content, which are most intimately known by workers doing the job, the natural level for negotiation is through shop stewards dealing in a highly decentralized way with supervisors and junior representatives.[5] Such decentralization further complicates adapting to incremental changes, because there is always an incentive for each individual work group to delay its agreement on new working practices, as the last group to agree has a strong bargaining position.

In Germany the more centralized pattern of enterprise negotiations enables the parties to focus more easily on the overall, longer-term objectives of such adjustment, and at the same time leaves much less scope for opportunistic behaviour by individual bargaining groups within the enterprise. The peace obligation binding the works council, and the union's effective exclusion as a collective body, as distinct from its individual members, from the workplace, together reduce the ability of either institution to pursue their members' interests by means of an aggressive bargaining policy. The rules of co-determination are such as to favour the adoption of cooperative bargaining strategies by workers' representatives (see Marsden 1978). The other advantage is that the basis of skill permits greater flexibility in job contents (although there are likely to be limits on this as even skills based on technical competence can become obsolete), and thus leaves management greater freedom in day-to-day labour allocation within the enterprise.

This is supported by Jacobs *et al.*'s (1978) study of technical change in British and German firms which suggested German managers indeed had greater freedom to redeploy their workforce, and that by doing so they had greater opportunities to avoid use of redundancies when faced with the need to restructure. There are nevertheless big variations between companies in both countries, and reactions to the need to restructure vary greatly. This was illustrated by different car firms in West Germany, some of which relied heavily upon layoffs and others more upon internal adjustments (Mendius and Sengenberger 1976; Shutz-Wild 1978).

France and Italy

In both France and Italy, company-based training and experience have traditionally played a more important part in the development of skilled labour, and this is reflected in their job classification systems. Both make extensive use of hierarchical job classification systems within the enterprise. In post-war France the pattern was established by the Parodi system of job classification,[6] which distinguished a number of job levels, defined in terms of the length of time required to learn the necessary skills, and assigned indices to them, expressed as multiples of the rate for the least skilled grade. In essence, such classification systems relate to hierarchically arranged jobs or work posts (*postes de travail*) rather than to individuals and the level of training which they have achieved. In their study of French and German manufacturing establishments, Maurice, Sellier and Silvestre (1982) found that use of diplomas as a criterion for defining job levels is rare in France. Employers have great freedom in the way jobs are classified into these job levels, although in the French engineering industry, when negotiating the reform of the Parodi system, the unions successfully established the principle that workers with the CAP (apprenticeship-level diploma) should not be engaged below a certain level in the classification. Nevertheless, the link between external training and job level remains fairly weak (Eyraud 1978).

In Italian companies also, great reliance is placed upon job classification systems which establish a hierarchy of job levels within the firm. In both countries, but particularly in Italy, workplace bargaining has focused a good deal on classification questions, and on how incremental technical changes affect the level at which certain jobs (and their holders) should be classified. Italian wage statistics reveal a clear 'inflation' of job classifications, especially in the early 1970s, when there was a marked decline in the percentage of workers in the less skilled grades (Saunders and Marsden 1981).

In principle, such job classification systems offer a good deal of flexibility in job contents, and indeed, it can be argued that they originated in the fairly centralized systems of pay bargaining in France and Italy in the early post-war period, associated with weak union organization at the workplace. They offer a different kind of flexibility to the British or West German systems. Because of the relative ease with which such systems can be adapted to relatively small additions of training or experience, employers can shape their labour force fairly continuously in response to changing demands. However, two factors can reduce this.

The first, mentioned earlier, is that such flexibility requires an implicit guarantee of job security for the groups of workers most affected. However, even with occupational labour markets, employers may wish to retain more skilled workers than immediately required, in order to avoid recruitment difficulties in an economic upswing.

Second, the flexibility of such systems depends upon the degree of managerial control that can be exercised over the rules governing job classifications, and it is here that some of the most significant changes have taken place in plant- and company-level industrial relations in France and Italy over the last fifteen years. The two landmarks were, in France, the events of May 1968 and the subsequent social legislation, along, possibly, with the 1981 Auroux reforms, which reinforced plant- and company-level collective bargaining and worker participation; and, in Italy, the Hot Autumn (*Autunno Caldo*) of 1969, when shop stewards and factory councils emerged as a new and major force in workplace bargaining. Subsequent developments and their impact upon the control over the process of adaptation to industrial change differ considerably between the two countries, in part because of the different role of the state in industrial relations. In France, a strong state has played a central role in establishing the key institutions of workplace industrial relations.[7] In contrast, in Italy, where the state has been much weaker, they have been established through collective bargaining. Crozier (1963) has argued that this is a power conflict between management and the work group, in order to gain control over uncertainty in the work environment, and thus to be able to shift the burden of adaptation to the other party. In Crozier's study, seniority rules, concerning access to vacancies arising within the organization, and for dealing with transfers and similar questions, were an important example of rules which the work group managed to gain acceptance by management.

There are clearly good reasons why workers should aim to achieve such rules, as they restrict managerial power, but the reasons why management should concede them is less obvious. One factor may be that management is often short-sighted on manpower questions. A rule conceded (or only half-conceded) in a period of rapid expansion may appear fairly harmless, and even a useful way of binding workers to the company and reducing wastage. Its effects upon labour force flexibility and the price management might have to pay in the future in order to achieve it, do not become apparent until the need to restructure arises. A study by Morel (1979) suggests that such rules could be fairly widespread in France.

A second factor affecting the regulation of internal labour markets in France has been the emergence of the workplace union branches after the 1968 law, the enhancement of their negotiating role by the Auroux reforms and the extension of the powers of the enterprise committee in questions of training and restructuring. However, the union workplace branches have only acquired limited influence within the workplace, nor have they as a rule developed any bargaining powers. Employers have preferred to deal with the enterprise committee, whose functions are described by law and of which the employer is himself a member (in strong contrast to the West German works councils). Despite their growing influence on questions of training and manpower reductions, the powers of the French enterprise committees remain a pale reflection of the powerful West German works councils, leaving French employers a good deal of freedom in the management of their internal labour markets.

The changes in Italy have been very extensive, and by the late 1970s many employers spoke of a 'crisis of the large enterprise' facing on the one hand a very high proportion of the total national tax bill, and on the other the full effect of the social legislation following the Hot Autumn and of greatly strengthened unions in the workplace. The latter developments have probably had a major effect upon the degree of managerial control over internal labour markets. During the first phase of worker militancy between 1968 and about 1974, the classification system came under very heavy pressure from workers who questioned both the reality of the skill differences behind the various job levels (and particularly that between manual and non-manual workers) and the hierarchy of authority of which it was part. In the engineering industry, for example, this resulted in an industry agreement in 1973 to reduce the number of job levels and to unify the pay scales for manual and non-manual workers. This particular agreement also sought automatic promotion after a certain time in a particular grade, and the development of training programmes to make this feasible. It has been suggested that the change of economic climate in the mid-1970s, and the very high costs involved, have limited progress in this direction (Scardillo 1977).

In Italy, unlike West Germany and France, but perhaps more like Britain, the new institutions of worker representation in the enterprise have been established through rank-and-file initiatives and collective bargaining rather than through the law. As a result, there is a great variety of arrangements governing the functions and powers of shop stewards (*delegati*) and the factory councils, and little clarity on the relationship between the different levels of bargaining. Having grown in the early 1970s on the wave of demands for change in factory organization and structures of authority, the factory councils now face a crisis of expectations among their constituents (Symposium in *Quaderni Rassegna Sindacale*, No. 86/7 Sept–Dec. 1980). The recession has left companies unable to meet the more radical demands of the factory councils, for example on the division of labour or on changes in authority patterns, so that bargaining demands have become more piecemeal, reverting to more traditional types of demand on pay and conditions, such as line-speeds. Despite the major defeat of the unions at Fiat in 1980, many of these institutions have retained considerable power in other industries. The councils have also become more institutionalized, and a greater separation has emerged between leading and other delegates. This in itself may make for a greater degree of 'incorporation' as the leading delegates, more isolated from their rank and file, come to look more to the economic constraints upon the enterprises in which they work. However, the factory councils probably remain a permanent feature of workplace industrial relations in Italy, and continue to exercise a major influence over many aspects of the regulation of deployment of labour, job classifications and other aspects of the functioning of internal labour markets.

Labour market segmentation and flexibility

One of the responses by firms to the increased regulation by law or by collective bargaining of relations within the firm has been to decentralize production, notably by subcontracting to smaller, less regulated firms, or by recruiting part of their labour force among weaker and less organized workers. Piore (1980) has argued that such strategies can enable larger, more bureaucratic firms to cope with economic fluctuations without having to lay off the more skilled sections of their labour force, particularly when they possess the non-transferable skills developed on their internal labour markets.

Of the four countries, Italy is the one in which the small-firm sector is probably the most developed, and the most tied into the production needs of the large firms, especially in Northern Italy. Paci (1973) has stressed the importance of these small firms, and of the casual labour market as a whole, to the pattern of Italian development, but has also pointed out that the nature of the secondary sector has changed with each major recession. One factor particularly in Northern Italy, has been the structure of labour costs. Social charges are a much higher proportion of total labour costs than in any of the other three countries. In manufacturing industry in 1975 they represented 28 per cent of total hourly labour costs, compared with 18 per cent in France, 15 per cent in West Germany, and 12 per cent in Britain. Because of their size, their more insecure existence and the political difficulties of taxing them, many of these small firms do not pay social charges, and so can offer attractive rates as subcontractors (Piore 1980).

In the other three countries, evidence of this type of dualism is more limited, and while labour market segmentation may be relevant to the study of the social situation of certain groups of worker, its relation to the problems of adjustment discussed in this chapter and particularly those of bypassing regulation within the firm is more limited, and its relevance perhaps confined to certain branches. For France, Michon (1981) has argued that the emergence of 'non-standard job forms', such as the use of temporary and agency staff, cannot simply be explained by firms' attempts to bypass legal and bargained rules within the firm. They affect too small a proportion of the labour force to provide a viable alternative to layoffs of permanent staff in a recession. Sellier (1979) has also argued that the growth of non-established personnel in many parts of the public sector and in some firms owed more to local management search for a way through over-rigid rules imposed by central management, than to responses to union activity.

Thus, except in Italy, during the 1970s the division of the labour market into non-competing segments does not as yet appear to be a major factor in the adjustment process in the sense discussed in this paper, or a new dimension of flexibility developed in response to rigidities in wage structure and in quantity and quality adjustments in the labour force. This does not prevent it from functioning as a low-wage sector prolonging the existence of low productivity branches or firms. There is evidence for the 1980s that there has been a significant increase in less secure forms of employment for many workers, notably in the areas of part-time, temporary and self-employment. Indeed, the development of such forms has been advocated in Britain by the Engineering Employers Federation (Chronicle, BJIR March 1985). Such changes have led a number of writers to ask whether we are witnessing the emergence of new forms of labour market regulation.

7.7 Conclusions

Assessment of the contribution of these different structures to labour force adjustment in the 1960s and 1970s is complicated by the range of other factors at work. In the best of all worlds, flexibility of work practices and labour mobility is probably to the benefit of all, but in a world of often highly imperfect labour markets the distribution of benefits arising from such flexibility is highly uncertain. Under such conditions it is understandable that workers should seek to increase the stability and predictability of their work by imposing certain rules, and consequently that employers should seek other ways of promoting flexibility in the production systems and in their labour costs.

In principle, greater use of internal labour markets should ease some of the problems of adapting to incremental technical change more than reliance upon occupational labour markets. The latter depend upon the demand for particular skills and thus upon the continued existence of the types of job requiring these skills, while the former make no such demands and should facilitate adaptive training within the enterprise. On the other hand, transferable skills associated with occupational labour markets may reduce the overhead element involved in employing labour and so facilitate adaptation to shifts in the structure of final demand. However, the extent of managerial control and of collective bargaining over job-related issues may alter this balance of advantages.

It is clear that the patterns of labour force adjustment in response to market changes are different in Britain and Germany as compared with France and Italy, and that both models of adaptation are flexible in different ways. The occupational labour market model is likely to be better adapted to short-term changes in the structure of labour demand between firms, enabling firms to operate with a lower overhead element in their labour costs, while the internal labour market model may provide greater ease for qualitative adaptations of the labour force's skills within a particular firm. In view of the importance of productivity growth across all branches, and the small size of the contribution to aggregate productivity growth of shifts of labour between branches, it would appear that, on balance, the internal labour market model has been the more appropriate when faced with the kind of adjustment problem of the last two decades—that of adaptation to incremental changes in technology and products. If the pace of technical change increases, it may not be possible to rely upon marginal increments in training to maintain the required mix of skills. If technical change were to slow down in many branches under the impact of slow or zero growth, then the occupational model may prove to be the more appropriate, enabling labour to move between firms as demand fluctuates in different branches.

Notes

1. The earnings relate to a single week in October and thus may be subject to a number of temporary factors, particularly the timing of major wage agreements, which can distort greatly in a period of rapid inflation.
2. These were the Italian *Accordo interconfederale 5 maggio sui licenziamenti per riduzioni di personale* and the French *Accord interprofessionnel sur la sécurité de l'emploi*.
3. According to Eurostat's survey of labour costs in industry in 1978, among manual workers in production industries, apprentices represented 5.1 per cent in West Germany, 4.2 per cent in the United Kingdom, 1.3 per cent in Italy and 0.4 per cent in France. There is also an informal apprenticeship system in Italian small firms. The continued decline in apprenticeship training in Britain, if it persists, is likely to lead to some skill shortages and a change in skill organization in the future.
4. These observations may appear surprising when contrasted with the ECE's findings on the amount of structural change in employment discussed earlier. This showed that in Britain such change was the lowest in the four countries and had declined most in the 1970s. This probably indicates that in the 1970s the use of occupational labour markets had led to reallocation between firms within the same branch, but that the structure of labour demand as between branches had not changed greatly in the 1970s in Britain as compared with the other countries.
5. The language of such negotiations may well give a false impression of the rigidity of workplace custom. A shop steward's claim that a particular work practice which management wishes to change is customary may often be no more than a way of saying that the price management is offering to pay is not right. 'Custom and practice' is part of the language of a highly decentralized system of bargaining.
6. The Parodi classification system was named after the French Minister of Labour responsible for setting it up in April, 1946 during the period of wage controls after the war. Daubigney (1969) showed that its influence was still strong even in the late 1960s.
7. Notable among these were the legislation on shop stewards in 1936 (*délégués du personnel*), which differ greatly from their counterparts in the other countries, although often dealing with similar types of grievance (Dubois 1965); that on enterprise committees in 1945 (*comités d'entreprise*); and that on union branches in the workplace (*sections syndicales d'enterprise*) in 1968. The Auroux reforms, introduced by the Socialist government in 1981 to strengthen collective bargaining and workplace representation, also represented an initiative by central government.

References

Anderson, A. (1981), 'What provisions do companies make for redundancy?' *Manpower Studies*, No. 3, Autumn, Institute of Manpower Studies, Brighton.

Becchi, A. and Negrelli, S. (1984), 'Personnel planning and industrial relations. Fiat: a case study of Italy's auto industry' in W. Streeck and A. Hoff eds., *Workforce Restructuring, Manpower Management and Industrial Relations in the World Automobile Industry*, Berlin, International Institute of Management.

Brown, W.A. (1976), 'Incomes policy and pay differentials', *Oxford Bulletin of Economics and Statistics*, Vol. 38.

Bulgarelli, A. (1980), *La mobilita difficile*, Rome, Edizioni Politecnico.

Camerlynk, G.H. and Lyon-Caen, G. (1978), *Droit du Travail*, 9th edn. Paris, Dalloz.

Crozier, M. (1963), *Le Phénomène bureaucratique*, Paris, Seuil.

Daubigney, J.P. (1969), 'L'actualité du système Parodi dans les comportements salariaux des entreprises', *Revue Economique*, No. 53, May.

Delamotte, Y. (1969), 'L'Accord interprofessionel sur la sécurité de l'emploi du 10 février 1969', *Droit Social*, Nos. 9–10.

dell'Aringa, C. (1975), 'La struttura delle retribuzioni nel'industria II', *Economia del Lavoro*, Vol. 2, No. 3.

Dubois, P. (1965), *Le Recours ouvrier*, Paris, Armand Collin.

ECE—Economic Commission for Europe (1977), *Structure and Change in European Industry*, New York, United Nations.

——— (1979), *Labour Supply and Migration in Europe 1950–1975 and Prospects*, New York, United Nations.

——— (1981), *Economic Survey of Europe in 1980*, New York, United Nations.

Eyraud, F. (1978), 'La fin des classifications Parodi', *Sociologie du Travail*, No. 3.

Garonna, P. (1986), 'Youth unemployment, labour market deregulation, and union strategies in Italy', *British Journal of Industrial Relations*, Vol. 24, No. 1.

Gennard, J. (1979), *Job Security and Industrial Relations*, Paris, OECD.

Hicks, J.R. (1955), 'The economic foundations of wages policy', *Economic Journal*, Vol. 65, No. 259, September.

Hunter, L. (1978), *Labour Shortages and Manpower Policy*, Manpower Services Commission, London, HMSO.

Jacobs, E., Orwell, S., Patterson, P., and Weltz, F. (1978), *The Approach to Industrial Change in Britain and Germany*, London, Anglo-German Foundation.

Mackay, D.I., Boddy, D., Diack, J.A. and Jones, M. (1971), *Labour Markets under Different Employment Conditions*, London, Allen & Unwin.

Marsden, D.W. (1978), *Industrial Democracy and Industrial Control in West Germany, France, and Great Britain*, Research Paper No. 4, London, Department of Employment.

——— (1980) (with the assistance of L. Redlbacher) (1980) *Study of Changes in the Wage Structure of Manual Workers in Industry in Six Community Countries Since 1966*, Report for the Statistical Office of the European Communities, July, Eurostat C2/80032.

——— (1981a), *Collective Bargaining and Industrial Adjustments*, Paris OECD.

——— (1981b), 'Vive la différence: Pay differentials in Britain, West Germany, France and Italy', *Employment Gazette*, July, London, HMSO.

——— (1985), *Occupational Pay in some Major OECD Countries since 1970*, Paris, OECD.

Marsden, D.W. and Silvestre, J.J. (1986), 'The economic crisis and labour market regulation in France and Great Britain', paper presented to the 1986 conference of the International Working Party on Labour Market Segmentation, Cambridge.

Maurice, M., Sellier, F. and Silvestre, J.J. (1982), *Politique d'éducation et organisation industrielle*, Paris, Presses Universitaires de France.

Maurice, M., Sorge, A. and Warner, M. (1979), 'Societal differences in organising manufacturing units: a comparison of France, West Germany, and Great Britain', *International Institute of Management Working Paper*, IIM/79–15, Berlin.

Mendius, H. and Sengenberger, W. (1976), 'Konjunkturschwankungen und betriebliche Politik: zur Entstehung und Verfestigung von Arbeitsmarktsegmentation', in Mendius *et al*., eds, *Betrieb, Arbeitsmarkt, Qualifikation I*, Frankfurt, Aspekte Verlag.

Michon, F. (1981), 'Dualism and the French labour market: business strategy, nonstandard job forms and secondary jobs', in Wilkinson, F., ed., *The Dynamics of Labour Market Segmentation*, London, Academic Press.

Morel, C. (1979), 'Le droit coutumier social dans l'entreprise', *Droit Social*, No. 7–8, July–August.

Oi, W. (1962), 'Labor as a quasi-fixed factor', *Journal of Political Economy*, Vol. 70, No. 6, December.

OECD—Organization for Economic Cooperation and Development (1965), *Wages and Labour Mobility*, Paris, OECD.

—— (1979), *Economic Outlook*, No. 25, July 1979, Paris

Paci, M. (1973), *Mercato del lavoro e classi sociale in Italia*, Bologna, Il Mulino.

Phelps, E.S., ed. (1971), *Microeconomic Foundations of Employment and Inflation Theory*, London, Macmillan.

Piore, M.J. (1980), 'Economic fluctuation, job security, and labour market duality in Italy, France, and the United States', *Politics and Society*, Vol. 9, No. 4.

Pissarides, C. (1976), *Labour Market Adjustment: Microeconomic Foundations of Short-run Neo-classical and Keynesian Dynamics*, Cambridge, Cambridge University Press.

—— (1978), 'The role of relative wages and excess demand in the sectoral flow of labour', *Review of Economic Studies*, Vol. 45.

Reddaway, B. (1959), 'Wage flexibility and the distribution of labour', *Lloyds Bank Review*, October.

Reder, M. (1955), 'The theory of occupational wage differentials', *American Economic Review*, Vol. 45, No. 5.

Reynaud J-D. (1969), 'La conventional sociale de la sidérurgie lorraine', *Droit Social*, No. 4.

Robinson, D., ed., (1970), *Local Labour Markets and Wage Structures*, Aldershot, Gower.

Routh, G. (1980), *Occupation and Pay in Great Britain, 1906–1979*, London, Macmillan.

Salter, W.E.G. (1969), *Productivity and Technical Change*, Cambridge, Cambridge University Press.

Santi, P. (1981), 'I differenziali retributivi occupazionali nell'industria italiana e la politica sindacale negli anni '70', *Rivista Internazionale di Scienze Sociali*, Vol. 89, No. 4.

Saunders, C.T. and Marsden, D.W. (1981), *Pay Inequalities in the European Community*, Sevenoaks, Butterworths.

Scardillo, P. (1977), *I sindacati e la contratazione collettiva*, Milan, Etas Libri.

Schutz-Wild, R. (1978), *Betriebliche Beschäftigungspolitik in der Krise*, Frankfurt, Campus Verlag.

Sellier, F. (1979), 'Les nouvelles analyses de l'offre de l'emploi', *Revue d'Economie Politique*, No. 1, January–February.

Silvestre, J.J. (1973), *Les Salaires ouvriers dans l'industrie française*, Paris, Bordas.

Thomas, B., and Deaton, D. (1977), *Labour Shortage and Economic Analysis*, Oxford, Blackwell.

Webb, S. and Webb, B. (1920), *Industrial Democracy*, London, Longman.

Wragg, R. and Robertson, J. (1978), *Post-war Trends in Employment, Productivity, Output, Labour Costs and Prices by Industry in the UK*, Research Paper No. 3, June 1978, Department of Employment, London.

8 Policies for a wider world

François Duchêne

Industry is complex, yet most declaratory policies are deceptively simple. This is not to say they are always insignificant. It is relevant that the Germans invoke free trade, the French mercantilism and the British sometimes one, sometimes the other, while the Italians are rarely explicit. Expressions such as these provide useful clues. But to make much sense of them one has to know the unspoken dictionaries behind the short-hand terms. Labels can be particularly misleading on the unwritten rules. To listen to the Four, they are all contrasts. Basic resemblances, such as the Common Market or the nationalism of public procurement, are simply taken for granted. Where contrasts do occur, they often turn out to be rooted in differences of situation or history, such as the opposite predicaments of first- and late-comers to industry. It is at points lying well downstream of Mount Sinai that most industrial practices are situated. This chapter seeks (i) to summarize national policy paths, (ii) to compare them and finally (iii) to attempt some evaluations.

8.1 National policy paths

West Germany

The first spectacular event in Germany's post-war economic history was the monetary reform of 1948 and the sudden burning of controls by Ludwig Erhard. Yet Erhard's daring coup has distracted attention from what was arguably the more important fact that his policy could rely on the kinds of responses which had already secured the rise of German industry from the 1850s onwards.

Despite massive bombing, the war inflicted relatively superficial damage on German plant and even less on the human skills sustaining traditional performance. Events soon showed that German manufacturers retained their old skills as producers and salesmen. There was high initial unemployment, so that, as in the late nineteenth century, wages, though rising rapidly, lagged well behind the increase in productivity (Lewis 1978, p. 122). Profits were good, and government encouraged investment by generous depreciation allowances set against taxes. The Deutsche Mark exchange rate was fixed at a level which, whatever the original intent, rapidly proved undervalued. Allied with strong anti-inflationary policies at home, this reinforced the familiar bent of German industry towards exports. This was ironic as free trade: it served one of the classic ends of mercantilism, to secure a quasi-permanent, positive balance of payments. Thus, if Erhard's Germany reacted against Nazi and Allied economic controls, the underlying feature was continuity with strengths consistent for a century.

Free trade may have helped to exploit the booming export markets of the 1950s and 1960s and to favour good strategic judgements when they began to flag. The steel and textile producers were already devising strategies to guard against decline in the late 1960s, whereas the French and British came to them only when crisis broke in the mid-1970s (Messerlin and Saunders, 1983). Such alertness demands not just flexibility in the face of accomplished fact, but foresight, since investments, reorganization and shifts of manpower take years to accomplish. Not surprisingly, interviews with industries ranging from textiles to telecommunications suggest that German firms are extremely sensitive to markets.

Yet there are difficulties in overemphasizing free trade as the root of German industrial strength. One is that it is only a post-war policy, while the exceptional record on export markets is rooted in a century during most of which Germany was notoriously cartelized and protectionist. In any case, free trade is relatively costless for firms which have often been consistent world leaders. Significantly, wherever that has been cast in doubt, the authorities have shown they will not allow the industrial base to be undermined. Since the banks dominate the capital market and many of the biggest firms, they have also been able to prevent takeover bids from abroad. Free trade, then, is a form of hygiene to keep leaders young, a reinforcing factor rather than an explanation of why they are strong.

In so far as one seeks the sources of that strength in policy, three features seem to stand out. The first is that Germany provides by far the oldest and most powerful system of general support of any of the Four to what one might call the industrial culture. The classic case is the attention paid even before 1850 to scientific and technical education as well as vocational training. Firms themselves finance substantial training—even in recession and though they cannot always retain the workforce—on the grounds that they benefit from a general raising of standards of skill. The unions' commitment has been equally important. The system is superimposed upon a historic guild tradition in which rigorous standards of quality have always been emphasized.

The second feature is a strong preference for general incentives rather than official leadership or favour given to particular sectors or firms. Government incentives to manufacturing are usually tied to functions across the board, such as investment, the encouragement of small and medium enterprises, or the broad regional dispersion of activity. The preference, in the post-war

German tradition, is for leaving responsibility to the firms themselves. Admittedly, credit controls in the 1950s and government aids for R & D (especially the usual trio of nuclear power, aerospace and micro-electronics) after the mid-1960s, have favoured a minority of big enterprises. But R & D has been financed and autonomously undertaken by firms much more than in Britain or France. When the fuss and fury over particular much-publicized projects, such as *le plan calcul*, subside, one tends to find, as in the semiconductor industry, that Germany's R & D has been carried out in greater breadth and depth and with more attention to commercial criteria than in her sister countries (Dosi 1983, pp. 226–7).

The third feature since the war, at least till recently, has been a high degree of consensus on production goals coming prior to—but not necessarily higher than—those of distribution. Before Hitler, 'the conventional wisdom was that the German workers' movement, with a high proportion of Marxist leaders, was more militant than the British workers' movement' (Lewis 1978, p. 127). Except for the aftermath of the Erhard experiment, between 1974 and 1977, and perhaps since 1984, management and labour have sought a consensus on production, new technology and even anti-inflationary macro-economic policies. They have narrowed their differences down to the way in which incomes are distributed within that frame. The implied condition has been the massive rise in the standard of living. Especially since the establishment of full employment around 1960, Germany has become a high-wage, high social security economy with an extensive range of fringe benefits.

It has sometimes been suggested that Germany also has a superior policy-making, even planning, environment in the industrial primacy of the banks, which control crucial shares in half the hundred biggest companies (see Chapter 3). This, it has been argued, ensures the main creditors of industry have the intimate acquaintance with its needs essential to long-term development. Connections through the banks make it easier for firms to cooperate: Germany is the historic home of both industrial banks and cartels. Control by the banks also facilitates vertical integration: it is often easier to reorganize activities by shifting them downstream or sideways within the firm than by cutting capacity. Finally, the banks are more commercial in outlook than government and less likely to throw good money after bad results, not least in reshaping firms in trouble (which they have often done).

This makes a plausible thesis, and could well be the case. Unfortunately, our research has failed to find much support for active leadership by the banks. In fact, it has increasingly been argued in Germany that they have become an obstacle to competition (Bruce 1987). Evidence for their strategic as distinct from formal control of industry, remains elusive.

None the less, the general effect of the post-war German system has been of a long-standing, cooperative effort between the various parties to policy and industry of impressive depth, breadth and relevance. The complement of this efficient corporatism has been a determination to keep the civil service as far as possible out of the business of management. Germany has profited unintentionally from her failure to acquire a major colonial empire: her civil service does not overshadow industry in attracting the brightest talents.

All the same, it would be hard to show that Germany's relatively successful industrial record has been due to official policy: an association with success is not by itself proof of cause and effect. There are signs that some of the presumed advantages of German industrial policy rest on traditional patterns of behaviour inherited from the nineteenth century which have proved well adapted to current conditions. Where they have not been so strong, one can make a case for a certain erosion of Germany's advantages.

The Germans have proved less effective in areas where the challenges have been really new. Their record in micro-electronics, while good by European standards, is not distinguished by those of Japan. The increasing importance in world trade of sectors, like telecommunications, where public purchasing is crucial at home, has sometimes shown giants like Siemens at less than their reputed best. Germany lost a large world market share in manufactures between 1973 and 1984 (see Table 2.3, p. 24).

There are also signs that social values possibly at the root of manufacturing may be changing. The steep increase in university intakes, especially since the early 1960s, has seemed to make vocational training less attractive. The tendency to seek first-class citizenship and self-determination through the university system rather than accept hierarchical subordination in worker-training streams of education seems to be spreading. It could be linked with the appearance for the first time, since 1973, and despite high unemployment, of shortages of labour skills.

German manufacturing remains immensely powerful. But there are signs that it is relatively not quite as strong as it was. The decline in population, which could slowly limit the potential of the domestic market, constitutes an added handicap to overcome. In some ways, Germany could face, *vis-à-vis* Japan, problems equivalent to those of Britain against Germany herself and the United States a century ago. It could prove crucial for the whole of Western Europe that she adjust to the changes better than Britain after 1870.

France

In 1940 France plumbed a nadir of weakness *vis-à-vis* Germany. French industrial policy since the war has been at the heart of a pervasive effort to regain strength. At the liberation, the old family businesses were discredited, partly because of pre-war lack of enterprise, partly for collaboration with the Germans. Though family business still accounts for a large proportion of the largest firms, the state stepped massively into the breach after 1945. Ever since, when it has discerned an urgent industrial priority, the political leadership has tended to intervene. France has been as explicit as Germany in her industrial policy, but at the opposite end of the range, as the West European model of *dirigisme*.

Upon liberation, only the state had the resources to reconstruct the basic industries. Before 1914, budget spending on industry was negligible. Between the wars it hovered around less than 0.5 per cent of GDP. Since 1945 it has averaged nearly 3 per cent, peaking in 1947 at 7 per cent, of GDP (Delorme and André 1983, p. 207). Moreover, there was such a shortage of capital in the early years that the state's control of credit was virtually absolute. This is tantamount to a change of system, with power shifting from family business to technocratic officials.

The brightest of the young, chosen in mandarin-style by national exams for the upper echelons of the civil service, later graduate in significant numbers and in quite early middle life into industrial management. This creates a considerable congruence of outlook between the state and business (Ehrmann 1957, p. 269; Marceau 1977, p. 150). The post-war change was not sociological since the new technocrats tended to come from the old bourgeoisie. But for the first time government behaved as if manufacturing was central to the future of state and society.

It has been argued by a participant in French industrial policy that its main preoccupation has been with security (Stoffaës 1986, p. 44). This would explain why in the 1940s the Monnet Plan, the attempt to annex the Saar to balance the Ruhr and finally the Schuman Plan, all stressed coal and steel, then still considered as the sinews of power (see Chapter 4). In the 1950s the armaments, aircraft, oil prospection and nuclear industries were all launched, or relaunched. In the 1960s de Gaulle's eye was drawn to data processing when the United States withheld IBM technology from the French nuclear deterrent. In the 1970s came two vast programmes: for nuclear power to gain energy independence and for telecommunications as a key to the micro-electronic future. France has stressed the power aspects of industrial policy more explicitly than any other of the Four.

The most obvious symbol of state enterprise has been the three phases of nationalization of firms—immediately after the war, in the 1960s and again, by the Socialists in 1981–3—so that by the latter date about 30 per cent of French manufacturing, in terms of value added, was publicly owned. Yet the hold of the state depends more on control of markets than on ownership. As a result, its practical influence has been greatest either through exploiting public purchasing to promote strategic goals, or when firms or whole branches (like steel in the 1970s) faced major crises and turned to it for rescue. It has used these opportunities broadly to build up 'national champions' as monopolists at home in order to give them the scale regarded as the passport to competition on world markets.

The technocratic impression all this gives is reinforced by the lack, in ordinary times, of obvious countervailing centres of power. There has been virtually no Green opposition, of the German type, to what is relatively the largest nuclear power programme in the world. Despite brief exceptions like 1968, the divided labour unions have rarely raised a decisive voice.

Yet, arguably, the most powerful shaping influence on French industrial strategies since the war has been not state intervention as such but the underlying drive for growth (to which the state has certainly contributed). It was realized in 1945 that industry's pre-war failure was linked to 'defeatist' and 'Malthusian' attitudes. Once growth got under way during the economic 'miracle' of the 1950s, and imports rose, winning export markets became imperative. Exports required efficiency, and efficiency competition. The last Fourth Republic governments in 1956–8 pushed through the Common Market, despite the enormous break with tradition they represented and a widespread fear of German industry; while General de Gaulle, who could have rejected European integration on coming to power, confirmed the choice. Significantly, in reaction to industry's traditional weakness compared with Germany, there was widespread agreement among leaders otherwise opposed on many issues that the country's revival demanded a more competitive economy.

Since Germany was the strongest, or second strongest, industrial exporter at the time, accepting German competition in the Common Market in effect meant accepting competition in general. Starting from the gradual introduction of the European customs union in the 1960s, there was a cumulative opening up of the French economy. Moreover, during most of the booming 1960s, when the Common Market was being progressively opened, French policy was relatively 'German' in that it emphasized broad incentives to mergers, investment, R & D and exports (Balassa 1986, pp. 98–9). By 1983 France was proportionately four times more dependent on imports than in 1950 (see Table 2.5, p. 30).

Once growth began to open markets and the 'technology gap' impinged on French perceptions in the mid-1960s, the priority turned to exports to the world. Again, French officialdom preferred to set priorities and goals rather than delegate responsibility to business and trust to competition. The height of this approach was reached with the Giscard–Barre strategy of conquering larger world market shares. This consisted in subsidizing a few big firms' exports of massive turn-key projects to middle-income countries, such as the members of OPEC or Comecon (Aujac 1986, pp. 32–4). Markets such as these suited a political approach in which the President himself often acted as a glorified travelling salesman.

The method worked in the boom years of the 1960s, and even in the 1970s when middle-income countries provided buoyant markets. French growth slightly exceeded German in both decades. France steadily broadened the initially narrow range of her industries and created new ones mostly in electrical and electronic engineering, which were presumed to matter most for the future. She succeeded beyond the wildest dreams of any immediate post-war optimist, and became for the first time a highly industrialized society. From 1970 to 1984 she even made up for declining net motor car exports by a substantial shift to capital goods (Freyche 1986, pp. 84–5).

But since the second and deeper recession, triggered by the energy crisis of 1979–80, the shortcomings of the traditional policies have shown up more and more. The decline of purchasing power in the middle-income markets has exposed the weakness of France in industrial ones and led to a sharp fall in her share of world manufacturing exports. The decline in competitiveness, which goes back to 1975 (Boyer 1986, p. 96; Barou and Keizer 1984, p. 288), has reduced the country's room for growth. The failure of the Socialist experiment in expansion in 1981–2 led to a questioning of the whole post-war approach. Since the later Socialist years, there has been a quite new emphasis on the need to provide more environmental support to industry and not to interfere with the operational initiative of the firm. More surprisingly still, these ideas have spread across the political spectrum.

Looking back, this evolution seems consistent and natural. French industrial policy was state led at first, partly because of the perception of the weakness of French business. Yet, in an increasingly competitive climate, state-promoted enterprise has ultimately proved a constraint on growth because it places output first and markets second. France seems to have reached the end of the road of protected growth. Gradually, this conclusion, though going against the grain, has gained more and more ground in the establishment.

From this point of view, the crisis of the 1980s, however serious, could be seen as a sign of growing maturity rather than of failure. Imitative techniques which are adequate enough in catching up are no longer valid once producers come in sight of the leaders and must, like them, cope with uncertainty. The need for innovation and quality takes over and demands a more open approach.

From another point of view, though, this means France still has major weaknesses. Even in areas of concentrated effort like nuclear reactors and telecommunications, her exports do not compare with Germany's. She tends to be strongest in industries where the foreign competition is itself highly dependent on public purchasing: armaments and aerospace. In other branches, her 'national champions' barely belong to the dominant world oligopolies. She lacks the breadth, depth and solidity of the German industrial 'fabric'. She is now either the 'strongest of the weak or the weakest of the strong' in Europe, a long way behind Germany (Bellon and Chevalier 1983, p. 20; see also Table 2.2, p. 23).

France, then, has probably reached a cross-roads in industrial policy and performance. She could now mature as a producer and graduate into the top league, at least by Europe's standards. If so, she would in effect join the Deutsche Mark Zone, or extended German economy, and strengthen the European core. Or she may begin to face British-style problems, with the downward cycle of constriction that makes recovery doubly hard. Though the French political consensus proclaims the need to diminish state supervision, really to divest technocratic networks of the authority they have savoured so long would be the most radical change of all.

Italy

Italy after the war displayed some characteristics superficially like those of France and others of Germany, but in an environment uniquely her own. She was even weaker and poorer than France; she had a powerful Communist Party, high post-war inflation and semi-revolutionary conditions; she too was consciously an industrial follower and for a time instituted far-reaching industrial policies. However, she had, in the fascist era, experienced autarchic controls associated with dictatorship, shortages and corruption. The economists who filled the policy vacuum tended to favour free markets as the economic face of political freedom, rather in the Erhard manner.

However, whatever parallels there may have been with others they were bound to be limited from the beginning by the Italian environment. This was rooted in an economic backwardness typical of the Mediterranean at the time. The dominant symptom of it was dualism. Dualism applied even in the North, where industry had 'taken off', mainly in the Turin–Genoa–Milan triangle at the turn of the century (Lenti 1973, p. 13). It contrasted still more sharply the relatively developed North from the pre-industrial South.

The dualism within the North has been primarily between firms of different sizes. Italy is industrially both concentrated and decentralized. It has a minority of large private firms which are virtually monopolists in their fields and four state holding companies, the biggest, IRI, inherited from the fascist period. Between them, these control a high proportion of the country's industrial assets. On the other hand, there was, and is, a relatively far larger mass of small and medium firms than in any of the other three countries (see Chapter 2). This polarization between extremes has strongly influenced industrial development.

The dualism of North and South has been if anything more important. Its most obvious result has been the need to divert investment to the South. Unfortunately, the returns on the heavy investments in the Mezzogiorno legally imposed in 1957 on the 'para-statal' firms were relatively disappointing. Most large plants built under this regime failed to generate downstream activities. The gap in productivity per head between North and South narrowed only to a small extent (see Chapter 5). This sluggish response may well have been rooted in resistance by local power structures to new activities which might undermine traditional hierarchies and privileges (Wade 1982). And yet, while plans have fallen short of expectations, industrialization has crept down the Adriatic coast in an unplanned way, so that today it is no longer possible (if it ever was) to speak of the South as a single problem area.

Two other consequences of North–South dualism may have been still more pervasive. The first is that the South is more than proportionately present in the *classa politica* and civil service. This has given the state a distinctly pre-industrial personality, with an administration signally weak for a country of Italy's level of development. Decisions are influenced by relations between political patrons and their favoured electoral or corporate clients, with administration often a source of 'jobs for the boys'. The resulting styles of accommodation and compromise between groups blur the programmatic approaches and predictable behaviour congenial to industrial strategies and easily degenerate into abuse of patronage.

Weakness in the state has had considerable influence on industrial policy and practice. For instance, the widespread evasion of taxes and official controls by small business has meant that an almost Victorian sector of untramelled free enterprise developed from the 1950s onwards. A large sector of small and medium firms, some deliberately too small to enter the legal net of social security costs, has gradually spread across much of the North and Centre. In places such as Prato, the old wool town near Florence, miracles of decentralized cooperation have produced major export industries in supposedly unpromising branches like textiles. Italy provides perhaps the most spontaneous instance of entrepreneurial vitality in Europe since the war.

This has undoubtedly added flexibility to the Italian economy, promoted exports and increased employment. But costs reminiscent of the nineteenth rather than twentieth century have also had to be paid. Low wages and lack both of welfare for workers and of job security are obvious instances. There are also industrial disadvantages. Small-scale manufacturing tends to operate best in sectors some of which may add high value (machine tools, designer clothes) but most of which do not. This helps to explain the relatively heavy weight of low-value-added sectors in Italy's manufacturing (see Ch. 2, fn. 2).

Second, the South provided a deep reservoir of landless labourers who migrated to the cities of the North during the two-and-a-half decades of the boom. After the war, they undermined the bargaining power of the trades unions. It was weakened anyway by divisions between Communists, Christians and Socialists and by fascism's long interruption of trade-union traditions. Management, therefore, with roots in the fascist period, was highly paternalistic. As rapid industrialization drew the migrants into the Northern cities, often in slum conditions, serious problems began to pile up. In the 1960s, with full employment virtually achieved, the Southerners filled the rank-and-file of an increasingly militant labour movement.

As one might expect, these special conditions have strongly affected Italy's industrial policies and performance. In the first fifteen years after the war, the patterns of policy were superficially reminiscent of France. First, both countries were protectionist well into the 1950s, though there was never any fear, as with France in 1954–6, that Italy might jib at a Common Market. Second, the state built up basic industries and infrastructures—if anything more widely than any of the other three countries—through the giant public holding companies and 'para-statal' agencies, especially IRI and ENI. The investments were deliberately designed to forestall potential bottlenecks to growth in energy, steel, fertilizers and later in basic chemicals (see Chapter 5). Third, policies which at first were almost speculative were legitimized by the economic 'miracle'. This was greater than in France, almost as intense as the German, and more 'miraculous' than either because of the much lower starting-point.

Yet there were major differences with France. One was a much less state-orientated outlook. The Italians curtailed their nuclear energy programme in 1961. They made no objection to the acquisition of Olivetti's computer operations in 1964 by an American multinational. There were no Italian *grands projets* in the 1960s when the 'technology gap' was fashionable.

Further, once full employment was attained in the early 1960s, Italy's industrial policies gradually lost coherence. Possibly because of unfamiliarity with industrial constraints, and certainly as a result of the social conditions around the factories, the radicalism of the Hot Autumn of 1969 and the last boom years fell on exceptionally receptive ground. The contradiction between aspirations and context turned to crisis almost immediately when radicalism fell foul of recession after 1973.

Instinctively, the 'weak' state rode the resulting crisis rather than tackled it. Large enterprises, public and private, were exploited as sources of unproductive jobs, disguised social security and electoral support. Public-sector firms in particular ran into spectacular loss. Inflation rose annually in double figures for twelve years running from 1973 to 1984. As the Communist Party, in response to electoral pressures, moved slowly towards the centre, Trotskyist and Anarchist groups appeared on its revolutionary flank. Their militancy and lack of parliamentary expectations soon degenerated into a campaign of terror, extending to within the factories. The resulting 'crisis of large organizations' almost brought the public-sector firms and Fiat to their knees at the end of the 1970s.

The reaction that duly followed was symbolized by the 'March of 40,000' Fiat workers in Turin on 14 October 1980 demanding work not violence. Subsidies to industry rose to new heights (Table 5.1)—like the budget deficit and unemployment—but to a significant extent to allow the state to take over the financial costs of redundancies. It began to pursue more deliberate industrial policies. Most were general. As elsewhere in Europe, stress was laid on more competition, markets and balanced accounts. From 1983 inflation fell, while industrial productivity, profits and output all rose. Though fluctuating in international comparisons because of unstable exchange rates, Italian value added per worker in manufacturing began to overtake Britain's. Italian groups began to establish multinational positions by buying up firms elsewhere in Europe. The state paid more (protectionist) attention to sectoral policy. Public procurement was used to build up telecommunications. Fiat's national monopoly in cars was completed by frustrating Ford's attempts to buy up Lancia (1979) and Alfa Romeo (1986). From 1973 to

1984 exports, especially of consumer goods, rose notably faster, and output a little faster, than in the other three countries, and in contrast to them, world export shares were maintained. On balance, Italy seemed to have worked through to a more secure industrial balance.

If performance had been worse, it would have been easy to tot up Italy's industrial weaknesses into an 'English disease'. Yet her problems have always seemed to be growing pains rather than those of the sclerosis of older industrial regions. Italy profited more from high growth and competition in the Common Market in the boom years than did Britain. Entrepreneurship carries more prestige and management has proved resilient. The small-firm sector has been particularly quick to adjust to markets. The capacity for export-minded self-regulation of sectors like machine tools belies the national reputation for individualism. Performance has defied apparently crippling structural weaknesses for four decades with less than the general European loss of impetus.

As with France, though in another way, the picture is very mixed. Italy has rarely tried to foster 'national champions'. She has not displayed state-led ambitions to compete in 'hi-tech' world oligopolies. She has few firms on that scale. She is well represented in sectors where value added is rather low, EC protection is rather high (textiles and clothing) and sales are potentially vulnerable to competition from NICs. Her environmental support for industry, such as education, is weak. These are massive limitations. On the other hand, if the scale and focus of the French effort are lacking, the commercial performance seems more convincing. It involves more organic growth from below—more market awareness—and is less imposed from the top. The Italians have consistently done better than expected, which cannot always be said of the French, nor even of the Germans. At the turn of the century, Germany's most vital industrial and commercial partner might turn out to be a congenitally pragmatic Italy rather than an ambitious France. On the other hand, as Pippo Ranci points out (see Chapter 5), long-term progress could well depend on the raw face of capitalism being less naked than in the 1950s.

Britain

Of all the Four, Britain has had the most trouble in formulating and pursuing industrial policies. An element in this was a failure of perception after the war. The Germans, French and Italians all had fairly realistic views of their practical options. The British, in contrast, long seemed unwilling to recognize their changed context and limitations.

At first this was reasonable. The British ended the war as victors and the contrast with the ruins on the Continent made them seem a force in their own right. In 1959 Britain was still the biggest producer of the Four (OEEC 1960, p. 4). There was a sense of self-reliance in memories of Britain's leading role in pre-war trade, taken as a norm to which the country should return. Britain, it was felt, had only failed between the wars through stubbornly wrong-headed deflation. Now, expansionary macro-economic policies would stimulate manufactures in growth sectors. Nationalization would ensure investment in the basic industries.

Recurrent export crises, beginning in 1947, soon showed this did not suffice. Though all sorts of remedies were subsequently proposed (incomes policies to restrain costs; devaluations of the pound to improve export incentives; membership of the Common Market as a draught of competition; and so on), none halted the relative slide of British manufacturing. In 1983, for the first time since the Industrial Revolution, Britain imported more manufactures than she sold (see Chapter 6).

Yet the dominant preoccupation with macro-economic policies did not fade. At first sight this might seem to rest on the prestige of Keynesian economics. In fact, the political balance confirmed in 1945 would have made it difficult to stress supply rather than demand policies even if the need had been perceived; and this political balance in effect prevented a perception of the need from emerging. Both sides of industry were involved.

Employers were used to protection, at home and abroad. Imperial Preference tended to perpetuate a vertical (i.e. non-competitive) division of labour between colonial suppliers of raw materials and British suppliers of manufacturers. This was prolonged by the British failure to enter the European Community in the 1950s and the forced restriction to EFTA with which British industry also competed relatively little. Domestically, between 50 and 60 per cent of manufactured output seems to have been subject to cartel regulations during the 1950s. When legislation on restrictive practices eroded cartels in the 1960s, a wave of mergers increased the size of firms without changing average size of plant. Mergers thus seem to have been designed to recreate the old protection in a new form. It was only with entry into the European Community in 1973 that competition began to bite. Unfortunately, 1973 was precisely the year that world recession broke out.

The trade unions, for their part, were traumatized by the unemployment of the 1930s coming as a climax to endemic tensions at least as old as the 1870s.[1] They were determined after the war to achieve full employment and 'fair shares'—the first reinforcing the second by improving labour's bargaining power. This set of priorities could, and did, downgrade the importance given to raising productivity, which might in the short-term subordinate wages to profits and jobs to machines. The willingness of the German trade unions in the 1950s to do just that was widely regarded as 'reactionary' in Britain.

Accordingly, the post-war political consensus was reached around a model of distributive justice which assumed that production would deliver the goods. But when production failed to deliver the goods, priorities proved hard to shift. Class conflicts having been tamed in restrictive practices and low productivity, disturbing the compromise was as likely to prise open old divisions as to generate a consensus on industrial policy.

However, by the early 1960s it became impossible to ignore Britain's relatively poor performance. A slowly maturing crisis began. In the next twenty years Britain responded in parallel ways to the same external stimuli as her European neighbours—the 'technology gap' in the 1960s, 'restructuring' in the 1970s and 'innovation' in the 1980s—but always with the special twist of cumulative decline by comparison with competitors.

Until 1979, except for the first two years of the Heath government, the accent was on intervention. Initially, under Wilson, there was a rather French ambition to industrial policy. True, it was justified, defensively, by the threat of 'industrial helotry' at the hands of US 'multinationals'. But it was energetically promoted. Mergers were to produce firms large enough to enjoy American economies of scale and act as national champions on world markets. Big R & D projects were to 'leap-frog' the present generation of technology to the next and seize the commercial initiative. Large projects, like Concorde, were launched. However, if the ambition was French, the results were generally less encouraging. The reason seemed to be that though the decisive parties to the game in each country resembled one another, they were all in limited but crucial respects different.

Britain entered the Common Market only in 1973, when recession began. Unlike France, she missed both the earlier heady growth and the competition. That was a major handicap in itself. Then the two states varied. The French set ambitious goals through public procurement and did not always pay too much attention to finance. The British, with empire not disaster behind them and less sense of urgency, were more prudent and closer to the balance sheets. Nor were the firms the same. Initially, the British were much larger and more prestigious. On several occasions they overreached themselves by assuming they were still world oligopolists when they had ceased to be. Last but not least, there was nothing comparable in France to British labour's resistance to technological change.

The politics behind this problem cannot be ignored. There was an implicit and in the end explicit struggle in Britain between opposing political conceptions of where society should go beyond the post-war settlement. When it became obvious, after the disillusions of the Wilson era, around 1970, that consensus approaches were not succeeding, the rival models of society lurking in the background came into the open to battle for political supremacy. Governments backed by electoral trends, wanted to make the mixed, or social-democratic, economy work more effectively. But in key parts of industry the initiative was held, as in Italy by determined socialists in search of more equality through political controls.[2] They were strongest in branches with a long-standing militant tradition (the mines, motor cars, printing, the docks, etc.). In 1974 a miners' strike led directly to the fall of the Heath government.

Given the obstacles, it was not altogether surprising the system worked poorly. British manufacturing grew at half the average rate of the European Community (of Ten) between 1960 and 1973 and only a third as fast, despite declining growth thoughout Europe, in the recession between 1973 and 1983 (Commission of the European Communities 1986, Table 9). Unit values of exports—usually taken as a measure of technological performance—were low relative not only to Germany but to France (NEDO 1977, Table 1; Saunders 1978). As for industrial policy, it became increasingly defensive. Cars, machine tools, aerospace, shipyards and data processing, all sectors under pressure, loomed large in rescue operations (see Chapter 6). The nadir came in the first two years of the Thatcher government, when North Sea oil came on stream. The exchange value of the pound rose steeply. Industrial exports fell. Output dropped a fifth between 1979 and 1981, with a loss of 1.5 million jobs in manufacturing.

Yet the 1970s may in retrospect be seen as having laid the seeds of reform. The Heath government took Britain into the EEC in 1973 and forced a new level of competition on British firms. The Labour government of the late 1970s began a trend towards greater stress on eliminating bottlenecks in high technology and training and towards small business as a source of employment and flexibility (see Ch. 6, p. 172). This has been continued under the Conservative Governments since 1979. The resistance of the trade unions to industrial adjustment, radical in ideological terms, but increasingly defensive to preserve jobs as recession worsened after 1980, has been weakened in important respects by high unemployment, by trade union legislation, by political confrontation with the miners and, not least, by social and cultural shifts in the workforce.

From 1983 onwards, a third phase may, or may not, have opened. True, the implied shift in priorities away from income distribution and demand stimulation towards incentives for entrepreneurship and production has been based on massive redundancies and some of the highest unemployment in Europe while wages still outpace productivity. But productivity and profits in manufacturing have improved. Investment has revived. There have even been signs of recovery in persistently weak industries such as automobiles and machine tools. In the three years from 1983 to 1986 the growth of manufacturing output rose to 85 per cent of the (modest) European Community average. Prior to the elections of June 1987, the Government, very traditionally, reflated the economy. Less traditionally, however, this showed few signs of greatly fuelling inflation; while growth early in 1987 did not seem to produce the usual surge of imports. The balance of trade, after a 20 per cent devaluation against the DM in a year, held up relatively well. This was new. If this were confirmed over a longer period, the Thatcher years might yet prove a watershed.

Looking back over the post-war period, a number of conclusions stand out. A central one has been the political consensus on generally open trading. Even most of the left wing of the Labour party accepts that the internationalization of the economy has gone too far for Britain to expand the domestic economy on its own. Britain has also been more inclined to accept inward investment, notably by Americans and Japanese—but also by the French automobile producer, Peugeot—than other European countries. Second, state-backed intervention has mostly failed to promote industrial dynamism. Third, British environmental support for industry, of the German kind, has been and remains, singularly weak, and the Thatcher government has done little to remedy it. The links between manufacturing and education or academic science are poor and there is a shortage of engineers. This seems to have a critical impact on industry's capacity to invest in new technology and to raise productivity (Daly, Hitchens and Wagner 1985).[3] Recent cuts in education budgets have created a serious shortage of science teachers (Harvey-Jones 1986).

If, in these circumstances, the Thatcher years were to prove a watershed, they would provide an interesting piece of evidence on the dynamics of industry. They would suggest, as Italy does, that institutional weaknesses are not necessarily crippling, so long as the conditions, both of competition outside the firm and of policy formation within it, are favourable to entrepreneurship. If so, environmental support of the German kind could be a reinforcing, rather than basic, factor behind industrial success. However, in Britain at least the case remains to be demonstrated.

8.2 Comparisons

The industrial policy styles of the Four are both markedly different and closely related. To situate the complex balances that result, the material below is broken down into half a dozen aspects: (i) the importance of the choices made in the relatively fluid period immediately after the war; (ii) the responses to the internationalization of the economy that followed; (iii) the implications of the relative strengths of the different national industries; (iv) the decision-making environment behind the formulation of industrial strategies; (v) the societal influences that form the milieu in which policies are conceived and implemented; and finally (vi) the learning curves in industrial policy-making in Europe over the period.

Crystallization

Because of the slowness with which industrial policies work, the way in which collective attitudes crystallize at a moment of fluidity around a more or less appropriate policy pattern can condition choices for decades afterwards. Just as failure in war is one of the classic breeding grounds of revolution, in which new power networks may take over, so the ruins of 1945 in Europe in many ways broke the pre-war mould. They gave reformers the chance to step into the breach with new policies.

In practice, three types of situation can in retrospect be seen to have obtained. The first and easiest case was where the material and psychological assets of a society, including its industrial structures, social assumptions and institutional frames of reference, already happened to be well adapted to the context or, by tradition, to adjustment as such. Among the Four, this category corresponded most closely to the position of West Germany: a number of her giant firms had been, pre-war, clear industrial leaders. It needed courage to bank on that continuing; but the background and record gave confidence and set a familiar standard.

The second case arose where established networks of social authority were so shattered that new generations and elites could make a new state. This fitted the case of Germany again but, perhaps more important, also of France and Italy, both of them with weak industries and systems in trouble, who henceforth dedicated themselves with some success to catching up.

The third case arose where pre-existing social formulas happened not to be too well adapted to evolving conditions nor subject to major upheavals which renewed personnel and outlooks. In this situation, elites tied to particular ways of doing things and the patterns of privilege built up in the past could constitute major obstacles to adjustment (Olson 1982). This category, of continuity in what was to prove a comparatively unprofitable pattern of behaviour, has covered the predicament of Britain. In many ways it can be said that she has been a neo-follower among industrial powers handicapped by attitudes from top to bottom of society derived from past leadership.

Though the choices made by the Germans on the one hand and the French and Italians on the other were different in their approach to government–industry relations, they were at one in placing priority on production rather than distribution. In a semi-revolutionary situation, these choices were at first far from assured. Even in Germany, Erhard's free-trade coup was highly speculative and faced strong opposition. In the event, the policies were legitimized by the economic 'miracles' of the 1950s, which depended on US more than European policies, huge unused supply capacities, especially of labour, and insatiable consumer demand. All three countries profited abundantly from the quarter century of *belle époque* that followed.

Significantly, Britain, the one wartime victor in the quartet, was the one country not to break with the past. On the contrary, in 1945 she fulfilled frustrated pre-war aspirations to a priority not of production but of distributive justice which assumed a strong productive system. Later, when this proved not to be the case, the enormous ideological and institutional pressures behind the priorities chosen made it difficult to shift them. As before 1914 and again between the wars, Britain only half benefited from the boom years before confronting her structural problems in the lean ones of recession after 1973.

In retrospect, it seems clear that once policy patterns were shaped in the fluid period after the war, they tended to last, because it was round them that the power networks and political forces crystallized.

Internationalization

From the 'miracles' of the 1950s onwards, the dominant feature for industrial policy has been the internationalization of production and trade. Throughout the 1950s the economies of all Four, especially on the import side, were almost as autarchic as in the 1930s (see Table 2.5, p. 30). But it soon became apparent that autarchy hampered high growth. As a result, even the weak protectionists, France and Italy, accepted the European common market; and in the twenty years that followed, the economies of all Four became more and more integrated in international trade. This primarily meant membership of an intense regional network of trade covering the whole of Western Europe, but it also involved greater openness to the rest of the world.

Competition was felt in the 1960s to come primarily from the United States. The United States was then joined, and in some respects surpassed, by Japan in the 1970s. The new competition was also linked to new technology and a new form of organization, the 'multinational' firm for which the world markets are the frame of strategy and operations. As a result, there could be no return to traditional protection. The new form it took was the mercantilist action of the state behaving as a kind of shadow entrepreneur and financier of firms regarded as 'national champions' in competition for world markets. Protection might be conceivable for Western Europe as a whole. But there was no consensus on this. In any case, each country, seeing the competitive problem as a national rather than European one, had too small a domestic market to offer any alternative base. The Common Market and the world ones have thus constituted the same decisive context for all the Four.

International ranking

Nevertheless, the ways in which the Four reacted to international pressures provide one of the main symptoms of differences between them, and these seem to have been related to the relative strengths of their industries. Industrial policies are applied in specific situations to promote strengths and correct weaknesses which are equally specific. When industry is strong, firms can look after themselves and are independent. This is true even for nationalized firms in countries reputed to be interventionist: Renault in its palmy days, working to consumer markets, was pretty free of interference from the French state that owned it. It is when industries are weak, or non-existent, that the state is tempted to step in. It can, of course, be claimed that strength or weakness is to be explained by the policy, not the other way round. But if all Four, except perhaps the British, were weak after the war, France and Italy were traditionally much weaker than the others, and highly conscious of the fact.

That the distinction between free traders and interventionists may be between the strong and weak rather than doctrinal opposites, is suggested to some extent by Germany. Germany has been a relative free trader since the war. Germany was not forced to free trade in 1948 (see Chapter 3). Politically, though, she had strong reasons for it. In a divided country, the legitimacy of the regime depended on ideology not nationhood. Choosing capitalism under American auspices gave a strong bias towards free trade. Yet the choice was controversial when Erhard made it. Had inherited confidence in German industry been lower, it would have been harder for him to gamble on the *Sozialmarktwirtschaft*. Similarly, Britain after the war still had confidence in her industries' potential. The Conservatives in 1951 raised the flag of free trade in opposition to Labour's controls at the time. It was only later, in the face of the 'technology gap' and commercial failures, that Britain experimented widely with direct state intervention in industry.

On the other hand, Germany's policies, on entry into Nato in 1955, for the sectors from which she was initially excluded after the war, and therefore weak, were also interventionist (and in parts—aerospace, data processing—only moderately successful). In declining industries, she has not held out against the European Community cartel for steel, or protection against imports of textiles from the NICs. And Germany has also prevented foreign interests from acquiring control of major firms like Krupp, VW or AEG when they were in trouble (see Chapter 3).

In general, intervention has occurred most frequently in fields that touch the state or society where it feels vulnerable: in basic infrastructures when these have been damaged, as in 1945; or in security, which can cover anything from energy and defence, through competitive capacity at the technological frontiers to the socio-economic plight of declining sectors. The judgement of Stoffaës that the French state's industrial policies can usually be traced to security concerns, may not be far from the mark for the rest of the Four, though they are much less explicit about it. Intervention thrived in these sectors when a qualitatively new and general European handicap was first perceived in the 1960s.

However, approaches also differed according to times and the nature of the state. In France, Italy and even Britain, in contrast to Germany, after the war, nationalized firms and state holding companies were mainly responsible for basic infrastructures or reconstruction. When the 'technology gap' became fashionable in the 1960s, Italy used the state sector much less than the other three countries to promote 'national champions'. At the other extreme, France had striking success in building up new, and often advanced, industries. But this was achieved partly by avoiding competitive markets either through state-led domestic programmes or variants of state-trading with *nouveaux riches* middle-income countries in the 1970s. When these began to shrink in the 1980s, so did French world-market shares. British industrial policies, because of relatively low growth and protectionist habits in managements and trades unions, tended to be defensive almost from the start.

Strategy environments

Whether markets operate freely or are subject to intervention, the focus of decision-making has to be the formulation of effective strategies. These may be short-term for small firms reacting to decentralized markets, but as the size of firms increases, a larger proportion must be longer term. Strategies may variously be devised by firms or by collective forms of consultation, including industry associations, banks, labour unions and states, including in federal Germany the provinces (*Länder*).

Reflecting a long and successful exporting tradition, Germany's political and administrative establishment tends (outside public procurement) to stand back and leave responsibility to the firm. Emphasis on free trade does seem to impress on entrepreneurs that they may receive no help if they fail. The Germans normally prefer to stress functions (e.g. investment, incentives to small business) rather than specific aid to sectors or firms. They have an old tradition of broad and powerful basic support, notably for research and manpower training. However, this is not lack of a framework, but a view of what kind is desirable. Just how decisively the system can intervene when it wants to was demonstrated for steel in 1982–3. This went as far as the forced dissolution of Estel, the combine of Hoesch (German) and Hoogovens (Dutch), in order to rebalance the German industry itself. On the whole, industrial policy is presided over by a cohesive, corporatist establishment, extended by *Mitbestimmungsrecht* to include the labour unions.

The grand gesture is the hallmark of the self-conscious state. From Versailles to Roissy and Beaubourg, the tradition in France has been alive and well. The same high definition is apparent in the *grands projets* of industrial policy. The scale of nuclear reactor building has been a monumental response to lack of domestic energy. Establishing major priorities and programmes to meet them are part of the decision-making environment in France. In this sense, the state has politicized industrial action and given a lead.

Once programmes are under way, state control is less clear. Public agencies have often become powers in their own right. French economic policy has probably owed as much to the institutional imperialism of, say, the Commissariat à l'Energie Atomique and others, as to political *gaullisme*. Studies of firms also show that some are adept at turning official policies to their own purposes (see Chapter 4; Jublin and Quatrepoint 1976; Cawson, Holmes and Stevens 1986). Behavioural strategies then become quite distinct from declaratory policy. French governments have often spoken of European industrial policies only for their firms to team up with American partners instead.

Mobilizing energy on priority programmes also distracts attention from the more diffuse and unglamorous tasks of building up the industrial fabric. Outside the state's incestuous relations with 'national champions', too many sectors of French industry have remained weak, mechanical engineering notably so. They might have been anyway. But concern for correcting basic weaknesses has only really appeared since the 1970s and more particularly in the last few years.

Italy has probably had a more decentralized development than any of the other countries. This is not for lack of a formally centralized administration, nor of abundant legislation on industrial matters (see Chapter 5), nor of activity by the 'para-statal' agencies. It is due essentially to the ganglionic nature of the political system and the lack of a uniformly effective civil service.

The strengths and weaknesses of such a broad-based and apparently ill-coordinated system can be gauged by comparison with French elitism. It certainly involves high costs. Advanced technology sectors are poorly developed. Environmental supports are weak. The 'crisis of large organizations' (both state and firms) reflected it too. On the other hand, it has given prestige and rewards to entrepreneurship, which the small-firm sector has diffused very widely. The industrial export record seems more solid, and by 1984 only marginally smaller, than the French. (Italy, that year, slightly exceeded Britain.)

The British 'disease' cannot be said to be due to weak institutions. The civil service, the City, the universities, even agriculture and distribution circuits, all stand international comparison relatively well. But Britain appears not to have been geared to industrial success along either of the well-tried paths of competition or *dirigisme*.

As regards competition, low growth since 1870, and protection of markets since 1931, have created webs of resistance to change. As regards *dirigisme*, most of Britain's institutions and attitudes seem to have developed in the past century to exploit industrial success (an imperial civil service, a world financial outlook, the divide between the 'two cultures', literary and technical) more than to promote it. The state itself has, for historic reasons, been wont to act as referee in society, rather than as the embodiment of the 'national will' as in France (see Chapter 6). In these conditions, it has proved very difficult to generate leadership for industry that is both strong, focused and appropriate. Yet the latent strengths should not be underestimated. Britain, for all her failures, had a slightly higher world market share of 'high technology' exports in 1984 than did France.

Societal attitudes

Societal attitudes are the democratic face of strategy environments. One of the basic difficulties about them is the uncertainty as to how far they are objective constraints and how far reflections of the quality of decision-making and leadership. In most industries, for instance, the main constraint is probably the amount of skills available (Patel and Pavitt 1986). This seems an effect of education policies. True, popular demand can resist industrially appropriate studies. But here again there can be links with leadership attitudes. In France and Britain, where prestige is geared to mandarin values, vocational training at lower levels can seem a mediocre option (Ardagh 1982, p. 480). Economic activity is a much greater source of social prestige in Germany and Italy, where the state competes less with industry.

However, prosperity has bred attitudes that are 'post-industrial', in the sense that they are increasingly critical of the social and environmental costs of industry. The Green movement in Germany has blocked a large number of industrial projects, estimated at the end of the 1970s to be equivalent to a fifth of national annual fixed investment (Horn 1982, p. 63). On the other hand, the demand for more sensitivity to the environment has helped a strong anti-pollution industry to emerge. Environmentalism has had least impact in France. Even Chernobyl has only moderately diminished the popularity of nuclear power, which has greatly reduced electricity bills.

Traditionally, the most obvious societal influence on industry has been the relationship between management and labour. The labour unions are potentially part of the strategy forming environment and could well be discussed there, but their role outside Germany has been primarily reactive. Capacity and intent are both involved in the relationship between management and labour. Either side can be strong or weak. Each can also seek consensus or confrontation.

In Germany, where the status of industry is high, both management and labour are strong. With few exceptions, they have been bipartisan on production and new technology, and narrowed their differences to income distribution. There have been signs since 1984 in the crucial metal-workers' union (2.5 million members) that an ideological gap could open up again. In all the other countries under review, the movement would seem rather the other way. The doctrines of organized labour have tended to confrontation in the past, but there have been some signs since the second energy crisis (1979–80) of a certain shift, even in doctrine, to cooperation.

In France the labour unions have been divided and, usually, weak. Political schisms are the most obvious aspects of this, but similar fissures did not prevent the Italian unions from acquiring substantial power in the 1970s. Social factors may be a more abiding reason. After the war, more than half the working population was accounted for by small peasant owners, artisans, shopkeepers and workers in tiny plants, all of whose mental outlooks turned round property and family relationships rather than class struggles based on the factory. After the mid-1950s, net labour transfers were directed mainly from agriculture into services. It is not altogether surprising that labour unions in France have had difficulty mobilizing the rank-and-file.

In Italy the labour movement has been marked by the mass post-war migration to the North of landless labourers from the South, often in very poor conditions. In the first 'miracle' years, this weakened the unions, then it helped to radicalize them in the 1960s and 1970s when full employment was more or less achieved. Deepening recession and high unemployment in the 1980s, along with weariness of radical violence, have led to another swing of the pendulum. Relations between management and labour have settled somewhere between the right-wing domination of the 1950s and the left-wing anarchy of the 1970s. The small-firm sector exists in part to circumvent responsibilities to labour and often works on a family basis.

In Britain the official trade-union leadership has leant towards accommodation in a corporatist system with employers and government, but real power has often been concentrated in the hands of shop stewards close to the rank-and-file on the shop floor. In the 1970s, shop-floor militancy reached a point of near breakdown in some sectors. Yet the most pervasive feature of British unionism has been the defensive character of arrangements to protect traditional jobs, even in non-militant sectors like textiles (see Chapter 7). There is little doubt that until the 1980s, union attitudes were a major handicap for many firms and sectors. On the other hand, some of the worst labour problems arose in companies which also had the least effective market strategies (such as British Leyland).

Learning curves

If one looks at past policy patterns, two major distinctions seem to divide the Four. The first relates to authority in generating industrial policy. On the whole (and in very different ways) both Germany and France have displayed a far higher concentration of power at the top than Britain and Italy, where (again in very different ways) societal factors have in effect decentralized decision-making much more. The second refers to the role of the state. The state has played a more overt centralizing part in industrial policy-making in the old nation states, Britain and France, than in the two relatively new ones, Germany and Italy, where firms have usually been left more to their own devices and entrepreneurs enjoyed more independent prestige. It will be noted that the two pairings do not coincide, so that each country is in a category of its own in relation to the two criteria combined. Many of the differences between the national industrial approaches can be summarized under these heads.

Along with this, however, there has been a high degree of commonality: in membership of the European Common Market, in the growing openness to regional and world trade, and even in the forms of partial reaction against them—joint protection for declining industries and separate promotion of the presumed high growth, high technology, sectors through national public procurement. Perhaps the most important aspect of commonality, however, is what seems to be the slow convergence of all four on a shared view of what constitutes appropriate policies. This is best seen in comparing Germany with the other three countries.

Whereas, after the war the state played a prominent role in Britain, France and Italy, Germany stood apart. Though her fiscal policies were highly directive in a broad way, sectoral intervention was played down. German firms were more expected than others to hold their own and less protected by government. Yet Germany also had by far the strongest tradition of environmental support for industry.

The 1960s, the top of the boom, the opening of the Common Market and the migration to it of American 'multinational' corporations, brought what might be called the first internationalization of the European economy. The initial response to the American challenge throughout Western Europe was to increase selective state intervention, on 'infant industry' grounds, in favour of 'high technology'. The emphasis on public support for social redistribution also grew everywhere. The gap between Germany and her neighbours remained, but converged on the interventionist norms of the majority.

The subsequent depression introduced a second stage of internationalization marked by the full impact of Japan's challenge, the first in a hundred years to the established industrial hierarchies. Germany returned to priorities based on production, and all her neighbours shifted in their declaratory policies towards her. By the time of the second energy crisis, from 1979 to 1983, Germany became the core of European orthodoxy, both by her competitive and financial power in the Common Market and because she had traditionally practised policies to meet Europe's major problem, as currently perceived: the quality of industrial performance. If imitation is the sincerest form of flattery, there is little doubt which country in Europe has had the clearest perception of industrial needs.

In theory, this trend might merely involve agreement between countries still evolving on parallel lines without coming closer together. In practice, however, there are signs of integration as well. Initially, after the war, the Four tended to go their own ways. Each bargained for Marshall Aid strictly on its own behalf even if the Americans forced a multilateral aproach on them. In the late 1950s the treaty for the Common Market clearly implied much greater fusion. But significantly, the hopes of the founding fathers that it would lead to an economic union were dashed in the 1960s. The reactions to the 'technology gap' and in the early phases to the recession after 1973 were essentially nationalistic. Yet the emphasis on competition, innovation and the inadequacy of state sponsorship of the 1980s implies a greater potential for transnational processes. These could be orientated to worldwide 'multinational' firm strategies, not primarily European ones. That is one of the questions for the future. Moreover, there is little doubt that national resistance to change will be enormous because of the stubborn attachment of power networks of all kinds to the status quo. The fact remains that the erosion of national concepts on which the European federalists counted too optimistically a quarter-century ago seems to be proceeding, though more gradually than they expected and on different lines.

8.3 Evaluations

To analyse industrial policies and performance is one thing, to establish connections between them is quite another. Governments, planners and banks cannot run firms themselves. Whatever their formal powers, in the end they have to rely on the managers. Their influence is inherently indirect. This arms-length quality is enhanced by other factors. One is the long gestation of most investment in human and material capital. Another is that industry is deeply embedded in society. Apart from a few exceptional periods, society is slow-moving. In the short term, industrial policies can only produce change at the margins. They rely for lasting effect on gradual influences over a period of time.

Once gradualism and time are admitted, it is clear that policies must be steady and cumulative. At least in retrospect, the steps must be seen to follow one another in fairly coherent progression. Moreover, specific actions are probably not the decisive items in the account. This is not because they are small against the scale of manufacturing, nor even that they may be misdirected. The main reason is that policies have to change the context of decision-making to affect it in breadth and depth. In the long run, they are probably more important through the influence they exert over the general climate among decision-makers than through this or that tangible issue that attracts immediate attention.

France provides an interesting instance. There is an air of coherence—certainly false in detail—about French industrial policy since the war. The country set out after the war against a background of weakness and protectionism, but with an establishment shifting priorities from the manoeuvres of great power to economic expansion. By the 1960s, this turned into state intervention to back up newly-formed national champions on world markets. By 1983, the limits of that too had begun to be evident. At least intellectually, the need to leave competition to firms had begun to be accepted. Over forty years a sea-change was accomplished simply by reacting as one's assets and the context evolved.

In these conditions, it is difficult to take sides once and for all in the perpetual debate between 'planning', as it was called when it dared say its name, and 'free trade'. *Dirigisme* seems as anachronistic as closed economies in a period of common and world markets, multinational corporations and, in advanced societies, abundance. But in the years of shortage, Italian reconstruction was no less state-orientated than French and virtually as rapid as German. If the Italians showed more flair than the French, this could well have been because they had no coal, almost no steel and fewer nightmares about the Ruhr. Further, in boom years, state stimulation cannot be conclusively written off as inefficient. Imitation can pay off, because backward economies that have plenty of room to catch up, benefit from an exceptional increase in the ratio of output and productivity obtained from given increases in investment. Even today, it is not clear that the attempt of the French to build up 'advanced' but not wholly competitive industries puts them in worse place for the future than Italy's more commercial but less technologically developed manufacturing. Perhaps both have suffered above all from a shortage of basic industrial structures at a time that could prove crucial in shaping world oligopolies. After all, Japan's giant multi-sectoral groups, spilling over in banks and trading houses, have done better than anyone by employing long-term strategies involving elements of collusion and, certainly at first, of government coordination (Kikkawa 1983). Whatever declaratory policies may convey, corporatism pervades all advanced economies.

This in no way denies the force of the arguments for a competitive environment. Though some countries are highly effective exporters and yet comparatively closed to imports (Japan, Korea, and before the war Germany and even the United States), most countries that are closed have had mediocre to poor trade records. Countries with open economies have done far better. Sweden, Switzerland and the Netherlands come to mind, with their apparent paradox of small domestic markets breeding major international corporations. Most exceptions to this rule seem to be, or to have been, marked by fierce competition on the internal market. This has been true of the United States. It is also true of Japan—and of Germany, certainly in the past—despite their traditional collusion between industrial groups. It is possible that a special ability to fuse high degrees of competition and cooperation is what defines a dynamic culture (Darlington 1969, p. 214).

More generally, there is at least one test which national economies, manufacturing sectors or individual firms that aspire to international market leadership appear to pass with flying colours. This is the consistent pursuit of clear market objectives based on searching out and meeting demand; and above all a flexible organization to turn external signals to good account within the firm. It is evident at one end in the success of the Japanese and, in the past, of IBM; and at the other of a number of relatively small Swedish and Swiss multinationals which have succeeded in expanding satisfactorily, and some rapidly, through the testing recession after the second energy crisis of 1979–80 (Dullforce 1985). Another instance, in Europe, among many individual cases, is those smaller Italian firms whose outstanding characteristic has been their commercial flair.

A second feature that recurs in industrial success is a powerful supporting environment. This is not a single quality. The promotion of human skills probably plays the largest part in it, from an appropriate educational system that spans the range between management and the shopfloor to intensive and commercially relevant scientific and technological research as a prime form of capital investment. Whether it is a root cause of competitiveness or a reinforcing factor is not clear. But it usually goes with another characteristic of successful economies: they offer industrial values and leadership great rewards in social respect and prestige. In European terms, these are more evident in Germany and Italy than in Britain and France, where mandarin values tend to predominate. The United States is an interesting case. Once the most dedicated of all societies to business values, it has now acquired an imperial role and a state with manifest attractions for many of the brightest young.

The conclusions drawn are predictable from the findings. First, supporting policies for industry must be as strong as possible, especially as regards training. Second, entrepreneurship and market awareness must be encouraged by cutting down on regulations, and on costs which reduce profits, and by giving incentives to innovation, defined not as invention but as the commercial exploitation of opportunity. Such goals are easier to state than to achieve. As so often, they imply changing the habits and sometimes even the essence of existing power networks and of social values associated with them. Hence, the frequency of large gaps between declared policies and behaviour. Nevertheless, bitter experience has turned these prescriptions into the orthodoxy of the 1980s.

Contemporary doctrine implies the downgrading of arguments fashionable in earlier periods. After the war, it was argued that if Europe had a vast, competitive domestic market like America it could achieve American economies of scale, output and specialization. In the 1960s, these arguments were extended to the attempt by European states to create their own 'multinational corporations'. This view has been devalued since by the frequent mediocrity and even failure of 'national champions'. The new emphasis tends to be that 'firms do not succeed because they are large, but are large because they succeed' (Ergas 1985).

Yet it does not follow, because economies of scale do not of themselves generate success, that they are never ingredients of it. There are a number of factors which suggest that governments, in still hankering after economies of scale, may not always be incorrigibly misguided.

In the first place, many sectors of importance at the technological frontiers, such as aerospace, armaments, telecommunications, power generation and health, are not open anywhere. (Recent US policy on telecommunications is an exception.) Second, in many activities, barriers to entry due to rising capital intensity have palpably grown (for instance, in semiconductors, telecommunications switchgear, pharmaceuticals and automobile distribution). Third, some of Japan's outstanding export gains have involved concerted campaigns by major groups to saturate markets, especially the American market, in successive specific sectors. If these do not explain Japan's competitiveness, they have certainly helped to exploit it.

In areas where economies of scale are the entrance ticket, they can hardly be the reason for failure. Much more plausible is the likelihood that the dwarfed nationalism of the larger European countries makes it impossible to combine economies of scale with competiton. Would-be American-sized firms in European-sized markets almost inevitably constitute monopolies. Limited markets also give inadequate scope for specialization. There is too little competition at home to prepare firms to compete internationally.

Because of nationalism, in Western Europe as a whole a plethora of 'national champions' face the Americans and Japanese. The automobile industry is an obvious but not a unique case. Leaving aside a host of minor firms (including failed former national champions), there are at least four big ones, three not implanted in America and none significantly in Japan, where the Americans and Japanese each have two operating world-wide. No European firm is securely placed in many of the oligopolies that dominate the most internationalized sectors, except in long-established branches such as food and chemicals. Even giants such as Philips and Siemens, for instance, are at best in the second league of manufacturers of a basic item like semi-conductors. There is argument over how much that matters. Yet the fact is the mediocrity has been suffered, it was not chosen.

In short, the industrial problems of the Four cannot be reduced to a choice of innovation or economies of scale. Policies must take account of both.

The core of the response in each case has to be competitiveness. In theory, one could conceive of a protected European economy. Western Europe as a whole is much less dependent on trade outside the borders than any European nation taken individually. But there would be no regional consensus on such a policy. The risk of a protected Europe being out-classed in the technologies of the electronic age would be too high. Such a Europe would be vulnerable, for instance, to further oil shocks if prices were to shoot up again and competitors better placed to pay them. Europe is virtually 'condemned', in the French phrase, to compete for world markets. This implies more than exports. Today, only 40–70 per cent of a major European company's turnover may be generated from within its domestic market, including exports (Bellon and Chevallier 1983, 36; Housego 1986). The rest comes from production in the rest of the world. It will often be necessary to become 'multinational' and operate world-wide.

If these goals are fairly clear, the paths towards them, however, can either aim directly at international operations from the present national home base, or seek added strength from a true European Common Market. In this sense, there is a race between the national and European approaches to world strategies.

Most European firms suffer from considerable handicaps in operating such strategies from a national base. Building up purely national capacity in hopes of acquiring long production runs, and so making exports competitive on world markets, does not have an encouraging history in the aircraft industry or latterly in the French nuclear and telecommunications sectors (OECD, Trade Statistics, Series C). To build up a multinational corporation from European national bases is also difficult, though some manage it successfully. The American market is so huge, and the Japanese one so hard, to penetrate that results are often mediocre. Partnerships with strong American or Japanese firms also present problems. Weaker European firms in particular seek to strengthen their technology and competitiveness by agreements with American or Japanese ones. These rarely provide the strength the Europeans hope to imbibe. Instead, they can lead to virtual absorption and strengthen the Americans and Japanese in Europe against the remaining local 'national champions'. Where the partners are not so strong, as in some of the link-ups to fight IBM, the new alliance remains on the defensive world-wide.

Even where the European firm is the senior partner, and its markets are dominated by governments, massive questions remain. For instance, will Alcatel—a merger of CGE (France) and ITT (United States)—be able to maintain ITT's old market share in Germany if Siemens fails to buy CGCT (ITT's former subsidiary) in France? If Siemens does acquire CGCT, this implies a sharing of market quotas between France and Germany not unlike the production cartel of European governments behind Airbus. Such solutions are not all doomed to failure. The row early in 1987 over Airbus between the sponsor governments and the United States seemed related to its threatened penetration of American domestic airline markets at the cost of Boeing and McDonnell Douglas. But in all countries, aerospace is directly or indirectly influenced by government purchases. Where markets are more open, such approaches are far too lumbering. They cannot work across the board.

The only strong solution of these difficulties would be a truly competitive European market including public procurement. This is the approach of the European Commission's proposals of 1985, which detailed some 300 measures to complete the 'internal' Market by 1992 (Commission of the European Communities 1985; Netherlands Scientific Council for Government Policy 1986). The purpose behind such a strategy must be to create a genuinely continental European market from which 'multinational' corporations of a world standard can emerge. In practice, this would have to mean that the more efficient European firms absorb the less. The root problem is the fears of the less competitive nations that they may end up as backward regions in a Europe dominated by the Germans and a few other surviving firms.

Another major issue would be whether to prevent American and Japanese firms from competing for European public purchases, at least at first. If not, they might acquire major long-term advantages within Europe. On the other hand, some of them are already installed in Europe and claim national status. To exclude them would add further bones of contention with the United

States and between the member states. It is not surprising that the efforts of the European Commission to break through the national purchasing monopolies have so far foundered and that in these areas the Common Market is a sham.

If the opening up of Community markets cannot be achieved directly, then it has to be approached gradually and indirectly by common European standards; by shared R & D and in some cases production; by cooperation in specific fields like major components; and by the establishment of different kinds of consortia. Attempts are being made along all these lines, and have acccelerated in the mid-1980s, with and without prompting from the European Commission, but progress tends to be slow. Time and the competition do not stand still.

A key area where Western Europe probably has more room for choice than it has been willing to exploit is macro-economic policy. Demand and supply are closely related, yet politically it seems difficult to maintain an optimal balance between them. In the boom years, when the political system leaned left, there was a bias towards distribution which assumed that supply would deliver the goods. Since the outbreak of recession, there has been a shift to the right, with an emphasis on supply-side policies, partly to re-establish production priorities, partly to squeeze domestic demand and so force manufacture onto export markets. Germany, which is the regulatory economy in Western Europe, has always tended to emphasize the supply side more than its neighbours. Useful in a boom, this can also reinforce recession and unemployment: between 1982 and 1985 demand in the United States grew by (an unsustainable) 18 per cent, in Japan by 9 per cent and in Western Europe by only 5 per cent (Marris 1986). Excessively prolonged, this helps create the supply-side inferiorities it seeks to correct. In the long run, the aim must be to achieve optimal sustainable balances of both demand and supply. This is needed to encourage investment and adjustment in industry itself.

It is not at present easy to tell which factors handicap Europe most: the qualitative weaknesses of rigidities which hamper entrepreneurship; or the two kinds of quantitative ones, the first a nationalism which holds up the establishment of a competitive continental market benefiting from the maximum economies of scale and specialization; and the second, hyper-cautious demand policies which slow up supply adjustment by reducing growth. Reform of all three seems crucial, if size of operations, specialization and competitiveness are to be combined in firms encouraged to pursue effective world strategies.

Unless European governments allow a genuinely competitive process to develop within the Common Market, present trends will continue. The weaker European firms will turn as juniors to American or Japanese partners and sooner or later be absorbed. The remaining Europeans will try to compete world-wide on their own, and some succeed, but not necessarily in the forefront of the oligopolies. There will be some half-hearted European cooperation and competition. The general outcome could well be a kind of integration into the world economy, in which the Europeans are unable to stay with the leaders across substantial parts of the spectrum.

Accordingly, European interest in industrial policies is driven by fear that the privileges conferred on the region for two centuries by the industrial revolution are being winnowed away. This is a real danger, though its meaning must not be distorted. It is not necessary to be *the* industrial leader to benefit to some extent from a generally rising ride of output; and some countries have achieved high standards of living without controlling the firms on their soil. At the same time, the diffusion of industry across the world implies that, to maintain relatively high levels of prosperity and to keep political options open, a semi-continent like Western Europe must compete in a range of the more sophisticated industries. It must make room for new societies below and not be overtaken too often. Adequate policies for industry are probably the outstanding investment the region can now make in its own future, and indirectly in international prosperity as well.

Notes

1. 'From 1870 onwards, the British economy moved from one deep slump to the next, punctuated only by brief booms, while the German evidence is of long periods of near full employment, penetrated by short recessions. The German economy also expanded fast enough to absorb all who wanted industrial jobs, whereas the British economy was expanding so slowly that British people had to emigrate right up to 1913' (Lewis 1978, p. 127).
2. Socialism, in this context, implies the presumed hegemony of the factory working class, with central controls to nullify the inegalitarian income effects of free markets. Social democracy accepts markets as the basic economic and social determinant but seeks to provide a floor for living standards by tax and social security measures.
3. A study comparing forty-five British and German manufacturing plants, with similar machinery and manning, found German labour productivity on average 63 per cent higher than British largely owing to the low technical competence of British managers and workers, which led to frequent machine break-downs; poor maintenance procedures; and inadequate British attention to quality control. British foremen, who mostly lacked any formal qualifications, were inferior to the German counterparts who nearly all had the higher certificate of *Meister* (which includes proficienty in staff supervision and work organization as well as technical skills). German production managers were normally graduate engineers whereas in Britain they were usually people who had learned on the job and had a sales or financial background. This played a big role in making German firms bolder than British in acquiring new equipment because they understood its potential better and quicker (Daly, Hitchens and Wagner 1985).

References

Adams, W. and Stoffaës, C. (1986), *French Industrial Policy*, Washington D.C., Brookings.

Ardagh, J. (1982), *France in the 1980s*, London, Secker & Warburg.

Aujac, H. (1986), 'An introduction to French industrial policy', in Adams and Stoffaës, op. cit., pp. 13–35.

Balassa, B. (1986), 'Selective versus general economic policy in postwar France', in Adams and Stoffaës, op. cit., pp. 97–102.

Barou, Y. and Keizer, B. (1984), *Les Grandes Economies: Etats Unis, Japon, Allemagne Fédérale, France, Royaume-Uni, Italie*, Paris, Seuil, (quoted Boyer, op. cit.).

Bellon, B. and Chevalier, J-M, eds (1983), *L'Industrie en France*, Paris, Centre de Recherche en Economie Industrielle (CREI).

Boyer, R. (1986), 'Industrial policy in macroeconomic perspective', in Adams and Stoffaës, op. cit., pp. 88–96.

Bruce, P. (1987), 'West Germany's banks: the political pressures are beginning to tell', *Financial Times*, 18 January.

Cawson, A., Holmes, P. and Stevens, A. (1986), 'The interaction between firms and the state in France: the telecommunications and consumer electronics sectors', in Wright and Wilks, op. cit.

Commission of the European Communities (1985), *Completing the Internal Market: White Paper from the Commission to the European Council*, June, Luxembourg.

Commission of the European Communities (1986), *European Economy*, November 1985, Brussels.

Daly, A., Hitchens, D.M.W.N. and Wagner, K. (1985), 'Productivity, machinery and skills in a sample of British and German manufacturing plants: results of a pilot inquiry', *National Institute Economic Review*, February, pp. 48–61, London.

Darlington, C.D. (1969), *The Evolution of Man and Society*, London, Allen & Unwin.

Delorme, R. and André, C. (1983), *L'Etat et l'Economie: Un Essai d'Explication de l'Evolution des Dépenses Publiques en France 1870–1980*, Paris, Seuil.

Dosi, G. (1983), 'Semi-conductors: Europe's precarious survival in high technology', in Shepherd, Duchêne and Saunders, op. cit., pp. 209–25.

Dullforce, W. (1985), 'Sweden and Switzerland: how small can be beautiful in Europe', *Financial Times*, 8 July.

Ehrmann, H.W. (1957), *Organised Business in France*, Princeton, Conn., Princeton University.

Ergas, H. (1985), 'Exploding the myths about what's wrong', *Financial Times*, 26 June.

Freyche, M. (1986), 'Export promotion as industrial policy', in Adams and Stoffaës, op. cit., pp. 82–7.

Harvey-Jones, Sir J. (1986), *The Listener*, 10 April, pp. 12–15, London.

Horn, E.-J. (1982), *Management of Industrial Change in Germany*, Sussex European Paper No. 13, Sussex European Research Centre, Sussex University, Brighton.

Housego, D. (1986), 'St Gobain aims to upgrade global image', *Financial Times*, 3 July.

Jublin, J. and Quatrepoint, J.M. (1976), *French Ordinateurs: de l'Affaire Bull à l'Assassinat du Plan Calcul*, Paris, Alain Moreau.

Kikkawa, M. (1983), 'Shipbuilding, motor cars and semi-conductors: the diminishing role of industrial policy in Japan', in Shepherd, Duchêne and Saunders, op. cit., pp. 236–67.

Lenti, L. (1973), *Grandeur et Servitudes de l'Economie Italienne*, Paris, Calmann-

Lévy, (translated from *Inventario dell'Economia Italiana*, Garzanti 1966).

Lewis, Sir W.A. (1978), *Growth and Fluctuations 1870–1913*, London, Allen & Unwin.

Marceau, J. (1977), *Class and Status in France: Economic Change and Social Immobility 1945–1975*, Oxford, Clarendon.

Marris, S. (1986), 'Don't freeze out fiscal policy', *Financial Times*, 3 July.

Messerlin, P. and Saunders, C. (1983), 'Steel: too much investment too late', Shepherd, Duchêne and Saunders, op. cit., pp. 52–81.

National Economic Development Office (1977), *International Price Competitiveness, Non-Price Factors and Export Performance*, London.

Netherlands Scientific Council for Government Policy (1986), *The Unfinished European Integration*, Reports to the Government 28–1986, The Hague, March.

OECD (annual), *Statistical Bulletins of Foreign Trade, Series C, Trade by Commodities*, Paris.

OEEC, Organisation for European Economic Cooperation (1960), *Industrial Statistics 1900–1959*, Paris.

Olson, M: (1982), *The Rise and Decline of Nations: Economic Growth, Stagflation and Social Rigidities*, New Haven, Conn., Yale University Press.

Patel, P. and Pavitt, K. (1986), *Is Western Europe losing the Technological Race?*, Science Policy Research Unit, Sussex University, Brighton, mimeo.

Saunders, C. (1978), *Engineering in Britain, West Germany and France: Some Statistical Comparisons of Structure and Competitiveness*, Sussex European Paper 5, Sussex European Research Centre, Sussex University, Brighton.

Shepherd, G., Duchêne, F., and Saunders, C., eds (1983), *Europe's Industries*, London, Frances Pinter.

Stoffaës, C. (1986), 'Industrial policy in high technology industries', in Adams and Stoffaës, op. cit., pp. 36–62.

Wade, R. (1982), 'Regional policy in a difficult international environment: the Italian case' (mimeograph), Institute of Development Studies, University of Sussex, Brighton.

Wright, M. and Wilks, S. eds (forthcoming), *Comparative Studies of Government Industry Relations*, Oxford, Oxford University Press.

Index